W9-ADO-394

THE CANNABIS GROW BIBLE

THE DEFINITIVE GUIDE TO GROWING MARIJUANA FOR RECREATIONAL AND MEDICAL USE

GREG GREEN

:: GREEN CANDY PRESS ::

PUBLISHED BY GREEN CANDY PRESS

SAN FRANCISCO, CA

www.greencandypress.com

COPYRIGHT ©2003 GREG GREEN

ISBN 1-931160-17-1

COVER AND INTERIOR DESIGN: YOLANDA MONTIJO

ILLUSTRATION: IAN PHILLIPS

EDITOR: S.T. ONER

EDITORIAL ASSISTANT: S. KAUDER

COLOR SECTION PHOTOGRAPHS © ANDRE GROSSMAN, PEPPER DESIGN

STUDIO, SERIOUS SEEDS, TRICHOME TECHNOLOGIES and

www.bubblebag.com

PHOTOGRAPHS © BIG ISLAND BUD, BUSHY OLDER GROWER, A MERRY

CANER, CHRISESQ, CHRONIC COUPLE, FOZ, GIYO, GREG GREEN, SHECKY

GREENE, ANDRE GROSSMAN, VIC HIGH, KRYPTONITE, RASTA LINUS,

MULLUMMADMAN, PEPPER DESIGN STUDIO, RATDOG, SAGARMATHA

SEEDS, SENSI SEEDS, STRAWDOG, www.bubblebag.com, X3N0 and MR. ZOG

This book contains information about illegal substances, specifically the plant Cannabis Sativa and its derivative products. Green Candy Press would like to emphasize that cannabis is a controlled substance in North America and throughout much of the world. As such, the use and cultivation of cannabis can carry heavy penalties that may threaten an individual's liberty and livelihood.

The aim of the Publisher is to educate and entertain. Whatever the Publisher's view on the validity of current legislation, we do not in any way condone the use of prohibited substances.

All rights reserved. No part of this book may be reproduced in any form without express written permission from the Publisher, except by a reviewer, who may quote brief passages or reproduce illustrations in a review where appropriate credit is given. Nor may any part of this book be reproduced, stored in a retrieval system, or transmitted in any form or by any means without written permission from the Publisher.

PRINTED IN CANADA BY TRANSCONTINENTAL

MASSIVELY DISTRIBUTED BY P.G.W.

ACKNOWLEDGEMENTS

My thanks to my family and friends for making this book possible.

This book is dedicated to growers all over the world. I would like to say thank you to Simi, Moni, Strawdog, Chris, Kryptonite, BushyOlderGrower (BOG), RealHigh, W.Y Evans-Wentz, Lama Kazi Dawa-Samdup, Vic High, ~shabang~, The Penguin, Bubbleman, Sir John Woodroffe, Mike H, Billy A, Sean C, Nick J, Paul M, John Mc, Mahoona, Cossie, Suz F, Emer D, Mary M, Eug D, Carol L, Arthur C. Clarke, Darra E and Mr. De Butler.

A special thanks to Serious Seeds, Sensi Seeds, Paradise Seeds, Spice of Life Seeds, Nirvana Seeds, Dutch Passions Seeds, Mr. Nice, Soma Seeds, Greenhouse Seeds, African Seeds, Flying Dutchman, Brother's Grimm, Homegrown Fantaseeds, KC Brains, Heaven's Stairway, Seeds Direct and all their breeders for keeping those genetics coming and making them available to all.

My ingratitude goes out to the CIA for refusing to be audited for activities relating to the drug war at the request of the General Accounting Office of America since 1960, making themselves the obvious profiteers of America's spiraling offshore illegal drug trade which creates adulterated cannabis products, the proceeds from which are used to train foreign guerilla forces for a 'cause' which eventually ends up with them rebelling and converting to terrorism that reaches every part of the globe. My ingratitude also goes out to their partners who spread disinformation about the cannabis plant across the world so that the profits can keep rolling in at the expense of human lives. These people should know better than to make money out of mischief.

It's only just cannabis!

I would also like to say a special thanks to my Publisher and Editor for their always welcome words of wisdom.

This is a book about growing cannabis, written by people who grow cannabis.

TABLE OF CONTENTS

FOREWORD

THIS BOOK IS A GROW BIBLE. You can find books on roses or orchids that are ten times as thick as this one with more information. But then roses and orchids are not illegal in most countries and cultivators and botanists are free to explore and share information about those plants. Sadly the same cannot be said for cannabis...until now. Admittedly, there is still much work that needs to be done to provide a complete reference to cannabis growers, but that will come in time. Despite cannabis-suppression efforts that have suspended cannabis information gathering over the past 60 years, we bring you *THE CANNABIS GROW BIBLE*.

THE CANNABIS GROW BIBLE is new and truly unique. Those who are willing to take serious risks in getting you this information have experienced most of what you will read and learn here. Although I am not personally putting myself at risk by penning this book, those who grew hundreds of plants in their basements and other 'secret locations' to provide data on this subject matter took grave risks. With their help I have been able to document what is real and what is not in the world of cannabis cultivation. They have provided the facts and figures presented in this book that will truly help readers grow bigger, healthier, more potent buds. The results have been outstanding and I am very thankful for their fearless contribution to *THE CANNABIS GROW BIBLE*.

In this book you will learn a number of things. Probably too many to remember all in one go if this is your first time growing. That is why I have broken the book into easy-to-follow, step-by-step portions. The book is designed to follow the same stages that a growing plant would. So you can imagine the life cycle of the cannabis plant being the foundation for the style and layout of this book. This is what makes *THE CANNABIS GROW BIBLE* so accessible and unique. It is equal parts theory and practice. Most grow guides are either too focused on theory or too lacking in information about the science of botany; they either ignore growers' practical concerns, or worse, contain information that is out-of-date or even incorrect. *THE CANNABIS GROW BIBLE* provides accurate, up-to-date information and practical experience from growers who know.

You only need a few simple tools to grow a cannabis plant and this book will explain those practices, but a great many other things go into growing a 'super cannabis plant.' *THE CANNABIS GROW BIBLE* clearly defines what you should and should not do to grow bigger, high-yield plants. Most of the time this has nothing to do with your growing experience, it has more to do with how much time and budget you are willing to invest, what cannabis strains you are working with and the environment in which you are growing.

A grower is not limited by growing experience. A grower is limited by legal constraints, grow space, money, information and plant genetics. We cannot help you with money or the law, or provide you with a safe grow space, but we can help you by providing good growing information and clear growing instructions — and we can also tell you how to obtain a good genetic base for your plants.

Don't ever let bad results hamper your new hobby. That is part of the process of learning. However, this book will point out some common mistakes that new growers make so you don't have to repeat them and learn everything the hard way.

Glance over this book and flick through the chapters. Get a feel for what is going on. Then read it all from start to finish. By the time you turn the last page you will probably have a bit of your own homegrown bud in a pipe. If you can do that then please tell people about this book. It is our goal to get everyone participating in growing the great herb.

This is not the final book on the subject either. This book has been designed in such a way that it will grow with the times. We will be adding new chapters, new pictures, new methods and new theories. That is why *THE CANNABIS GROW BIBLE* is the grower's handbook of choice.

We hope that you stick with us and we hope that this book will help you to get where you want to go. Happy growing and most of all remember to . . . HAVE FUN!

PREFACE

THIS BOOK WAS WRITTEN UNDER ADVERSE CONDITIONS. In most countries it is illegal to own cannabis seeds, or to grow or use cannabis. Maybe this will change for you one day if enough people make the effort to have their voices heard. Until that day comes, it is recommended that you verify what your country's legal stance is with regards to growing cannabis. This book was not created with the intent to encourage anyone to break the law. *THE CANNABIS GROW BIBLE* is about cannabis and how it is grown around the world. Even though the contents of this book may show you how to acquire seeds and grow very potent plants, ultimately, you are responsible for your own actions. We would like you grow bigger, better cannabis plants; however we don't want you break the law.

I would also like to say that many countries have permitted medical users to grow their own personal supplies of cannabis. If this is true of your country then this book will be of massive benefit to you and your health.

THE CANNABIS GROW BIBLE is part of a foundation series and is a developing project. We listen to and talk with 100s of growers every single year. It is with their advice that we can offer you the latest updates on growing techniques and strains. Where other books have followed, this is the one that will lead.

THE CANNABIS GROW BIBLE is a dynamic information resource. We hope that you stick with us and visit us online at www.cannabisbook.com to learn more about how to grow BIGGER BUD!

1 | THE CANNABIS PLANT

A BRIEF HISTORY OF CANNABIS

CANNABIS HAS BEEN GROWING ON THIS PLANET for thousands, maybe millions of years, quite some time before human intervention. Cannabis can be grown nearly anywhere as long as the temperature is not consistently cold and there is enough sunlight and food for the plant to flourish. In Asia, you can travel to various regions around Mongolia and visit the cannabis plant growing naturally on hillsides and across vast plains, sometimes covering entire hill faces and spreading across the valley below. The origins of cannabis are not entirely clear, but biologists and cannabis researchers generally agree that the plant first took root somewhere in the Himalayas.

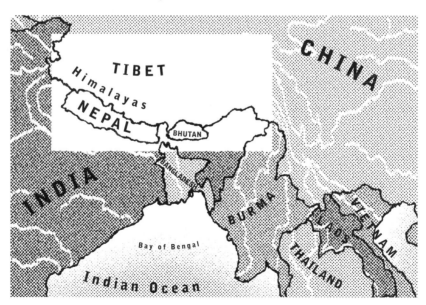

Map of Asia: the square indicates where cannabis is believed to have originated.

The cannabis plant has managed to travel across the globe without the involvement of humans. The seed has been carried by the wind, in bird droppings and has attached itself to animals that trek over long distances, thus globally dispersing the plant, naturally.

Today, human intervention has forced the cannabis plant to be grown under more controlled conditions and in areas where the plant would not have previously existed. It is estimated that there are between two and twelve different cannabis strains growing wild in countries that have not culled the plant, but there could be more. These wild strains, known as **landrace** strains, are often cultivated by local residents for their *hemp* material and herbal qualities. The *Afghani* plant, which has been used by many a cannabis plant breeder to create strains like Kush, Master Kush and the Hash Plant, is a well-known landrace strain. Farmed *hybrid* strains often make their way back into the wild, creating new landrace strains. In Afghanistan in particular, there are now several different strains of Afghani growing in the wild.

Wild cannabis plants are rarer in countries that have tried to eliminate the plant by burning fields and conditioning woodlands. In certain countries the cannabis plant has been identified as a dangerous drug and has been all but eradicated by government and law-enforcement officials. It is treated as a noxious *weed* that induces social, mental and physical problems. Despite the fact that the reasoning behind these attitudes is not well founded, the cull of cannabis continues. Highly adaptable, however, the cannabis plant has survived these attempts at eradication in secret indoor and outdoor grow spaces around the world.

Cannabis was used for many things other than the extraction of *tetrahydrocannabinol* (THC).* Until the late 1800s or early 1900s our ancestors used hemp to make clothing and various materials, from paper and rope to fuel. Hemp is a strong, durable material that can withstand large amounts of stress and is widely regarded as one of the best materials for producing fabrics. A pair of pants made from hemp will stand the test of time and be far superior to cotton. This should provide some clues as to why the fabric industry wanted to stop the cultivation of *marijuana* in the late 1800s. Hemp-fabric products last longer than cotton-fabric products; thus buyers purchase less over a longer period of time.

Although cannabis prohibition is a booming industry that creates jobs and capital, if cannabis were decriminalized these lost jobs and profits could be derived

---

*For step-by-step information on THC extraction, please refer to Chapter 17.

from a new cannabis industry. It will take a huge groundswell of support for legalization to overturn 70 years of suppression, however. Governments that have prohibited cannabis cultivation and made a concerted effort to outlaw the drug and punish users would most certainly lose face if they turned around now and admitted they were wrong. Governments rescinding their cannabis policies would also have to release people from prison, radically change their justice department's stance on cannabis and even compensate those imprisoned for cannabis-related offenses.

THE HIGH
THC

Cannabis plants produce psychoactive ingredients called *cannabinoids.* The main ingredient in cannabinoids that gives the high effect is called delta-9 THC. All strains vary in THC levels and quantities or percentages. The difference between THC levels and THC quantities is that THC levels are genetically determined: they cannot be influenced by the grower. THC quantities, on the other hand, are related to bud mass and how much resin can be collected from that *bud* mass. By way of example: some bud may only contain 20 percent THC, with a THC level of 5. The same plant grown under better conditions could produce 70 percent THC, with a THC level of 5. The level is genetic. The quantities of 20 percent and 70 percent are under the grower's control.

CH3

9

OH

H3C

O

H3C

C3H11

Tetrahydrocannabinol (THC) is the active chemical in cannabis and one of the oldest drugs known.

Genetic THC levels correspond to the ratio of THC to other cannabinoids contained in the trichomes of the pistils of a flowering female plant. Although this ratio varies depending on the strain, how it is grown, when it harvested and how it is cured, under optimal conditions a stable strain should produce a consistent THC level that is genetically inherited. Once the THC level is genetically set in the seed it can not be increased past this point during the plant's life. Likewise, the maximum quantities of bud that the plant can produce is also genetic and can not increase past this point during the plant's life. The grower should endeavor to create a growing environment which optimizes both these traits to their full potential. Emphasis should be made here on choosing good genetics. You can't improve on something that isn't there in the first place.

An optimally potent plant will have both high levels and quantities of delta-9 THC. Cannabis plants also produce a compound called delta-8 THC. This ingredient is found in low levels but does contribute to the high. When we mention THC levels, we are referring to both delta-8 and delta-9 THC. There are also other ingredients that add to the high, such as CBD, CBN, THCV, CBDV, CDC and CBL. Since these are minor components compared to THC they will not be discussed in this book.

When examining a strain in a seed bank catalogue you can check the THC levels of that plant to understand the **potency**. Many seed retailers and breeders measure their plants' THC levels and offer accounts of how much THC their plants have. Of course, breeders may be tempted to embellish the THC levels their plants produce. If you want to know more about the THC level of a specific strain, you should consider consulting the seed bank or breeder for details.

Another interesting fact is that some cannabis plants do not produce any THC at all. These plants have been genetically engineered to produce very low levels of THC and are mainly used by farmers in countries that permit the growth of cannabis for hemp production only. It is best to keep away from these seeds and strains, as they do not produce a high.

The myth that birdseed food contains cannabis seeds is true but birdseed food usually contains the low THC level hemp seed that we are referring to above. It is the author's opinion not to waste your time with these and to buy better genetics instead.

Resin

Some female plants produce resin glands that contain lots of resin but are not considerably potent. Other plants may have little resin but be highly potent. Optimal growth gives rise to a plant that has both a considerable amount of resin and is highly potent. Resin glands are produced all over the female flowers and new leaves, and can be seen clearly with the use of a magnifying aid. These resin glands are called *trichomes.*

Trichomes

Resin can be rubbed off the bud using your fingers and then rolled into the palms to create small balls of hand-rubbed *hashish.* The main concentration of produced cannabinoids and THC exists within these glands. When a plant is in full flowering some of the resin glands may explode or break, drooping resin onto the leaves below, giving these leaves an extra shiny potent look during flowering. Toward the bottom of the plant are the *fan leaves.* These leaves are generally large, outstretched and are used to collect light for plant growth. Because these leaves are far away from the top of the plant and the furthest away from the light, they produce the least amount of resin glands and collect the least amount of burst resin from the tops. They are considered to be not very potent. It is best to consider separating the fan leaves from the rest of the plant after harvesting as these leaves will not provide the best high.

Zero Zero

Cannabis can be cured into various forms. A popular form is hashish.

Some freshly made hashish.

Hashish can also be graded, and one of the most famous grades of hashish is called **Zero Zero.** Hashish making can improve but sometimes degrades the overall potency of marijuana. The grades of hashish are as follows: 00 (Zero Zero), 0, 1, 2, 3. Zero Zero is by far the purest form of hashish and comes from plants that have high levels of THC in conjunction with a good hash-making technique. Sometimes the technique may be good yet the levels of THC in the plant are low. This may produce a hash grade of two or three.

The potency of a plant depends on a number of factors. It should be the goal of every grower to produce a potent, high-grade product. Hash making is discussed in greater detail in Chapter 17.

THE PLANT

When the word cannabis is uttered, the image of the famous leaf shape is immediately recalled. Leaves are in fact the least potent part of the plant next to the stem and the roots. The cannabis plant can be divided into six main sections; they are the bud, stem, branches, *nodes*, leaves and main *cola*.

The next thing to note is that plants have genders. They can be male, female or a mixed gender (*hermaphrodite* condition). There is also a condition of the female plant called *sinsemilla* that growers and breeders alike need to understand.

Male Plant

The male plant contains low levels of THC and does not taste very good, but it can produce a high. Growers only cultivate male plants for pollen so that they can make seeds.

Female Plant

The female plant, when *pollinated*, produces THC but also produces seeds, which prevents larger quantities of bud from growing.

Female flowers growing at various node regions during the early stages of flowering.

Close-up of the female's pistils at the early stages of flowering.

Hermaphrodite Plant

Hermaphrodite plants contain both male and female organs. If the *pollen* is viable, the plant will automatically pollinate itself (selfing), resulting in a crop that can never be sinsemilla. Although most strains have the ability to become hermaphrodites under poor growing conditions, there are some cannabis plants that are genetically hermaphroditic and this disorder can not be reversed—even under optimal growing conditions. Avoid growing these genetically hermaphrodite plants because they do not help the cannabis gene pool.

Sinsemilla Plant

A non-pollinated female (sinsemilla) plant will produce more flowering buds and more quantities of THC than the male plant or a seeded female plant. The buds produce resin, which contains THC and can drop down onto the leaves. When fully mature, it should produce a very pleasing high, depending on the grow method, the strain of plant and time of harvest.

It should be the goal of every cannabis cultivator to grow non-pollinated female plants because these produce the best yield. The goal of a cannabis breeder is to produce quality seeds and plants. How breeders and growers achieve these goals is the subject of this book.

The result of a good indoor harvest, by Kryptonite.

STRAINS AND SPECIES

There are three main species of cannabis: *Sativa, Indica* and *Ruderalis.* Each species carries different characteristics and has its own subset of strains. Each individual strain has its own special identity.

Most strains that you will come across are the result of human intervention. Breeders try to produce strains that are tasty, smell good and give the user different types of highs. Good strains are widely sought after by growers because you can be guaranteed that the seller of the seeds knows a great deal about the plant and its particular history.

Sativa
Height — Tall, averaging between 4 and 15 feet
Nodes — Long *internodes* between branches, 3 to 6 inches
Leaves — Thin, long and pointy leaves with no markings or patterns
Blades — Usually between 6 and 12 blades per leaf

Indica
Height — Small, averaging between 6 inches and 4 feet
Nodes — Short internodes between branches, 3 inches and less
Leaves — Wide, short and rounded leaves with marble-like patterns
Blades — Usually between 3 and 5 blades per leaf

Ruderalis
Height — Small, averaging between 6 inches and 4 feet
Nodes — Very short internodes with much branching
Leaves — Small and thick
Blades — Usually between 4 and 6 blades per leaf

Ruderalis is hardly used today. Sativa and Indica are extremely common and these two species will be the main focus of this book. Indica and Sativa species produce different forms of high. The high of each species can be controlled by the time at which you harvest. In addition, the species can be crossed to produce Indica/Sativa hybrids. This may sound confusing, but it is in fact quite simple and will be further explained in Chapter 15.

A Word About Male Potency
In general, the male plant is considered inferior. This, however, may not be true in all cases. Male plants from some strains can produce more THC or be more potent than females from weaker strains. Most male plants from good genetics are stronger than the Ruderalis female. Males can also be smoked or made into *hash oil*. Simply wait until the plant shows its sex during the flowering stage of the life cycle, described in more detail below, and then clip the top 6 to 12 inches of the male plant away and remove the leaves. Throw away any stems and branches. Cure these leaves and find out for yourself if the male is any good or not. You could be in for a surprise.

THE LIFE CYCLE OF THE MARIJUANA PLANT
The marijuana plant grows in three main stages: *germination, vegetative growth* and *flowering*. There are also three additional sub-stages in the marijuana plant's life cycle. Here we describe the complete life cycle of the cannabis plant in brief.

Germination
Germination is the initial stage of growth and occurs when the seed's *embryo* breaks through the shell, the *testa*, and the seedling produces its first initial root,

the *plumule*. This root fixes itself into the germination *medium* and pushes the newborn seedling up and over the surface. Following surface contact, two embryonic leaves, the *cotyledons*, open outward to receive sunlight, pushing the empty *testa* away from the seedling. It takes anywhere between 12 hours and 3 weeks for seeds to germinate.

Seedling embryo breaking through the outer shell, the *testa*.

Sometimes the shell can be removed by hand if it appears to be obstructing the seedling's growth. In nature the wind helps to shake the seed shell away. Since artificial wind is not initially used in your germination environment some seedlings find it harder to shed their shell although most do not have a problem doing so. Be careful that you do not damage the seedling if you need to remove the shell.

Seedling

After the first pair of embryonic leaves receives light, the plant will begin to produce another small set of new leaves. These leaves are different from the first two and may have some more noticeable marijuana characteristics, such as the three-rounded, finger-shaped points. As the seedling grows, more of these leaves are formed and bush upward along with the stem. Some stems are very weak at this stage and need the support of a small, thin wooden stake tied to the seedling with some fine thread. The seedling stage can last between one and three weeks. At the end of the seedling stage your plant will have between four and eight new leaves while some of the original bottom leaves and cotyledons may have dropped off.

Some seedlings after 2 weeks of growth.

Vegetative Growth

The plant now begins to grow at the rate that its leaves can produce energy. At this stage the plant needs all the light and food it can use. It will continue to grow upward and produce new leaves. It will also develop a thicker stem, thicker branches, develop its maximum finger (blades) numbers on the leaves and will eventually start to show its sex when mature enough to do so. Then it is time for the plant to enter pre-flowering. The vegetative growth stage can last between one and five months.

A cannabis plant in vegetative growth, by GIYO.

Pre-flowering

At this stage, the plant's upward growth slows. Instead of growing taller,* the plant starts to produce more branches and nodes. The plant fills out during this stage and will start to show a calyx where the branches meet the stem (nodes). This calyx is the ultimate indicator that your plant is in the pre-flowering phase of growth and is mature enough to flower. Pre-flowering can last anywhere from one day to two weeks. During this stage, plants start to exhibit signs of their sex and more calyx development takes place at other node points.

Flowering

During this stage the plant continues to fill out. The plant's sex is now clearly evident. The male plant produces little balls that are clustered together like grapes. The female plant produces little white pistils that look like hair coming out of a pod. Each of the plants will continue to fill out and their flowers will continue to grow. It can take between 4 and 16 weeks for the plant to fully develop its flowers depending on the strain. During this time the male's pollen sacks would have burst, spreading pollen to the female flowers.

Female plant flowering.

Seed Production

The female plant will produce seeds at this point if she has received viable pollen from a male plant. The seeds grow within the female bud and can take anywhere between 2 and 16 weeks to grow to full maturity. The female pistils may change color before finally bursting the seedpods, sending them to the soil below. Breeders like to collect seeds before the seedpods burst.

---

*As soon as the plant is flowered it continues to grow rapidly in height again. For Indica the 'vegetative growth to flowering height ratio' is usually around 1:2. Indica plants that are flowered at 2 feet usually finish at 4. For Sativa this ratio can go as high as 1:5. Some Sativa strains that are flowered at 2 feet can sometimes finish at 10 feet. Most breeders work on the 1:2 or 1:3 'vegetative growth to flowering ratio' for their strains.

If, during the flowering stage, there are no males present to pollinate the female plants, the buds will grow larger and develop more resin glands. Resin may drop down on to the leaves making the plant very sticky. The pistils on the buds will begin to thicken and cluster into balls. The reason for the high increase in bud growth is that the female plant is trying her best to attract male pollen. This is the Sinsemilla condition. Toward the last days of flowering, the pistils will change color, indicating that the plant is ready for harvest.

Cycle Times
Given the various stages it can take between 10 and 36 weeks for a plant to grow from a seed to full maturity. The most common grow time is three to four months. All this is dependent upon the strain that you have selected. Pure Sativa can run anywhere into the six to nine month bracket. Indica can flower in six weeks. As you can image, a Sativa/Indica hybrid plant will fall into the two to four month flowering period.

THE DECISION TO GROW
The following issues are important to bear in mind before you decide to grow cannabis:

- What do you hope to achieve—high potency, high yield, one or many plants?
- Which species/strain best meets your needs?
- Are you willing to spend over $100 for 10 seeds?
- Will you grow indoors or outdoors?
- How do the people you live with feel about this?
- Do you have time to take care of your plants?
- Do you have someone you trust to take care of your plants in your absence?
- How secure is your grow area?
- Are people going to walk past your grow site?
- Can you hide the smell when the plants start to flower?
- Do you have the patience to wait a few months before sampling what you produce?
- Are you prepared to spend money on lights and other grow items?
- Are you prepared to pay the costs of a higher electricity bill?
- Are you aware of the risks for the amount you plan to grow?
- Are you sure you really want to do this?

- Can you afford a good attorney if you think there could be legal consequences to your grow?
- Have you any previous convictions which could be used as a legal prejudice against you if you are charged with growing cannabis?
- Do you know what your legal rights are?
- Can gun ownership be used against you if you are caught growing cannabis?
- Can other drug possession in your home be used against you if you are caught growing cannabis?
- Can your children can be taken from you and put into social care if you are caught growing cannabis?
- Is your home safe to grow in?
- Are there any pets around which can damage your crop or start a fire?
- Can you deal with a fire?
- Are you a relaxed tight-lipped person?
- Can you keep it a secret?
- Do you really want to be another dull cash-cropper who wastes their lives just selling cannabis or do you want to be a new wave frontier grower who grows to rid themselves of the connection to the black market in order to enjoy their favorite herb?
- Do you want to grow?

If you are hesitant on any of the points above I suggest you resolve those issues before growing. Reading on should help you answer most of these questions.

Let's Get Growing
You should now have a general idea of what to look for in a plant to produce a good-quality smoke. We are looking for non-pollinated female plants that have flowered, producing lots of buds with resin glands containing high levels and quantities of THC. We are also looking for plants that have been well cured and processed in a way that allows us to sample the full flavor, smell and potency of the plant. Some people prefer plants that provide a high but do not cause drowsiness. Other people like plants that give a down effect and cause the body to become less responsive to stimuli.

Another thing to note is that street cannabis may contain added drugs. In most clinical cases, a person who complains about cannabis addiction and shows physical signs of addiction is not actually addicted to cannabis, but to the other drug substances that the supplier has added to the marijuana to make it stronger. For example, animal tranquilizer is a popular adulterate used to make black market hashish more potent. One hundred percent homegrown, clean cannabis does not contain physically addictive properties. People who add other drugs to cannabis are not doing the cannabis community a favor. This is a good reason to grow your own pot.

Great bushy plant picture by X3n0.

2 | SEEDS

THERE ARE APPROXIMATELY 450 SEED VARIETIES of cannabis on the market today. Out of the 450 seed varieties, 200 are worth considering and out of the 200 about 50 are truly outstanding. Each variety is either a pure species strain (two plants of the same species that have been crossed) or a crossbreed of two species (two plants from different species that have been crossed).*

Cannabis seeds by Kryptonite.

Before we go on, let's clarify what we mean by *hybrid* and *strain*.

A hybrid is the offspring of two different strains. A strain is simply a stock line with common parents. Stable strains have stable genetic traits, which means that the offspring will all be very similar. In fact, most strains are called strains because of their uniformity in growth and reduced variations in the offspring. Hybrids tend to be unstable, or genetically unpredictable, because of their 'new-ness'. A good stabilized hybrid eventually goes on to become a strain.

Out of the 450 seed varieties we said that 200 were good. This leaves 250 that

---

* For more information on breeding cannabis, refer to Chapter 15.

we have disregarded. Those 250 are usually very unstable hybrids. These hybrid plants are so unstable that they cannot be properly classified as either Sativa or Indica species because the variations they exhibit are too wide ranging.

Most unstable hybrids do not find their way into the market and are found only among breeders who are experimenting with plant genetics. Seed producers tend to only produce strains in the following categories:

- Pure Sativa (pure species)
- Sativa (mostly Sativa species with some Indica)
- Pure Indica (pure species)
- Indica (mostly Indica species with some Sativa)
- Indica/Sativa (50/50 cross between an Indica and a Sativa species)
- Ruderalis (pure species)

Ruderalis is a problematic plant. It does not produce large quantities of THC or flower like the other species. Ruderalis is considered substandard by most grow- ers because it flowers according to age, not according to the *photoperiod.* This means that the Ruderalis cannabis plant will flower when it is mature enough to do so and this flowering action of the Ruderalis plant is 'out of the growers hands', so to speak. Ruderalis is grown in countries that experience cold weather conditions — Russia, Eastern Europe and Alaska are places where Ruderalis grows wild. It is an extremely sturdy plant for outdoor growing — however the autoflowering properties of this plant make it hard to control. Trying to *clone* a Ruderalis plant is nearly impossible because it is extremely hard to force the clone to remain in the vegetative growth stage of the plant's cycle. Photoperiod manip- ulation — the way growers control cannabis flowering with Indica and Sativa plants — does not work with Ruderalis plants. Photoperiod, an extremely impor- tant part of cannabis cultivation, is further explained in Chapter 7. The only rea- son to grow Ruderalis is if you must grow outdoors, where the photoperiod is of no concern to you.

Pure Sativa is a total head high. Pure Indica is a total body stone/couch-lock. A 50/50 cross will give a 50 percent head high and a 50 percent body stone. If an Indica plant is crossed slightly with a Sativa plant it will give a 60 percent body stone and a 40 percent head high. A Sativa plant that is crossed slightly with an Indica plant will give a 60 percent head high and a 40 percent body stone. The 60/40 ratio is the most common but breeders can also alter the ratio.

Equipped with this knowledge, you are now ready to choose a plant that fits your needs in terms of height, potency and high. Your choice of seeds will also depend on whether you will grow indoors or outdoors, as well as other characteristics of your grow space. There is no point trying to grow an eight-foot Sativa indoors if you don't have the space and a two-foot Indica plant may not survive outdoors if other plants compete with it for light. As a rule, we can always shorten the plant through *pruning*, but it is impossible to double the plant's height if the plant's genetics only allow two or three feet of growth. Indoor and outdoor grow spaces will be discussed more in later chapters. The rest of this chapter will focus on selecting, acquiring and handling quality seeds.

A small grow room, by Mr. Zog.

SELECTING SEEDS

Now you have an idea of the species and strain of plant you want. The next step is to verify if the seeds are for indoor or outdoor use. There is a saying that all cannabis seeds can be grown indoors and outdoors. This is true, but for the best results, growers should consider what the breeder intended. If the breeder created a plant that does well indoors then it is suggested that you only grow these seeds indoors. If you grow outdoors and the plant does not produce that well, then you know that you should have followed the breeder's advice. Of course, there is nothing stopping you from experimenting, and some growers have produced excellent results this way, but if you are new to growing it is best if you follow the advice you're given.

When selecting a seed, check to see if it is pure or if it has been crossed. Most seed sellers will have this listed along with their seed type. When you look at strains that are crossbreeds you must understand which species the plants lean toward. Along with the cross, you can expect the plant to look different. Some Sativa plants may be shorter because of their Indica genetics and some Indica plants may be taller because of their Sativa genetics. In Chapter 15, we will see that as breeders, we can control the plant's appearance and growth and can influence height and particular features. We can also harvest the plant in a specific way to produce a different high. The later you harvest the plant, the more you'll help produce a couch-lock effect. Harvesting just before peak growth will induce a more cerebral high. If you are working with strains that are for either cerebral or couch-lock highs then you can use harvest time to augment these properties.

Outdoor Sativa. By MullumMadman.   Indoor Sativa. By MullumMadman.

Both of the above pictures, show a mostly Sativa strain: one growing outdoors and the other indoors. As you can see, this would probably be labeled an outdoor strain because of its size. The grower has been able to grow it both ways.

The next thing to look at is the flowering period. Each strain's flowering period can vary. It is toward the last days of flowering that you should begin your harvest. If the seed bank says Skunk#1, flowering time seven to nine weeks, then you should be able to know roughly when your plant will be ready for harvest. In this case it will be seven to nine weeks from the time your plant starts to flower.*

You may also find that a number of similar strains have been produced by different breeders. When you look at the seed bank list you may see as many as four or more listings for the same strain. Take Skunk#1 for example. Skunk#1 is a mostly Sativa plant but there are about seven breeders who have provided a certain seed bank with Skunk#1 seeds. Each breeder tries to develop the best plant possible from that strain, but some breeders are better than others. Make sure that you check with the seed bank and confirm which strains are the best. The reason for choosing the best is that later on you can produce your own seeds from that optimal strain. Welcome to the wonderful world of marijuana growing.

HOW TO GET SEEDS

The best way to get seeds is from another grower who has developed a plant that you enjoyed smoking. This, by far, is the best way because,
(1) you may get the seeds for free and
(2) you know what the high will be like because you have already sampled it.

The next best way is through the Internet. The Internet is full of seed banks that want to sell you seeds, but you may encounter problems. Firstly, some of these seed banks are not legitimate and will rip you off. Secondly, some of these seed banks do not ship worldwide and their products may be unavailable to you. Thirdly, some of these seed banks misrepresent their stock. Finally, seeds can be very expensive. Some seed banks charge anywhere between $80 and $300 for 10 to 16 seeds. There are rip-off artists out there, but there are also seeds that are worth the money because the strain is excellent in both vigor and production. So, how do you choose a seed bank?

Choosing a Seed Bank

After locating a seed bank the first thing you should do is to research what people have to say about that particular seed bank. The best way to find this information is to check one of the more popular sites on the net, like
www.seedbankupdate.com
www.yahooka.com
www.overgrow.com
www.cannabisworld.com

---

* Flowering times commence at the start of the flowering photoperiod (12/12) and not at the start of calyx development (pre-flowering). This is covered in detail in Chapter 7.

www.cannabis.com
www.cannabisculture.com

Some web sites give listings and ratings on seed banks. You can also do a search on the Internet using a search engine, like Google or Yahoo.

Find a good web site that is used by a number of people. A community of growers is a great place to go for message-board forums and to chat.

www.seedbankupdate.com

Greenman's seedbank update is one the most useful seedbank review sites on the internet. It was one of the first review sites ever established and still remains the most popular to this day.

www.cannabisculture.com

www.cannabisculture.com is the home of Cannabis Culture magazine—a Canadian marijuana publication run by Marc Emery. It has lots of information on cannabis news and marijuana growing. It is also home to emery seeds and has an on-line message board system aimed at growers who cultivate the good herb.

www.overgrow.com

www.overgrow.com tend to have the largest attendance of cannabis growers currently found on the Internet. Consider maintaining your anonymity by using an email account or ID that cannot be traced to you. Using a proxy will also help you surf safely on the net. www.overgrow.com has lots of helpful information for growers on proxy services, general web surfing and anonymity.

Also confirm that the web site you are buying from has a registered URL, like a Dot.com site. If they use a free web-site service then consider avoiding it because it could disappear overnight. Once you have found a web site, run a search on seeds and seed banks.

Next, check out the reviews on each seed bank by the public. Then, visit the URL of each seed bank and check out their prices. Make sure that the seed bank has a quick turn-around time. It should only take up to 30 days for delivery. Some seed banks have been known to create back orders that take over two to three months to clear. I have personally witnessed Christmas seed orders arrive in the

---

* Counterfeit goods are seeds released under a breeder's name which are not originally from the breeder but are the result of seeds bred from the breeder's original seeds which where purchased by the counterfeiter who used them to make the fakes. These seeds are less stable and are generally non-uniform in growth when compared original breeder's line. These counterfeit seeds can also be called F2 seeds although F2 does not necessarily mean that the line is counterfeit. Breeder's now practice sealing their original seeds in breeder's packs to help prevent counterfeiting. Consult Chapter 15 for more information on F2 offspring.

following March. This is a problem usually associated with counterfeit* goods. Avoid seed banks that have a large turn-around time gap. You want a snappy service and delivery within 30 days is the norm. Some seed banks have a 1 to 2 day shipping policy as soon are your money has cleared. These seed-banks are generally very popular with most growers.

Some seed banks offer deals on seeds and you will also find that prices fluctuate from bank to bank. Before buying anything, send them an email and inquire about their services, the seeds you like, delivery options, postage, packaging and security arrangements. Wait until you receive a reply. If you do not get a reply then do not use that seed bank. These individuals are salespeople and should communicate with you and answer all of your questions.

Most seed banks sell their seeds in batches of 10 to 20 but anything can happen in transit. A misplaced foot in the postal office can kill the seeds, making them not viable. Quality seed banks should provide good protective packaging.

If your seeds do not arrive in a reasonable amount of time, send an email to the seed bank and ask them what happened. If they do not reply or if your seeds are lost write them a complaint and then post that complaint in one of the web boards mentioned above. If you receive your seeds in good condition then it is always considerate to post a positive review of that seed bank. This will improve your communication with the seed bank the next time you purchase seeds. If you do not have access to the web then you will have to write to the seed banks to request more information. Information about some seed banks is provided in the back of this book.

Always consult the seed bank about your strain — you never know, they may even be able to recommend something better to suit your needs.

STORING SEEDS

You should receive your seeds in a stealth package. You will probably find them inside a clear, heat-sealed and labeled plastic bag. Check your seeds to make sure that none are crushed. If some or all of the seeds are crushed, send them back to be replaced explaining to the seed bank that this particular package was damaged. Do not open the bag if you are sending them back.

If the seeds appear to be in good condition, then the first thing you should do is to remove the seeds from the bag. Make double sure that these seeds do not come in contact with anything damp or wet or they may start to germinate. Once you have removed them from the bag you should place the seeds in a small, clean and very dry film canister. Seal the canister and make sure that you LABEL it. I can not stress how many times I have heard of people storing seeds only to forget what they were and when they were stored when the time came to use them.

The film canister is a short-term solution to seed storage. It will prevent your seeds from coming in contact with light, bacteria, moisture and air — all of which can cause either germination or damage to occur. If you are going to store your seeds for more than a year, you should store them in an airtight container in a freezer.

WWW.SENSISEEDS.COM

Always look for the official Breeder's pack when you receive your seeds from the seed bank.

3 | PROPAGATION AND GERMINATION

WHAT IS PROPAGATION?

Propagation: 1) The action of breeding or multiplying by natural processes: procreation, generation, reproduction. 2) The action of spreading an idea, practice, etc., from place to place. 3) Increase in amount or extent; enlargement; extension in space or time.

Propagation is *The Grow*, however some growers treat propagation only as the events that occur between the planting of the seed and the **transplanting** of the seedling to the main grow environment. We will correctly treat propagation as the entire process of growing from seed to harvest, including the logistics of the grow: in short, propagation represents the events that occur over the entire life cycle of the plant. This Chapter focuses on the first stage, germination, but first we'll discuss propagation logistics. You will hear the term propagation used to describe elements of the grow that may be seen as one-time actions like seed towel propagation, but we ask you to bear in mind that propagation is the continuous growing process.

Propagation Logistics

So, what are you going to do? Are you going to buy a batch of 10 seeds and grow them all in one go? Are you going to then kill the males and just use the females? Are you going to keep the males and produce more seeds from the females? How many seeds can a female plant produce? What can you do to guarantee that all your seeds will grow? This is where propagation logistics come into play. The answers to these questions depend largely on the size of your grow area and your budget.

Let's say you have about $200 to spend on seeds. You can buy an expensive strain, like a G13 cross, grow the G13 and produce more seeds from it. You could get between 100 and 2000 seeds depending on plant size and grow conditions. If you produce lots of seeds this season, you may never need to buy seeds for this strain again.

There is something else you can do to prevent the need to ever buy or grow from seeds again, called *cloning*. Cloning is a technique whereby you grow a number of plants and select a quality female. You then take cuttings from that female plant and grow these cuttings into new plants. Clones always retain the same sex and vigor as the *mother plant*, so it is possible to create a garden of plants through cloning that will last for decades from a single mother plant. Cloning is described in detail in Chapter 11.

Clones in rockwool.

For the new grower it is advised that you buy 10 seeds and only germinate three the first time, followed by another three and then the last four. This will allow you some degree of experimentation as you may fail on your first attempt to germinate the seeds.

For people who have germinated seeds in the past, it is advised that you germinate five followed by another five the next week. Only if you are a long-time grower with a good amount of growing experience should you germinate all the seeds at once. In this way, you can reduce the risk of failing some, or all, of your seeds because of bad germination methods.

During your plants' growth you may decide to pollinate only a few of your females. You will need two grow areas to do this: one for growing all your female plants; and another for growing one or more females mixed in with males. As stated before, this depends on the size of your grow space and your budget. It is important that your pollination room be kept well away from your all-female grow room because pollen can travel by air. Bees and other insects can spread pollen, and so can you. Always wash your hands and face after handling a male plant to prevent pollen from a male plant getting onto a female that you wish to keep for sinsemilla.

HPS lights hang down over this grow room.

So, now you have 10 seeds and your goal is to achieve 100 percent germination results. The following section on germination will help you achieve an optimal success rate.

GERMINATION TECHNIQUES

Seeds can be germinated a number of ways. Some guarantee more success than others. It is recommended that you consider the rockwool SBS (single block system) propagation tray method.

Germination shot, by BushyOlderGrower

Seed Soil Propagation

In this method, seeds are placed in moist soil about 3 mm, or the length of the seed, from the surface. The soil is kept moist (not soaking wet), by sprinkling water over it once a day. This has a moderate success rate: out of 10 seeds you can expect 7 to 8 to germinate.

++ Germination Soil

There are many soils advertised as germination soils.[*] They are basically the same as other soils except that they contain special blends of *micronutrients* and are kept somewhat clean (the soil is sifted and no *compost* is added). Ordinary *loam* soil with a *pH* of 7 and an *NPK*[**] of higher or equal amounts of N than P or K is good for starting seeds. Even ratios of NPK of 5:1:1 or 8:4:4 are good. Just make sure that the N is equal to or higher than each of the P and K factors on the label.

Seed Towel Propagation

Seeds are placed either on a damp towel or on damp cotton balls (cheesecloth may also be used). Cover the seeds with more damp cotton balls or a damp towel.

---

[*] Some germination soils are not suitable for cannabis because they contain higher amounts of P and K than N. Most growers find that an ordinary loam soil is just as good for germination as long as the N values are equal too or higher than the P and K values.
[**] For more information about soil and NPK, refer to Chapters 5 and 6.

If the material dries out it may damage the seeds, so keep it moist at all times. Every day, check to see if the seeds have started to produce roots. If they have, immediately transfer the seedlings to a grow medium, such as soil, using a pair of tweezers. Do not touch the roots as this can kill your seedlings. This method has a moderate-to-high success rate. Out of 10 seeds 8 to 9 may germinate. The problem with this method is that sometimes the transplant can cause the seedling to go into shock. This can terminate the germination process, leaving you with nothing. With practice you can get all your seeds to germinate using this method.

Propagation Kits

Seeds are germinated in small units inside a seed or clone propagator: a tray of sorts, designed to help plants germinate. One such kit is called a rockwool SBS propagation tray.* At the bottom of the tray is a small area where water or germination hormone can be poured. Small grow cubes called rockwool cubes are placed into slots in the tray, which automatically dips the rockwool into the solution. The seeds are placed into tiny holes in the cubes (the holes are filled with rockwool particles to prevent the seeds from being directly exposed to air in the environment) and the cover is replaced. Some propagation kits are even heated and look like miniature greenhouses.

Propagation kit and clones, by Strawdog.

This method has a very high success rate, however a disadvantage is the cost of the tray, rockwool and grow *fertilizers.* You should note that, although some seedling fertilizers contain growth hormones mixed into the nutrients in order to promote plant growth, it is recommended that you not use fertilizers or growth hormones with your seeds unless you have experience. Even the slightest amount of overfeeding can kill your seeds or burn your seedlings. In fact, you are better off just using water in your propagation kit to germinate your seeds. I have yet to find a cannabis strain that needed growth hormones or fertilizer to germinate properly. The price of the tray is about $10, the rockwool cubes $5, the grow fertilizers $5. If you have spent upwards of $50 on good seeds, why not spend the

---

*Propagation kits can also be used with growing mediums other than rockwool.

extra $20 on getting a small kit like this together and increase your chances of achieving a 100 percent success rate? The kits offer the added advantage of serving two purposes: they can also be used to root your clones.

Overhead shot of seedlings germinating in rockwool, by Shecky Greene.

Scuffing Seeds

Most seeds that fail to germinate do so because their shells, the *testa*, are too hard to break open and allow water to seep in. At the end of your germination period you may have found that some seeds have not managed to break open. You can help these seeds to grow by using a method known as scuffing.

Simply get a small box, like a matchbox and line the inside of the box with sandpaper. Place the seeds into the box, close and shake the box for a few minutes. Now that the seeds have been scuffed, their outer shells should break open more easily and they should germinate.

Dangers when Germinating Seeds

During germination and transplantation, your plants are at their most vulnerable. Here are some tips to help you protect your future crop during germination.

Drafts are a killer and can stunt germination. Always make sure you keep your germinating seeds away from any open windows or fans. Also ensure that the room is warm. A cold room can inhibit your germination rates.*

Take care when using germination fertilizers or hormones to ensure that your mixture is correct. Do not use high doses of fertilizers with seedlings. Water is all seedlings really need. You do not need to add anything. Some people use germination solutions, but these solution strengths should be low. An incorrect mixture can burn your seedlings and cause them to fail.

Leave your seeds alone to grow.** You may be tempted to check on your seedlings and could run the risk of disturbing the soil. This is a bad move as too much tampering and shifting of the seeds can break and damage the young roots.

Some strains produce seedlings with weaker stems than others. In these cases, the seedlings may tend to lean to the left or right. If you find that your seedlings need support then use a small stick to brace your seedling. Tie the stem to the stick using a piece of thread. Never tie the thread above a growing shoot or the seedling will push up against the thread and may rip itself. You may continue to use a stick to support your plant as it grows. Never bring a stick from outdoors indoors as some bugs, such as spider mites, can go undetected in their incubation nests inside the wood. If your plant still has a weak stem during vegetative growth it is recommended that you give the base of the stem a gentle shake every morning and evening. This will help the plant to develop a more solid stem. Outdoors the wind shakes a plant and causes it to develop this solid stem. You can simulate the effect of the wind by doing this mildly every morning for two or three seconds. Indoor fans also help and are described in Chapter 6.

Seeds must be viable if they are going to germinate. Never use white seeds. They are immature. Find seeds that have white and gray markings or another color apart from white. Crushed seeds will not germinate. Old seeds may have trouble germinating. Always try to use the best seeds you can find.

---

*Consult Chapter 6 for details on temperature.
**Seeds take up to 3 weeks to germinate. After this time if no seeds have germinated check your seeds and your germination method. Usually seeds germinate together within a few days of one another. If all the seeds fail to germinate and your method was good then report this to the seed bank to see if their batch was faulty. Usually good seed banks keep records of germination rates and failures.

TRANSPLANTING SEEDLINGS

During the stages between germination and vegetative growth the grower may find that plants outgrow their pots. Transplanting to bigger pots should be done as early as possible.

Here is an example. When your seedlings are ready, simply lift them from the propagation tray along with the rockwool cube, and place the cube and seedling into a bigger container full of another grow medium, such as soil or a **hydroponic** setup (more about hydroponics can be found in Chapter 9). There is not much of a problem when transferring a cube and seedling to soil. Just dig a small hole in the soil for the cube and place it in. Then cover the cube with soil. The cube will not affect your plant's growth and will provide additional support as it grows into its larger container.

Even if you have started your seedlings in soil, transferring them to bigger pots need not be a complicated process. The problem you'll encounter is that, in order to move the soil and roots from one pot to another, the plant must be lifted out gently, with the soil in place. The most important objective of any transplant is to keep the roots intact while avoiding as much material spillage as possible. How is this done? There are three basic ways:

The first way is to simply cut away the base of the smaller pot and place it inside the bigger pot of soil. The roots will grow down through the hole in the bottom of the smaller pot and into the larger one.

The second way involves making sure that the soil is very dry. Delay watering your plant for a couple of days and let the soil settle until hard. Then you can use a clean knife to cut around the inside edge of the pot. Cut deep, but not so deeply that you risk damaging the roots. Then push your fingers down into the sides and lift the plant and soil out. Some soil will break away but this shouldn't affect your plant. Quickly place the plant into the larger pot and cover with soil. Give your plant some water so that it will take to the new soil. Although you can lift some plants out of their pots by pulling on the stem, this can cause problems down the line. You should always maintain a firm grip on the soil when transplanting.

If your soil is very compact, you may be able to turn the pot upside down and gently tap the whole medium out as one solid mass. This transplanting method — turning the pot upside down and tapping it out — is a very professional way of transplanting but you should try it out first on a plain pot of dry soil. A bit of practice will pay off in the long run. Simply move your hand to cover as much of the top of the pot as possible. The stem should be resting at the base between your fingers. Lift the pot and plant up with the other hand. Turn the plant upside down and use your free hand to pull the pot away from around the soil. You can also use the remains of an indoor harvest (if the cut stem is still in the soil in the pot) to practice this.

Transplant Shock

During some transplants the cannabis plant may go into shock, even if your transplant was done cleanly and quickly. If your plant is otherwise healthy, it should survive. If the plant hasn't been looked after it may fail quickly. Transplant shock results in delayed or slowed growth and is caused by damage to or a disturbance of the roots. This is why you must always make sure to keep a firm hold of the soil during transplants. Also refrain from feeding plants suffering from transplant shock for one week if you can. The reason for not feeding the plant is because shocked plants can not use fresh nutrients properly. The plant's poor health, coupled with its inability to uptake and use the fresh nutrients, usually results in plant burn, which can be fatal to a shocked plant.

Some growers like to clean down their roots before transplanting. Although this can be done with some plants — cannabis does not like it unless the root mass is small and undemanding. Cleaning cannabis roots is not needed but should you wish to attempt it then it is best to do it between the first and second weeks of vegetative growth. Root size and complexity is very strain dependent. Since cannabis mostly produces a complex root system, it is nearly impossible to avoid some root damage when cleaning the roots and in most cases where root damage has occurred, plant growth will be stunted. If the damage is severe, the plant could die.

There are some transplant feeding products available. One popular brand of growth hormone called *Superthrive* is used extensively by cannabis growers to help the plant through the transplant process and recovery from shock. Superthrive contains the **vitamin B1** better know as the hormone **'thiamine'** — a proven root and growth hormone.

For step-by-step information on THC extraction, please refer to Chapter 17.
For more information about breeding cannabis, refer to Chapter 15.
For more information about soil, pH and NPK, refer to Chapters 5 and 6.

4 | THE GREAT DIVIDE: INDOORS OR OUTDOORS?

WE NOW COME TO THE CORE DIVIDE in growing marijuana. At this stage you should know something about the history of cannabis, how it is smoked, various species, the high, seeds, the life cycle of the plant, propagation, germination and transplanting. With the exception of transplanting, all these things are generally pre-production methods. Now, you are ready to start growing: you're about to take your seedling and put it into your main grow area. This means that for the next three to nine months your plant is going to be located in a certain environment. That environment will be either indoors or outdoors. So let us talk about each environment in brief for a moment and also discuss the important issue of security before moving on to a more detailed description of indoor and outdoor grow spaces, environmental control and basic and advanced growing techniques in the chapters that follow.

GARDENING TOOLS
Here is a list of the basic items used to grow cannabis plants, both indoors and out.

- Light source
- Water source and delivery system
- Nutrients
- Fertilizers
- Soil/medium
- Propagation trays
- Rockwool cubes (Oasis cubes or Jiffy cubes are just as good)
- Pots
- Scissors and/or a sharp knife

- Small shovel or trowel
- Pest control
- Support sticks
- Thread

As we advance to the latter sections of this book we'll see that growers can equip themselves with many more items to help them on their quest for bigger buds. The above list of tools represents the basics.

PLANNING FOR INDOOR GROWING

Next to choosing your strain, lighting is the most important factor that you must consider when growing indoors. The first thing you should know is that indoor lights produce bigger flowers (more bud) than natural light coming in the window (the process of utilizing natural light indoors is often called a window grow). This means you get more THC quantity with artificial lights than you will with natural sunlight indoors. Even in countries that have relatively hot sun for six months of the year it is still hard to produce big buds indoors under natural light. Some people have grown plants under an attic window that's open during the dry days. This will grow you bud but not as much as an artificial lighting system will produce. The other side of the coin is that natural light is free, electricity is not and grow lights can be expensive to buy and run.

When using a window grow try to place your plant near a window that receives the most sunlight throughout the day and the seasons. If you plan on a window grow, remember that you want your plant to get most of its light during flowering. If July is the best month for sunlight then you may consider germinating your seedling back in April or May or even as early as early March. Try to estimate when you'll get the best weather and coordinate this with the flowering times directed by the breeder.

Also remember that people might be able to look up and see your plant if it is growing near the window. People washing your windows can also see in. Also, if you have a Sativa plant it will get big and very conspicuous. Take all these factors into consideration when you are growing your plants with natural sunlight indoors but keep in mind that even low wattage indoor grow lights will improve your yields tenfold to a window grow. Window growing can result in a vain attempt to grow bud and is one of the top reasons why first time cannabis growers discontinue growing cannabis. A window grow by no means reflects the cannabis plants' true potential.

If you are growing indoors then you may have a room or part of a room that you wish to use, such as an attic, closet, basement or spare bathroom. These locations nearly always require artificial light. There are many ways to set up an indoor grow room. We will discuss this later, in Chapter 5.

A window grow that gets plenty of natural light.

A basic indoor grow room with multiple air cooled lights.

OUTDOOR GROWING

Throughout the discussion that follows, we define outdoor growing as growing on your own property and guerrilla farming as growing away from your property, either in public areas or on someone else's property.

Some outdoor Sativa/Indica hybrids can produce more bud on a single plant than several indoor Indica plants.

Your grow patch, whether on your own property or public property, must be pre-treated and tended to regularly. Leaving seeds in the soil and coming back four months later is generally not going to get you good results. Two main things must be done to the patch to begin the grow — weeding and digging.

Planning for Outdoor Growing and Guerrilla Farming

The biggest problem with outdoor growing is keeping your grow area secure and private. Some people will rip off your plants in a second if they see what you have. Others will just create trouble for you. The risks are high and security is vital. I once heard about a small community that lived near a forest and grew their marijuana near a stream. They eventually had to stop growing as their plants where being ripped off by the locals from the town nearby. And the thieves weren't just teenagers either. Adults will do this too. Some rippers are even professionals, using other people's grow as their main supply.

Perhaps the most affordable, low-key and best way to conceal an outdoor garden is to grow your cannabis plants among other plants that will mask the cannabis. If you have the advantage of living out-of-town and have a garden in which this kind of stuff can be constructed, you could also grow plants inside a brick cubicle with sheets of glass on top. This is much like a very small greenhouse without the glass sides and can be camouflaged to look like a small shed. The problem with *enclosed outdoor* grows like this is that light only really gets to the canopy of the plants and very little bud is produced under this canopy. The advantage is that this setup does not look like a greenhouse or anything that is housing plants. If you want to use a greenhouse instead, then it is suggested that you paint the sides of the greenhouse white to prevent anyone from looking in. The white will also help reflect the sunlight that enters in above through the glass around the grow area promoting growth on lower leaves and bud areas.

Whatever method you choose: Hide your crop well. Not everyone can easily spot marijuana, but someone who is trained to watch out for the plant will know it right away for what it is.

Guerrilla Farming

Guerrilla growing is hard work and often prone to rip-offs. By planting in a forest or in someone else's field or property, you are not in any danger of being caught with the plants *on your property.* However, the person's property you plant on is put at risk. Be a nice grower and do not plant on someone else's private property. It is not nice and reflects badly on the cannabis-growing community. Find a public area, such as a forest or a hill slope. Look for an area that is away from the public eye, but will receive plenty of light. There are lots of places for this sort of thing, but you will have to spend time finding the right spot. Finding a good patch is the key to successful guerrilla growing. A patch near a river is ideal because it offers ready access to water and can help your crop survive a short draught.

Outdoor Sativa Guerrilla plant.

Most guerrilla farmers prefer to keep it simple and favor the following method. They start their seedlings in small plastic pots indoors. When the seedlings have developed, and the plants are ready to enter the vegetative growth stage of the life cycle, the grower cuts the bottoms of the pots away and tapes a small piece of cardboard to the bottom of each pot. The plants, in their pots, are then taken to the grow patch where the grower digs holes in the ground, removes the cardboard and places the pots and plants in the earth. Then the holes are filled in with soil. This way the grower has germinated the plants and only needs to worry about secondary factors such as light, security and pests. The roots will find their way out of the bottom of the pots and into the soil below. Don't worry about the roots not finding a way out of the pot. They always do, that's their job.

SECURITY
The Most Important Advice Ever About Growing Cannabis
What I am going to tell you is the most important thing you will ever learn about growing marijuana. It is a simple rule, but can be difficult to actually commit to.

Never Tell A Soul that You Are Growing Cannabis!

If you do this then you greatly reduce the risk of detection, other than someone accidentally stumbling into your grow area. *Never tell anyone anything.* This rule has helped some growers live their whole lives cultivating cannabis without ever having an encounter with the law.

Loose lips cause 99.9 percent of all security-related issues. The remaining 0.1 percent of security breaches are due to poor preparation and growers neglecting to take the time to conceal the area well enough. If you intend to share your crop with friends do it by another means. The only people who should ever know that you grow are the people who live with you and even then, only if it is absolutely necessary.

Security is always an issue whether you are an outdoor or indoor grower. We have learned that to secure your grow area you must prepare yourself for any future eventuality. Pre-production security arrangements are very important. A sudden peak in your electricity bill may attract unwanted attention from certain authorities that look for these things. This may seem odd to you, but it does occur.*

---

* In most countries a high electricity bill is not grounds enough for a search warrant. Electric heaters use just as much, if not more, electricity than grow lights. If your grow is well hidden but the authorities suspect that you grow then all they can do is look through your trash for evidence of a growing operation. If they find anything it can be used to obtain a search warrant. Do not use your trash for getting rid of growing materials. Find another way to dispose of unwanted growing rubbish. Create a compost heap in your garden for most organic waste materials.

It is now common practice in most countries that support cannabis prohibition to set up special task forces to track down growers. The most frequently used technique is tracking purchasing orders. Many agencies keep tabs on grow shops and the items being sold to customers. Tracking requires special court orders, but law enforcement agencies can obtain these with ease. If someone has been identified as buying suspicious grow products, the agency will also try to find out what other items have been bought using the same credit card or other accounts. Many growers have been caught this way. The best way to avoid this trap is to *always pay with cash.**

Seed banks are also sometimes tracked by agencies that watch for incoming mail with certain stamps and envelope headers. Sometimes it isn't the agency that does the tracking but people in the post office. To get around this, most seed banks don't head their mail anymore. If your seed bank does, it is best to keep away from that seed bank in the future.

If you have done the right thing then you should have all your growing tools and kits bought using cash and your seeds purchased from a seed bank that offers good seeds and a safe, secure way of sending you their product. Many seed banks use great stealth to get you your seeds. It is advised that you *never have seeds sent directly to your grow area.*

Indoor Security

When growing indoors try to consider certain short-term security factors, like visits from service people. Some growers have a grow room that can be swept clean in under a minute. They have a closet nearby where they can quickly move their plants if visitors do drop by.

Always keep your security closet near your grow area. It's no good walking around your house with five or more plants in your arms. It's a bad idea to use a bathroom as a backup security area unless you have another one that guests can use.

Another thing you must consider with indoor security is odor. Now Super Skunk and Skunk#1 are very smelly plants, especially during flowering, hence the name Skunk. If you live in an apartment complex there's no way you'll be able to hide the smell unless you have some form of extraction fan or an ozone generator.

In some indoor setups fans can be used to extract unwanted smells away from

---

*Check to see if your country or state has granted law enforcement officials with the legal right to track purchase orders from grow shops. A quick search on the internet will reveal news items about this. In most countries it is illegal for law enforcement officials to trace purchase orders as a means to track down indoor cannabis cultivation operations.

An Activated Carbon Filter is the professional way to stop smells and odors from leaving the grow room.

corridors and high-traffic areas. Air can be pumped through a window or filter to another area where the smell will not be noticed. Not only that, but plants love fresh air and wind, so the fan can do two things at once for you. An ozone generator is a device that helps to get rid of cannabis odor problems and can be purchased from most grow shops.

Fire is another major security issue for growers. Some people growing indoors use second-rate lights and/or fixtures, creating a very real fire hazard. *Never use any lighting kit or fixture that is either damaged or unsuitable for indoor use.* Taking shortcuts with lighting and electricity is a big no-no — you could be risking your home, and everything and everyone in it. I have heard of and met people who have come home only to find the fire department outside just finishing putting out the fire that engulfed part of their house. The same thing happens in every case: The grower approaches and sees a number of police officers looking around the area. The fire officer points to the cause of the fire — a half-melted light fixture with burnt-out sockets. They all know what this is all about because they have seen it all before.

New marijuana growers nearly always make the mistake of creating inferior lighting setups. Needless to say this is because of three factors: either they don't have the right information; they don't have the money to invest in a proper lighting system; or they just want to grow their pot quickly and cheaply. Proper lighting systems are discussed in Chapter 5.

Outdoor Security

As previously stated, the best way to secure your outdoor garden is by using a shelter. You must also remember that some outdoor plants do smell and this can carry over a short distance given the right wind conditions and climate. Most people won't know what the smell is but *some will!* Many growers get around this problem by growing cannabis plants that have very little smell during flowering. Ask about these strains when you contact your seed bank. They should be more than happy to recommend a less smelly strain for you. All cannabis plants smell to some degree, however, during flowering.

The other thing to make sure of is that you can harvest your crop as quickly and as privately as possible. Standing over a small shelter putting cuttings of cannabis into a big black bag is not exactly the most secure way to go about this. Some people go to their garden with black plastic bags and drop the bag over the plant before pulling it up. This way you won't expose your crop to anyone. Some people do their harvesting at night. This is not recommended though as it can draw unwanted attention to you and your setup. A flashlight rummaging around in the darkness is not very stealthy at all. Also during the day you have a clearer view of what is around you. It is much wiser to do your harvesting during the day unless for some reason there is less activity in your area at night.

If you are growing your plants outdoors without shelter and away from the general public then you may want to create a pen for your plants. A pen made from chicken wire will prevent any unwanted predators, such as deer or rodents, from eating your plants. Predators are a big problem for outdoor growers and will be further discussed in Chapter 12.

Guerrilla Growing Security

Tracks left behind from your ventures to and from your grow area are the worst giveaway for any guerrilla farmer. People just love to walk through the woods and say: Oh, look a nice track, I wonder what's down there? Do not create a track when you go to your grow area. Even by visiting the same spot once every two weeks you will leave a trail, which hikers might see and use. Try to access your grow area through several different routes.

As a guerrilla grower you probably don't want to hack through 100 feet of bram-bles to access your grow site. When choosing a spot, look for an area that is nei-ther too dense nor too sparse. Some guerrilla growers have even created small grow baskets that hang from trees away from the public eye. If the baskets are well camouflaged then you can get away with loads.

Hanging baskets are easy to make. You need a three-gallon wire hanging basket, a plastic garbage bag to fit inside the basket and some wire. Simply line the inside of the hanging basket with the garbage bag and lightly perforate the bottom of the bag to allow water to drain through. Fill the basket with soil and transplant your seedling to the basket. You can then suspend this basket high up on the branch of a tree. Hanging baskets need to be used in conjunction with slow release fertilizer types like granular foods. All the plant's nutrients should be stored in the soil throughout the plant's grow. Slow release feeding products do this. A pop-ular brand of slow release food is 'Fish, blood and bone'. Slow release foods are not as controllable as normal feeding products because the nutrient break down in the soil occurs over weeks and months in different quantities, but the foods per-mit the grower to feed the hanging plants less often. Although hanging baskets are a stealthy way to grow they can be hard to access and maintain. Watering is also a consideration that must be taken into account. It is advised that if you try grow-ing cannabis in hanging baskets that you have a little experience with growing cannabis beforehand.

As a guerrilla grower you should always wear gloves when handling your grow and tools. If you have buckets nearby don't leave fingerprints on any of these. Also, you will want to consider having a good excuse for being in your grow area. Imagine that you're walking back from your path with nothing incriminating on you and someone jumps out and asks what you are doing here? Of course, you know that there's a river nearby so you show your fishing rod or your binoculars and bird-spotting book. There are many things you can take with you to make you look like somebody other than a cannabis grower. I have heard cases of grow sites being staked out by people you would definitely not like to meet. Always check the area around your grow site for suspicious-looking people.

The worst security time for any guerrilla grower is during the harvest. This is when you must go from your grow area to your home or another location with your growing rewards. Always do this in the morning, as early as possible. Double-check the area for any suspicious-looking people. Pack your buds and plants into bags (brown paper bags are better or alternatively, use black plastic bags) and then put these into a backpack. Before you approach your vehicle, drop your bag against a bush and cover it up. Walk toward your vehicle and look around again. You may even want to drive for about five minutes and look out for anything suspicious or anyone who might be following. Remember, you can always leave the bag and go to a nearby town (not home — leave that until the situation is well under control again). If things look okay, you can drive back to where you left your bag, pick it up, stow it out of sight (the trunk for example) and drive home carefully.

Some people can get away with guerrilla farming lots of pot. This is commercial growing on a risky scale but still occurs in various parts of the world where cannabis is banned. The growers usually live deep in the forest miles away from the nearest town. They may spend up to seven months on their own, cultivating the crop. Recent grow busts by the police have identified several tons of bud being grown by as few as three people living in a remote region of British Colombia.

There isn't much more to guerrilla growing than this. Most of the elements that you need to complete your outdoor and guerrilla grow site are in the indoor growing chapters of this book. Read through this and it should give you ideas about how to treat your outdoor grow patch.

Guerrilla growing is so popular in some places around the world that it has become competitive and dangerous. Remember that not all growers are nice people. Some of them don't even smoke cannabis and just want to make money. Check your local news media for information relating to seizures of Guerrilla grows and if those arrested were armed. This is huge problem associated with cannabis prohibition.

Ruderalis Indica hybrids from Sensi Seeds.

5 | THE INDOOR GROWING ENVIRONMENT

A successful indoor garden.

THERE ARE MANY WAYS to grow cannabis plants indoors. The two core methods are soil growing and hydroponics. Chapter 9 is dedicated to hydroponics. The next three Chapters deal with soil growing: from basic setups, to controlling the environment, tending your plants throughout the life cycle and advanced techniques. Although these Chapters focus on indoor soil grow, the hints and tips provided can be used to improve plant health and growth in any growing environment.

There are many ways to grow an indoor soil garden ranging from basic setups to advanced setups. The most common indoor basic setups are:
• Soil growing
• Hydroponic growing

The most common advanced indoor setups are:
• SOG growing
• ScrOG growing
• Cabinet growing

Hydroponic growing is covered in Chapter 9. The common advanced indoor setups are discussed in detail in Chapter 8. First we will look at what all indoor growing setups have in common.

LIGHTING

Your choice of lighting is the second most important growing decision you will make next to selecting your strain. Lights come in all shapes and sizes with varying levels of wattage and *lumens*. A full indoor lighting kit should contain the following items: bulb, reflector, *ballast*, timer and electrical inputs/outputs.

Most lighting kits are open, meaning they have no glass cover or hood to shield the bulb. Instead, the bulb is fixed into a socket that is attached to the inside of the reflector and hangs directly underneath the reflector. That socket is in turn connected to the ballast, which can be either internal or external.* If external, there will be a cord leading to the ballast from the bulb's socket. If internal, the ballast will be attached directly to the bulb socket and may even support the reflector. The ballast plugs into a domestic light socket like the ones in your home. Some ballasts have built-in timers.

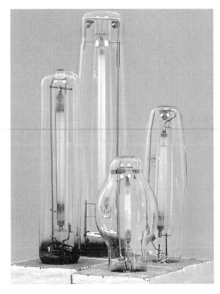

A variety of High-Pressure Sodium (HPS) bulbs.

---

*Professional growers choose lighting kits with an external ballast because it is easier to move the light and keeps temperatures cooler. Internal ballasts make the light heavier and cause extra unwanted heat on your plants. External ballasts are highly recommended.

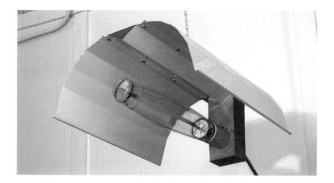

When purchasing a lighting system it is recommended that you look for a complete system and buy an extra bulb. Check to make sure that the lighting system meets safety regulations and has some sort of guarantee or warranty.

An external ballast with a timer.

Color Bands and Plant Growth

When a beam of light is split by means of a prism or diffraction grating, it produces a number of color bands which represent the colors of the rainbow: red, orange, yellow, green, blue, indigo and violet. The bands correspond to the frequencies emitted by the heated light source.

The electromagnetic spectrum is a term used to describe the distribution of electromagnetic radiation by reference to energy. The table below roughly gives wavelengths, frequencies and energies for different regions of the spectrum. You may want to refer back to these later if you are interested in analyzing your bulb's qualities. On the bulb's packaging you should be given data on the bulb's use of the electromagnetic spectrum. Your bulb should mention wavelengths and frequencies somewhere between the 'Infrared', 'Visible' and 'Ultraviolet' regions. Each bulb manufacturer has different specifications with regards to the bulb's abilities to cast artificial light.

SPECTRUM OF ELECTROMAGNETIC RADIATION

Region	Wavelength (Angstroms)	Wavelength (Centimeters)	Frequency (Hz)	Energy (EV)
Radio	109	>10	<3 x 109	<10-5
Microwave	109–106	10–0.01	3 x 109–3 x 1012	10-5–0.01
Infrared	106–7000	0.01–7 x 10-5	3 x 1012–4.3 x 1014	0.01–2
Visible	7000–4000	7 x 10-5–4 x 10-5	4.3 x 1014–7.5 x 1014	2–3
Ultraviolet	4000–10	4 x 10-5–10-7	7.5 x 1014–3 x 1017	3–103
X-rays	10 - 0.1	10-7–10-9	3 x 1017–3 x 1019	103–105
Gamma Rays	0.1	<10–9	>3 x 1019	>105

Light color depends on the light source. It also is a visual indicator that a number of different factors important to plant growth are present in the light. Artificial grow lights are designed to provide an intense and clean white light that meets certain color and temperature requirements so that the bulb can be classified as a 'grow bulb'.

The Correlated Color Temperature (CCT), the thermal temperature, of a light source is usually expressed in degrees Kelvin (K). When certain basic elements that are used in light bulbs are heated, they start to glow. As the elements get hotter, they change color. This occurs within a certain range and peaks when the bulb is fully heated. At this peak the color holds and this is the CCT rating of the bulb. Bulbs that have a CCT rating of 3000 are referred to as 'warm' bulbs. A CCT rating of 4000 is a 'neutral' bulb and a 6000 CCT bulb is a 'cool' bulb. The color of the bulb at CCT is a combination of the many different colors being emitted by the hot elements in the bulb.

Although the CCT gives us an indication of the bulb's color temperature it does not tell us much about how well each of the color bands are represented. For this we need to refer to the lamp's Color Rendering Index (CRI). This is done under laboratory conditions by comparing the bulb's CCT with a darker material at the same CCT. It is generally understood by the growing community that the higher the CRI rating of a bulb, the better the quality of color distribution.

Outside daylight measures around 5500K for most of the daylight hours.

The next table shows the colors you will come across most often when using artificial light sources and the effect that each one has on cannabis plant growth.

IMPACT OF LIGHT COLOR ON PLANT GROWTH		
CCT in Kelvin (K)	Light Color	Effect
5000 to 8000	Deep blue	Encourages excellent leaf and stem growth
4000 to 5000	Light blue	Encourages good leaf and stem growth
4000	Neutral white	Promotes normal growth
3700 to 4000	Warm neutral	Promotes rapid growth
3000 to 3700	Warmer yellow neutral	Highly active photosynthesis for all stages of growth
1500 to 3000	Hot orange or red	Promotes flowering

Plants are green, which means they reflect green light. This is due to fact that cannabis, and most other plants, does not use green light for photosynthesis. This has to do with *chlorophyll*. High intensity discharge (HID) bulbs are designed to cast as much useable light as possible. There are two different types of HID grow lights that we will discuss in a moment. Each type is designed to lean towards casting a warm or a cool type of light. HID grow lights are the most common type of indoor lighting used by cannabis growers.

Basics of Photosynthesis
It is important for us to understand the basics of photosynthesis because it is at the heart of the cannabis plant's energy system. Plants are the only organism with the biological ability to synthesize complex foods for themselves from simple substances.

++ Chlorophyll
Plants naturally produce chlorophyll, which gives them their green color. Chlorophyll is a group of magnesium-containing green pigments that act as an absorber of light energy for specific wavelengths. The plant converts this light energy into chemical energy.

++ The Process of Photosynthesis
Photosynthesis means 'combining with light'. Photosynthesis is a 'reactant - product' process which occurs wherever chlorophyll is found in the plant, which is mostly in the leaves. The symbolic equation for photosynthesis is:

$$6\ CO_2 + 6\ H_2O - \text{sunlight \& chlorophyll} - C_6H_{12}O_6 + 6\ O_2$$

If there is no light then there is no photosynthesis. At night plants cease photosynthesis. If there is not enough nutrients then chlorophyll will not be produced by the plant and photosynthesis will cease. Temperatures are also important for photosynthesis. If the temperatures go out of the normal range for good cannabis plant growth then photosynthesis will slow down or even stop. See Chapter 6 for more on temperatures.

Common Lighting Types
++ Domestic Lights
These are the lights you find in use around your house. They come in all sizes and generally range from between 15 and 150 watts. These lights are unsuitable for growing because of their low light intensity and poor CRI rating. Standard domestic bulbs have a CCT rating of about 2700 K.

++ Fluorescent Tube Lights
These lights are the long, tube-shaped, lights commonly used in industrial and commercial buildings. They come in a variety of lengths and sizes, but 2 to 10 foot-long bulbs are the most common. They also range from between 10 and 300 watts. These lights are okay for growing but they provide a low light intensity and are difficult to set up properly. They are also not in the best light spectrum for the growth of cannabis plants because, like domestic lights, fluorescent tubes have poor CRI ratings.

++ Halogen Lights
Halogen lights are small and often used for flood lighting during the night. These lights can range from anywhere between 75 and 4000 watts. Halogens get extremely hot and this creates a completely unsuitable condition for growing cannabis. They are not recommended because they can be dangerous for indoor growing use. They also have a low CRI rating. Halogens have a CCT rating of about 3000 K.

++ Fluorescent White Tube Lights
Similar to fluorescent lights, fluorescent white tube[*] lights have a higher CRI rating. These lights do not range high above 100 watts and are only recommended as 'cheap to buy and run' grow bulbs. They can, however, be invaluable for rooting clones and starting seeds. Fluorescent white tube lights are usually found in the following wattage levels — 10W, 30W, 60W and 100W. You should aim for 30W and above if you want to induce some form of floral development. Less than 30W lights are only sufficient for rooting cuttings and starting seedlings. Cool white fluorescents have a CCT rating of about 4200 K.

++ Horticultural Lights
Commonly called HID (high intensity discharge) lights, professional horticultural lights are designed to promote indoor plant growth. These lights are available

[*]Fluorescents tend to produce buds that are airy and less dense than buds produced under HID lights.

in kits complete with bulb, reflector, ballast and timer. They also come in different wattage levels, shapes and sizes. If you want to grow good bud, you should use HID lighting. HID lights have three distinct subcategories: metal halide (*MH*), mercury vapor (MV) and high-pressure sodium (HPS).

++ Metal Halide (MH) and Mercury Vapor (MV) Lights

MH lights are HID lights that are used for the seedling and vegetative growth stages of your plant. They can also be used for flowering. They come in all shapes and sizes and range from 75 to 4000 watts. These lights are very commonly used kits and are ideal for the indoor cannabis grower. MH lights mostly lean towards a blue color meaning that the bulb is a 'cool' type. Daylight MH lights have a CCT rating of about 5500 K. Standard clear MH lights have a CCT rating of about 4000 K. 'Warm' MH lights also exist and have a CCT rating of about 3200 K. Opt for the daylight halide, as it provides the best possible type of MH light for cannabis.

MV lights have been almost replaced by MH lights. If you have a choice between the two it is best to opt for the newer MH kits. MV has a tendency to be slightly out of the optimal spectrum range, being too blue.

++ High-Pressure Sodium (HPS) Lights

HPS is the lighting choice of many a cannabis cultivator. HPS lights come in all shapes and sizes and range from 75 to 4000 watts. They are in the perfect spectrum for growing cannabis and come highly recommended, particularly for the flowering stage of the life cycle. HPS lights lean towards a red color meaning that the bulb is a 'warm' type. High-pressure sodium bulbs have a CCT rating of about 2200 K.

Wattage and Lumens

HID lights can range from anywhere between 75 and 4000 watts.[*] In general, the stronger the wattage the more light that bulb will produce. However, we must also consider another factor called *lumens*. Lumens are the correct way of measuring how much light per square foot a bulb emits. Lumens and wattage go hand in hand, but can vary to a large extent between systems. In general, the better the lighting kit, the more lumens it will cast. Lumens have more to do with the design of the light than the wattage of the light itself. Some 600-watt lights may emit the same lumens as a 400-watt light. The sample comparison table below shows the lumens emitted by four different lamps. Of note, the two HPS lamps both use the same wattage, but cast different levels of lumens.

---

[*]In general grow bulbs come in the following wattage amounts - 250W, 400W, 600W and 1K.

SAMPLE COMPARISON TABLE OF WATTAGE AND LUMENS

LAMP TYPE	WATTS	LUMENS
MV	175	8,000
MH	400	55,000*
HPS	600	85,000
HPS	600	55,000*

* The 400-watt MH system and the 600-watt HPS system both cast the same lumens. The 600-watt HPS lamp casting 85,000 lumens is by far the best of the four options for cannabis cultivation.

HID BULB BRAND COMPARISON CHART

BRAND	MAKE	CATEGORY	WATTS	INITIAL LUMENS	PAR WATTS*	CCT
Argosun	Classic	MH	1000	117,000	581	~3K
Hortilux	Super HPS TM EN	HPS	1000	145,000	535	~2K
Sunmaster	Warm Deluxe	MH	1100	133,000	505	~3K
Sunmaster	Warm Deluxe	MH	1000	117,000	470	~3K
Sunmaster	Warm Deluxe	MH	1000	117,000	470	~3K
Sunmaster	Natural Deluxe	MH	1000	117,000	442	~4K
Sunmaster	Warm Deluxe	MH	1000	110,000	441	~3K
Sunmaster	Natural Deluxe	MH	1000	110,000	416	~4K
Sunmaster	Cool Deluxe	MH	1000	80,000	340	~5K
Hortilux	Super HPSTM EN	HPS	430	58,500	220	~2K
Sunmaster	Super HPS Deluxe	HPS	600	85,000	205	~2K
Hortilux	Super HPSTM EN	HPS	400	55,000	205	~2K
Sunmaster	Warm Deluxe	MH	400	40,000	159	~3K
Sunmaster	Natural Deluxe	MH	400	40,000	151	~4K
Sunmaster	Cool Deluxe	MH	400	32,500	138	~5K
Sunmaster	Natural Deluxe	MH	400	36,000	136	~4K
Sunmaster	Super HPS Deluxe	HPS	400	55,000	132	~2K
Sunmaster	Warm Deluxe	MH	250	22,000	87	~3K
Sunmaster	Natural Deluxe	MH	250	23,000	87	~4K
Sunmaster	Warm Deluxe	MH	250	21,500	85	~3K
Sunmaster	Cool Deluxe	MH	250	19,000	81	~5K
Sunmaster	Natural Deluxe	MH	250	21,000	80	~4K
Hortilux	Super HPS Deluxe	HPS	250	32,000	77	~2K

This chart was compiled by a grower called Nietzche.

*Photosynthetically active radiation (PAR).

LAMP EFFICIENCY IN LUMENS

BRAND	MAKE	CATEGORY	WATTS	INITIAL LUMENS	PAR WATTS	CCT
Hortilux	Super HPS TM EN	HPS	1000	145,000	535	~2K
GE	Lucalox® Standard	HPS	1000	140,000		~2.1
Sunmaster	Warm Deluxe	MH	1100	133,000	505	~3K
Philips	Son Standard	HPS	1000	130,000		~1.95K
Philips	Son T	HPS	1000	130,000		~1.95K
Osram Sylvania	Lumalux® Standby	HPS	1000	127,000		~2.1K
Sunmaster	Warm Deluxe	MH	1000	117,000	470	~3K
Sunmaster	Warm Deluxe	MH	1000	117,000	470	~3K
Sunmaster	Natural Deluxe	MH	1000	117,000	442	~4K
ArgoSun	MS	MH	1000	117,000	581	~3.2K
GE	High Output (HO)	MH	1000	115,000		~3.8K
Osram Sylvania	Super Metalarc®	MH	1000	115,000		~4K
Sunmaster	Warm Deluxe	MH	1000	110,000	441	~3K
Sunmaster	Natural Deluxe	MH	1000	110,000	416	~4K
GE	High Output (HO)	MH	1000	110,000		~3.4K
GE	Multi-Vapor® Standard	MH	1000	105,000		~4K
Philips	Son T Plus	HPS	600	90,000		~1.95K
Sunmaster	Super HPS Deluxe	HPS	600	85,000	205	~2K
Sunmaster	Cool Deluxe	MH	1000	80,000	340	~5K
Hortilux	Super HPSTM EN	HPS	430	58,500	220	~2K
Hortilux	Super HPSTM EN	HPS	400	55,000	205	~2K
Sunmaster	Super HPS Deluxe	HPS	400	55,000	132	~2K
Philips	Son T Agro	HPS	400	55,000		~2.05K
Philips	Son T Plus	HPS	400	55,000		~1.95K
Philips	Son Plus	HPS	400	54,000		~1.95K
GE	Lucalox® Standard	HPS	400	51,000		~2.2
Philips	Son Standard	HPS	400	48,000		~1.95K
Philips	Son T	HPS	400	48,000		~1.95K
Osram Sylvania	Lumalux® Standby	HPS	400	47,500		~2.1K
GE	Extra High Output (XHO)	MH	400	44,000		~4K
GE	High Output (HO)	MH	400	41,000		~4K
Osram Sylvania	Compact Super Metalarc®	MH	400	41,000		~3.8K
Sunmaster	Warm Deluxe	MH	400	40,000	159	~3K
Sunmaster	Natural Deluxe	MH	400	40,000	151	~4K
ArgoSun	MS	MH	400	40,000		~3.2K

LAMP EFFICIENCY IN LUMENS (CONTINUED)

BRAND	MAKE	CATEGORY	WATTS	INITIAL LUMENS	PAR WATTS	CCT
Sunmaster	Natural Deluxe	MH	400	36,000	136	~4K
GE	Multi-Vapor® Metal Halide Standard	MH	400	36,000		~4K
Sunmaster	Cool Deluxe	MH	400	32,500	138	~5K
Hortilux	Super HPS Deluxe	HPS	250	32,000	77	~2K
Sunmaster	Natural Deluxe	MH	250	23,000	87	~4K
Sunmaster	Warm Deluxe	MH	250	22,000	87	~3K
Sunmaster	Warm Deluxe	MH	250	21,500	85	~3K
Sunmaster	Natural Deluxe	MH	250	21,000	80	~4K
Sunmaster	Cool Deluxe	MH	250	19,000	81	~5K

This chart was compiled by a grower called Nietzsche.

LAMP EFFICIENCY FOR MH & HPS

BRAND	MAKE	CATEGORY	WATTS	INITIAL LUMENS	PAR WATTS	CCT
Argosun	Classic	MH	1000	117,000	581	~3K
Sunmaster	Warm Deluxe	MH	1100	133,000	505	~3K
Sunmaster	Warm Deluxe	MH	1000	117,000	470	~3K
Sunmaster	Natural Deluxe	MH	1000	117,000	442	~4K
ArgoSun	MS	MH	1000	117,000		~3.2K
GE	High Output (HO)	MH	1000	115,000		~3.8K
Osram Sylvania	Super Metalarc®	MH	1000	115,000		~4K
Sunmaster	Warm Deluxe	MH	1000	110,000	441	~3K
Sunmaster	Natural Deluxe	MH	1000	110,000	416	~4K
GE	High Output (HO)	MH	1000	110,000		~3.4K
GE	Multi-Vapor® Standard	MH	1000	105,000		~4K
Sunmaster	Cool Deluxe	MH	1000	80,000	340	~5K
GE	Extra High Output (XHO)	MH	400	44,000		~4K
GE	High Output (HO)	MH	400	41,000		~4K
Osram Sylvania	Compact Super Metalarc®	MH	400	41,000		~3.8K
Sunmaster	Warm Deluxe	MH	400	40,000	159	~3K
Sunmaster	Natural Deluxe	MH	400	40,000	151	~4K
ArgoSun	MS	MH	400	40,000		~3.2K
Sunmaster	Natural Deluxe	MH	400	36,000	136	~4K

LAMP EFFICIENCY FOR MH & HPS (CONTINUED)

BRAND	MAKE	CATEGORY	WATTS	INITIAL LUMENS	PAR WATTS	CCT
GE	Multi-Vapor® Standard	MH	400	36,000		~4K
Sunmaster	Cool Deluxe	MH	400	32,500	138	~5K
Sunmaster	Natural Deluxe	MH	250	23,000	87	~4K
Sunmaster	Warm Deluxe	MH	250	22,000	87	~3K
Sunmaster	Warm Deluxe	MH	250	21,500	85	~3K
Sunmaster	Natural Deluxe	MH	250	21,000	80	~4K
Sunmaster	Cool Deluxe	MH	250	19,000	81	~5K
Hortilux	Super HPS TM EN	HPS	1000	145,000	535	~2K
GE	Lucalox® Standard	HPS	1000	140,000		~2.1
Philips	Son Standard	HPS	1000	130,000		~1.95K
Philips	Son T	HPS	1000	130,000		~1.95K
Osram Sylvania	Lumalux® Standby	HPS	1000	127,000		~2.1K
Philips	Son T Plus	HPS	600	90,000		~1.95K
Sunmaster	Super HPS Deluxe	HPS	600	85,000	205	~2K
Hortilux	Super HPSTM EN	HPS	430	58,500	220	~2K
Hortilux	Super HPSTM EN	HPS	400	55,000	205	~2K
Sunmaster	Super HPS Deluxe	HPS	400	55,000	132	~2K
Philips	Son T Agro	HPS	400	55,000		~2.05K
Philips	Son T Plus	HPS	400	55,000		~1.95K
Philips	Son Plus	HPS	400	54,000		~1.95K
GE	Lucalox® Standard	HPS	400	51,000		~2.2K
Philips	Son Standard	HPS	400	48,000		~1.95K
Philips	Son T	HPS	400	48,000		~1.95K
Osram Sylvania	Lumalux® Standby	HPS	400	47,500		~2.1K
Hortilux	Super HPS Deluxe	HPS	250	32,000	77	~2K

This chart was compiled by a grower called Nietzche.

Lumens and Marijuana Growing

You are probably wondering: How many lumens do I need? This depends on three things:

1. How much you want to spend
2. How many plants you have
3. The size of your grow area

You never want to use less than 2500 lumens, even for one plant. In general, one light that casts 45,000 lumens is enough to cover a grow space of about 3 feet by 3 feet. This is quite an average space and you'll probably get anything between 1 to 12 Indica plants in that area. Again we must keep in mind the strain that we're growing. One large Sativa plant can cover a nine square foot grow area in no time. Short Indica plants are different. If you really want to pump up your plants, then you could consider a lamp that casts 100,000 lumens or more. If you have a big grow area then you might consider two lamps that cast 100,000 lumens each. It's all relative to how much you want to grow and the size of your grow room.

Let's say that you would like to grow four Indica/Sativa hybrid plants. What you should aim for is a light that casts 45,000 lumens. This means you should buy a 600-watt HID system. If you want to pump up your available light to around 60,000 lumens, you should buy a 1000-watt HID system. If your area is bigger still, you might need two or more 1000-watt HID lights to achieve this.

++ The General Illumination Formula

You need roughly 50 watts of HPS or MH light per square foot of your grow area. The simple formula looks like this:

    250W HID = 2′ x 2′ area
    400W HID = 3′ x 3′ area
    600W HID = 3.5′ x 3.5′ area
    1kW HID = 4′ x 4′ area

This simple watts-per-square-foot calculation assumes that each square foot of space receives the same lumens but in reality bulbs do not cast lumens equally to all areas of the space. We need to include depth in our calculation. As light travels away from its source, its intensity diminishes by a factor of one quarter each time the distance traveled doubles.

There's nothing wrong with using a 1000-watt HID light on a few plants or even one plant — they will grow bigger and better for it — but you need to make sure that you choose genetics that can use all the available light. Lighting overkill occurs when a single strong HID light is used to grow a genetically poor yielding plant. You will find that a single 400-watt HID may have been more than enough to grow the plant to optimal maturity. Most strains available from reputable breeders are high-yielding plants, which is why growers can sometimes use a single 1000-watt light and pull sometimes two pounds or more of bud from the one plant.

The other issue is cost. Do you really want to spend all that money on lighting and electricity? HID lights range in price from anywhere between $220 and $700 for a full kit. A 600-watt HPS kit should cost about $250: money well spent if you want great plants with big buds.

Over time you will understand more about grow rooms and how to light them properly. With experience you should be able to tell intuitively which light suits your needs. As a general rule, when in doubt buy a 400-watt HPS or better. Even a 250-watt HPS can get you good-size buds, but going below that mark will yield you less than average results. Most growers use a 600-watt HPS for better results. 1000-watt lights provide the best yields indoors but consume more electricity.

What to Look for When Buying a Lighting Kit

What type(s) of HID/horticultural light will you use? Some growers will use a MH setup for seedlings and vegetative growth and a HPS setup for flowering. If you can only afford one setup, we recommend HPS lighting since it is best for flowering — the stage when cannabis produces the all-important bud.
Is the light kit certified; does it come with a warranty? For obvious reasons.
Is the light kit air-cooled?*

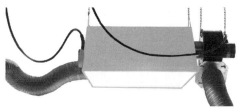

An air cooled light fixture.

---

*Air-cooled kits have openings in the reflector to allow for hot air extraction. Some of them even come with a built-in extractor fan.

Water-cooled light system — these inventions have been around for a while but have not caught on because they require a bit of work to maintain. A constant pump of cool water must be circulated into and out of the light system.

Good lights should be air-cooled. Some may even have built-in fans. Lights that are air-cooled tend to last longer and do not heat up your grow area as much. If your light is not air-cooled then you will have to include an air vent and fan in your grow room to keep the temperatures under control.

Remember that your plants can burn if placed too close to your lights. How will the system be supported? Will you use a light stand or suspend your lighting from the ceiling?

Do the electrical fittings suit your needs? Will they plug straight into your system or will you need an adapter or an extension cord? What wattage and lumens can you use with the kit?

Most HID kits can only accommodate a specific wattage of bulb and a certain type of bulb. If you have a 600-watt HPS system, then you should only use 600-watt HPS bulbs. Some lighting kits include a switchable ballast. This means that you can use both MH and HPS lights with the system.

Also, there is such a thing as too much power. A 4000-watt HID is overkill for any small grow room. A 1000-watt bulb is the maximum wattage you should purchase for a small space. Use several 1000-watt bulbs if you need more light. A 4000-watt bulb can bleach cannabis and is very hot.

How to Get the Most from Your Lighting System

Reflectors do exactly what their name implies — they reflect light. Growers use reflectors to ensure maximum lumens coverage over their plants. Basically, when light bounces off a reflector it is directed towards your plants, which absorb most of this light. Reflectors should be either white or made of polished metal. Some reflectors have a green plastic film covering the insides. Remove this, if possible.

Some grow guides mention Aluminum foil as a useful material to aid grow room reflection. Some have even mentioned using it to cover up anything that isn't reflective like electrical cords, sockets, reflectors and pots. Aluminum foil is actually a very poor reflector, highly heat conductive and very dangerous to use in a grow room. Aluminum foil only has 30 to 60 percent reflectivity at best, raises the temperature of the item it is used on (the reflector, pot lid, electrical cord, wall etc.), and can burn easily. Avoid using aluminum foil. It is also hard to keep clean and tears easily. Growers who line the walls with Aluminum foil will eventually find the place falling down around them. If you have no option but to use aluminum foil then it is suggested that you use the dull side rather than the shiny side. In the meantime, make sure that you place an order for a cheap can of flat white paint that will give you almost 99 percent reflectivity for a couple of years.

White-colored material is best for reflecting light: not shiny, glossy white, just plain matte white. A white wall will reflect more light than a mirror or foil. Many growers paint the walls of their grow space white. Others line their grow areas with Mylar: a substance that looks like a thick tinfoil sheet. Mylar is, in fact, very popular in cannabis grow rooms. Most DIY (do-it-yourself) and hardware stores sell Mylar in sheets.

It is also recommended that you keep a spare bulb on hand at all times in case the other bulb dies.* It's no good going to the local hardware store only to find that they are out of the bulb you need. You risk leaving your plants without light for a long time.

It is also wise to remember that plants need water and lights use electricity. When mixed, these factors can be extremely dangerous. Be safe and wise and keep your plants and any liquids away from all electrical outlets.

Nice Indica/Sativa Plant from Bushy Older Grower.

---

*Most grow bulbs have a lifespan of approximately 2 to 4 grows. This depends heavily on the bulb type and how long the bulbs are left on for. After the 3rd grow the bulb's quality tends to reduce overall.

Adjusting Your Lights

If you have a good stand or light support, you should be able to lower or raise your light to accommodate your plants at various stages of the life cycle. You should note that the closer your lighting is to the plants, the more light they will receive. However, get too close and you risk burning your leaves. To see if you are too close, try this simple, common sense test: if you can hold your hand under the light and not feel discomfort, then your plants should do okay. If you feel discomfort, so too will your plants. Use common sense and adjust your lights accordingly.

Your light should not be to close to the plant, as it is very hot and can burn the top of the plant

Some cannabis plants can grow as much as an inch a day. Pure Sativa varieties in particular can triple in height between the start and end of flowering. A four-foot Sativa bush can suddenly turn into a twelve-foot monster in a few months. You need to monitor growth carefully to ensure that your plant doesn't get too close to the light. If your plants do suffer a burn, use clippers to remove the burnt areas and either adjust your lights or cut back your plants to maintain a safe, healthy distance. Tying your plants back may be another option if you have out-grown your space and don't want to clip the plants because of flowering.

Your plants need all the light they can get during the vegetative growth stage. Leave your lights on 24 hours a day and enjoy watching your plants as they grow. During the flowering stage you will shift to the 12/12 light cycle, which is dis-cussed in detail in Chapter 7.

++ 24/0 and 18/6 - The Vegetative Photoperiod
Cannabis is a light demanding plant. Professional growers keep the light on their plants using the 24/0 photoperiod for this reason. Plants that grow under 24/0 flourish and do not need a quantity of darkness in order to rest and perform pho-tosynthesis properly. Plants that are grown in optimal conditions under the 24/0 light regime grow vigorously and the benefits of a 24/0 photoperiod can be seen actively in the results. More nodes are formed, more branches are created, leaf numbers increase, the plant is growing at its finest.

Some growers opt to use 18/6 as their photoperiod. This is an 18 hours of light, six hours of darkness light regime. Under these conditions the plant will grow quite naturally but not as vigorously as the 24/0 photoperiod.

The 18/6 photoperiod expels 3/4 the amount of light that a 24/0 photoperiod does. Although this does not mean that a plant produces 1/4 less leaves, branch-es and nodes under the 18/6 photoperiod, it certainly does show the correlation between light and cannabis growth. As we have said already, cannabis is a light demanding plant. There are no problems associated with 24/0 and although some have attributed cannabis sexual dysfunction (the hermaphrodite condition) to the 18/6 photoperiod these problems are actually the result of heat stress.

A 24/0 photoperiod requires that your grow room temperature be kept well mon-itored. The 18/6 option is cheaper to run. You use a quarter less electricity and this will have an impact on your electricity bill. Also the 18/6 photoperiod will generally extend the bulb's lifespan. During the 6 hours of darkness the grow room is allowed to cool down for this period but a well maintained good grow room setup should not require a cooling down period.

24/0 and 18/6 both share the same problem though. Once you start the photoperiod you should keep it that way especially when the plants near maturity— the pre-flowering phase. An irregular photoperiod can cause more males than females to develop. It can also cause sexual dysfunction to appear.* Whether you choose 24/0 or 18/6 as your vegetative photoperiod try to keep that photoperiod until your plants are mature enough to express their sex.

Electrical Costs

Everyone who starts out using indoor grow bulbs will probably ask how much they cost to run. The answer to this is — *it depends on how much your electrical supply company charge per watt or unit of electricity used.* There are also times in the day when electricity is cheaper or more expensive to use. In general, one unit of electricity is measured at about 1000-watts per hour. 1000-watts per hour usually works out at about 10 cents but can be cheaper or more expensive than this. Check your electricity bill for the correct price per unit. So in our example:

1kW x 24 hours = 1kW x 0.10 x 24 = $2.40 per day = $16.00 per week or $67.20 per month

A four month 1000-watt grow could cost up to $268.00. Average growers using the right genetics yield about 20 ounces from a 1kW single bulb. Experienced growers can go as high as 40 per 1kW bulb. Even though the cost of electricity may seem high, the end results easily justify the cost.

SOIL

Soil comes in many types and varieties. As you gain growing experience you will learn to add various ingredients to your soil in order to improve plant growth. The cannabis plant will grow long, winding roots into the soil. These roots absorb water and other minerals from the soil to promote plant growth. The soil also goes through dry periods when you don't water your plant or when the plant has absorbed most of the water. During these dry periods air is allowed to creep between the soil particles, allowing the roots to breathe.

Please note that you should NEVER bring natural outdoor soil into an indoor

---

*Although some growers can manipulate the photoperiod without sexual dysfunctions emerging it is not worth the risk. Once a dysfunction appears it can not be reversed. Sexual dysfunctions are covered in Chapter 7.

grow space. This is because the soil will contain bugs and pests that could compromise your grow. Always buy your soil from a gardening shop. Soil should be
the cheapest part of your grow.

There are three main factors to consider when selecting the right soil: pH, nutrients and composition.

pH

pH measures the levels of *acidity* and *alkalinity* in the soil. The pH scale runs from
1 to 14, with 7 being neutral, 0 very acidic and 14 very alkaline. Cannabis plants
like a neutral pH of 7. When choosing your soil you should be looking to achieve
a pH of 7, (it should be clearly marked on the bag). Going above or below this
mark can create problems for your plant during growth. Small pH meters can be
also bought in most gardening shops and used to measure and monitor the overall pH of your soil.

Nutrients

The three major plant nutrients, or *macronutrients*, found in soil are nitrogen,
phosphorous and potassium: NPK, for short. NPK can come in two forms —
either pre-mixed into the soil or as a stand-alone fertilizer (usually in a bottle).
The percentage of each nutrient should be clearly labeled on the packaging, in the
following manner: 20:20:20. This indicates 20 percent N, 20 percent P and 20
percent K. The remaining 40 percent are other elements that make up the soil. This
ratio can vary among different nutrient and soil brands so you need to understand
which nutrients cannabis requires, and in what amounts, during the various stages
of the life cycle.

Cannabis plants like high levels of N and moderate level of P and K during vegetative growth. You should select a soil that that has all three. When choosing a
chemical fertilizer you need a mixture with high N, and P and K levels that are
equal to or lower than N. Any of the following combinations would be suitable:
12:12:12, 20:20:20, 12:6:6, or 18:4:5. The 12:12:12 and 20:20:20 are best.

During flowering, cannabis needs a higher level of P so you should choose your
soil and/or fertilizers accordingly. Since the plants are usually not transplanted
between vegetative growth and flowering, you must plan to adjust the pH levels
for flowering.*

---

*Adjustments are made in the flowering phase of a plant's life by adding different nutrients to your medium.

THE CANNABIS GROW ROOM ++ KEY

(1) Trays. Easy to move in and out. Can hold water. Prevents spills.
(2) 12 female cannabis plants in pots in soil. Mostly Indica variety. Nearing end of vegetative growth.
(3) Thermometer. Can be moved according to plant height.
(4) Climate control Sensor. Attached to climate controller.
(5) Adjustable chains for suspending lights.
(6) Air-cooled HID light.

(7) Adjustable ducting pipes. Can move with light height.
(8) Junction box for ducting.
(9) Activated Carbon Filter. Suspended. Also contains main extraction fan.
(10) Window. Boarded up.
(11) CO_2 regulator. Pipe goes all the way to the back of the plants. Can be connected to climate controller (19).
(12) CO_2 tank.
(13) Oscillating fan.

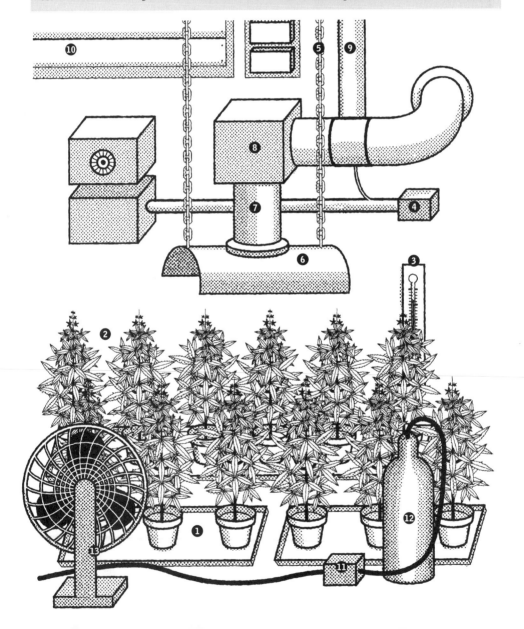

Composition

Ideally, your soil will have a balanced consistency: not too moist, not too dry. This will allow the roots to absorb the required amounts of both water and oxygen. The packaging should indicate whether the soil is wet or dry, and you should aim for a balance between the two. Wet soil will sometimes cause plant damage by blocking off airflow to the roots. Dry soil may dry out too quickly, starving your roots of moisture. Try to find a soil that is loose and feels fine but slightly heavy in your hands. Do not buy anything that is hard and bulky or soft and weightless. Aim for the middle ground: a balanced composition using a mix of the soil types below.

COMMON SOIL TYPES

There are many types of soil mediums available and we will briefly describe the more common types. Marijuana can be grown in most of these soil types. We have indicated where potential problems could occur.

Clay

Clay is a stiff, tenacious fine-grained earth consisting of hydrated aluminosilicates that become flexible when water is added. Marijuana roots don't really like clay. Clay can rarely be used on its own to grow cannabis. It is commonly mixed with other soil types to create a medium suitable for cannabis growth.

Humus

Humus is the *organic* constituent of soil, formed by the decomposition of plant materials, and can be bought in bags at local gardening stores. Most of these products claim to be free of bugs and other living matter, but sometimes this is not 100 percent true. Don't be surprised if you find a worm or green fly in the package. Humus is also sometimes known as compost, but compost is the final mixture of manure (which is of organic origin), loam soil and some other mediums, with added organic matter. Humus is that added organic matter.

Sand and Silts

Sand soils can be pure sand or a mixture of sand and soil. The problem with sandy soil is that it drains water and minerals out too quickly. It is a very dry soil and is not suitable for the cannabis grower's needs.

Silt soils are nearly the same as sand soils, except they have a consistency more like clay and are darker in color. Silts hold nutrients well but do not hold water very well. Like sands they are prone to quick drainage. Sands and silts are rarely used on their own to grow cannabis and are mostly mixed with other soil types.

Loam

Loam tends to be a mix of all of the above. The composition of the mix should be stated on the bag. In fact, in most cases, normal soil purchased in shops has humus, sand, silt and clay already mixed in. When you buy a bag of soil it is nearly always going to be a loam. Loam is a very fertile soil composed chiefly of clay, sand and humus, and is highly recommended for your grow.

Perlite and Vermiculite

One type of artificial medium on the market is called *perlite*. It's a good medium but doesn't come with any nutrients and generally needs to be mixed with another soil type. *vermiculite* is another product that should be treated the same way. Perlite and vermiculite are also called 'inert' soils because they do not contain any nutrients. In fact vermiculite is processed mica — a naturally occurring mineral. Mix them well with soil if it's your first time using them. Begin with one part *substrates* for every four parts of soil. With a bit of experience you should be able to control the mixture ratios, as high as a 1:1 ratio. Pure vermiculite mixtures or pure perlite mixtures do not retain moisture very well and thus can only really be used in pure format as a substrate support for hydroponic systems, which we will explain in a Chapter 9.

Moss

Sphagnum and peat moss are the two most common moss type substrates that you will come across on the market. This moss is gathered in bogs and dried out into green, gray, brown and black masses. It is then compressed into blocks and is used as a substrate by gardeners for its ability to absorb and retain nutrients. Moss tends to break down very quickly after successive watering though, and this may require you to add more moss to your mix before the end of harvest.

MIXING SOILS AND SOIL RATIOS

There is no perfect soil mix for cannabis plants. This is because all strains are different. Some cannabis strains prefer lots of nutrients. Others do not because they burn easily. Obviously a less nutrient holding soil mixture is preferable for the plants that burn easily. Here is a list of loam soil mixes to suit different plant needs.

Strains that require high levels of nutrients:
1. NPK loam soil (20:20:20)
2. Moss
3. pH up

Mix the soil and moss at a 3:1 ratio. Add pH to balance soil to 7. The high NPK ratio of the loam and added moss makes this a strong nutrient-retaining soil mixture.

Strains that require normal levels of nutrients:
1. NPK loam soil (10:10:10)
2. Perlite or vermiculite

Mix the soil and perlite/vermiculite at a 4:1 ratio. The average NPK ratio of the loam and added perlite makes this a good nutrient-retaining soil mixture.

Strains that do not require high levels of nutrients:
1. NPK loam soil (5:5:5)
2. Sand
3. Perlite or vermiculite

Mix the soil, sand and perlite/vermiculite at a 1:1:1 ratio. This soil mix does not hold minerals or water very well. This is good for a plant that does not need lots of nutrients, however light mixtures like this do require more frequent watering.

All soil mixtures can be changed to suit your plants' needs. In this section, we have looked at soils without focusing much on nutrient ratios or how the nutrients themselves work. Even though the above soil mixtures contain nutrients, they should never be counted on to feed your plants throughout the life cycle. To maintain the nutrient balance over time you must add nutrients to our mix. We will look at this in detail in Chapter 6.

Understanding the NPK Ratio

It is important to understand the NPK ratio that appears on soil packs, fertilizer packs and nutrient bottles. Consider a soil mixture like the following:
1. NPK loam soil (20:10:10)
2. Vermiculite

You would mix 4 parts loam to 1 part vermiculite to create a medium for a plant that needs just above normal amounts of nutrients. Instead of using a balanced 10:10:10 we have gone for the 20:10:10 because we need that little bit more nitrogen. 20:10:10 simply stands for 20 percent N, 10 percent P and 10 percent K. If we add them we get 20+10+10, or 40 percent nutrients. The remaining 60 percent is made up of soil particles, or in bottle foods, water unless otherwise stated on the packaging.

POTS

Pots come in all shapes and sizes. Marijuana plants are best kept in large pots (1.5 to 3-gallon pots) because cannabis grows long roots. You are better off buying a pot that has perforations (holes) at the bottom. Perforated pots should rest in small dishes (you should be able to buy these at the same time you purchase your pots). When you water your plants some of the water may drain down through the soil and come out through the perforations into the dishes. The dishes should be emptied to avoid water spills if you add too much water. Keep in mind that water on the floor can also be an electrical hazard.

Instead of using dishes you could use trays. Trays are more professional, can hold reserve water that is later soaked up by the roots, but are a lot harder to empty if you do have a spill. Although perforations do help to prevent overwatering, you should note that water does leech down some of the nutrients added to your soil. Overwatering can cost you time, wasted nutrients, and can even kill your plants.

More advanced growers use pots that don't contain perforations. This is because experienced growers don't overwater or overfeed their plants.

Before you bring a pot into your grow space, make sure you clean it thoroughly to get rid of any unwanted chemicals or dust that may have gathered in the shop or factory. Pots are very cheap to buy. Use only one pot per plant so that if there is a problem with the soil, watering or nutrients, only one plant will feel the effects.

Wide pots permit wider plant growth. This is because the roots are allowed to stretch out further, offering the plant more support for side growth. This plant has also been pruned to allow for the overall 'bushy' plant effect to flourish.

This is a method known as double potting, which helps create a thicker stem. During vegetative growth, the bottom of the top pot is cut away and is placed on top of a fresh pot of soil. Fresh soil is then packed around the edges to hold the pot in place. The roots grow down into the bottom pot. Look at the size of the cola in this picture by GIYO!

At this stage, you have the best soil you can get your hands on. You take a seedling, make the transplant and fill in the empty areas of the new pot with more soil. Pat down the top of the soil lightly and apply a stake if support is needed. Add a small amount of water to your pot and place the pot and plant under the light. You'll leave the light on for 24/0 or 18/6 hours a day and watch as your plants grow over the coming weeks.

Seedlings finishing their seedling stage and going into vegetative growth, by Vic High

By now, you should know how to set up your grow area and make your security arrangements. You will have your lighting kit set up to hang down over your grow area. You will also have some form of light reflection around your plants to help conserve and direct light. You will have obtained seeds, germinated them on a tray, and started preparing to transplant them into larger pots. The larger pots will house the plants throughout the rest of the life cycle, during which time you will provide the best medium possible in which your plants will grow. In the next chapter we will explore how to fine tune aspects of the indoor environment to maximize your yield and get the most from your plants.

6 | INDOOR ENVIRONMENTAL CONTROL

BY NOW YOU HAVE THE KNOWLEDGE YOU NEED to set up the basic environment for your indoor plant. As the grower, you have total control over that environment and you need to make sure it meets all of your plant's needs. This chapter deals with controlling four important environmental factors for plant growth: nutrients, soil, water and air. The most important environmental factor, lighting, was covered in detail in Chapter 5. With the right amount of care in all five areas, your plants with thrive.

NUTRIENT CONTROL

Remember nitrogen, phosphorus and potassium (NPK)? These macronutrients are the primary ingredients needed in soil to ensure a healthy marijuana crop. In addition, the secondary supplements Ca (calcium); Mg (magnesium); and S (sulfur), or CaMgS for short can be used to promote plant growth and health, and are also part of the macronutrient group. Secondary supplements are generally found in soil, but not always in sufficient amounts. There are eight additional plant micronutrients: iron (Fe), Boron (b), chlorine (CI), manganese (Mn), copper (Cu), zinc (Zn), cobalt (Co) and molybdenum (Mo). These eight micronutrients are less important for good plant health, than are NPK and CaMgS. Check your soil bag to see if it contains micronutrients.

The nutrients and nutrient levels in your soil can be monitored using either electronic or manual nutrient testers. Most growers however do not have the luxury of such expensive items and have to control everything by hand, using judgement. Don't despair! Growers the world over have successfully tended to plants long before the invention of electronic readers. The key to nutrient control is to plan your feeding in advance of growing your plant. This way, everything else you feed to your plants is simply a supplement to the plan. You can always adjust your plan for future grows of the same strain based on what you learn the first time around. Remember though that each strain is different and will probably require changes to the following basic routine.

1. For seedlings, use a soil with an even NPK ratio, such as 10:10:10 or 5:5:5. No nutrients should be added, but if you do find that need to, add them in very small doses (no more than 1/8th of the strength of what it says on the bottle).
2. After germination do not feed for three weeks, unless seedlings show signs of yellowing. In either case, feed them a dose of NPK with an even ratio (10:10:10) or a higher N than P and K ratio (20:10:10) at 1/4 of what is recommended on the label for the first week and continue this once a week until calyx (pre-flowers) show on the plant.
3. If your plant shows any yellowing, increase the feeding strengths until yellowing stops. Increase in small steps from 25 to 33 percent before trying 50 percent or higher. If plant health does not improve, consult chapter 13 on problem solving a nutrient deficiency.
4. In the second week of growth you should be adding secondary nutrients to your plants. Mix secondary nutrients at 1/4 strength of what it says on the bottle. Continue adding secondary nutrients once every other week.
5. Once every 2nd week add micronutrients at 1/4 strength of what it says on the bottle.
6. As soon as calyx development shows, switch to a food with a higher P than N and K ratio (10:20:10). Continue to feed your plants as usual, exchanging the older vegetative food for this new flowering food.

Remember that cannabis burns easily and does not need full strength nutrients. It is better to increase the frequency of your feeding rather than the strength of your foods if you discover that your plant needs more food. This may be more time consuming, but it reduces the risk of plant burn immensely.

Some plants require more foods in higher doses than others do. The frequency of your feeding and food strengths will vary from strain to strain; however the basic elements of these foods and their composition will not. Your plants need NPK as the basic building blocks of their diet. You need to know how to select for these in soil and you need to know how to keep them in your soil type. Some soils also diminish in nutrients more quickly than others do because of the soil's composition and its nutrient- and water-retaining qualities. Whenever you select a soil type for cannabis try to find one that has an even NPK balance like a 10:10:10. It is easier to maintain this balance if you use a balanced NPK vegetative growth feed. If your soil is higher in P or K then it is hard to balance it using other foods.

FOR EXAMPLE:
A soil type of 10:20:10 needs to be balanced back to 10:10:10 or else the high levels of P will cause the plant problems accessing the other N and K nutrients that it also needs for vegetative growth (also a condition known as 'Nutrient Lockout'). In order to balance it back you need to wait until the next time you feed and only add 10:0:10 to the soil. This is because you would expect the remaining nutrients in the soil to be already high in levels of P. The hard part is *finding* a bottle of nutrients that have 10:0:10 on the label. So in order to avoid this problem we select a balanced soil in the first place.

Growers mainly have four types of nutrients at their disposal: vegetative primary nutrients, flowering primary nutrients, secondary nutrients and micronutrients. The list below contains classic examples of food types that you may find or work with.

1. N10:P10:K10 – This is an example of a balanced **vegetative primary** nutrient pack.
2. N10:P20:K10 – This is an example of a **flowering primary** nutrient pack.
3. N0:P20:K10 – This is an example of a flowering food without N.
4. N10:P0:K10 – This is an example of a vegetative food without P.
5. N10:P20:K20 – This is an example of a flowering food that is not suitable for cannabis because of its equal P and K values but lower N values.
6. a1:Mg1:S1 – This is an example of a balanced secondary food.
7. Ca2:Mg3:S4 – This is an example of a **secondary** food.
8. N10:P10:K10:Ca1:Mg1:S1 – This is an example of bottle of food that contains both primary and **secondary** nutrients.
9. N10:P0:K0 – This is a pure N supplement.
10. N0:P10:K0 – This is a pure P supplement.

Micronutrients are sometimes listed in ratios like NPK values but it is more common to just find micronutrients measurements. One good brand of micronutrient that is used by nearly every grower is called Formulex®.

Growers ensure that at least some secondary nutrients are added to the soil mix or in with feeding routine because some secondary problems are hard to find. Ca problems are awkward to detect because a Ca deficiency only stunts growth and does not appear to display anything else usually associated with a nutrient disorders like: leaf discoloring, *rusting, blotching,* leaf curling or any other chlorotic condition that one would expect. To solve problems like this, growers always try to prevent instead of cure. Ensure that your soil or feeding routine has some sort of secondary nutrient plan incorporated into them.

Professional growers get their supplements in separate packs of N, P and K. That way they have total control over their primary macronutrients. Using these separate packs, they can mix vegetative foods, flowerings foods, pure N, pure P and pure K supplements — whatever they want and in whatever strengths they want — 20:10:10, 20:5:5, 5:20:5, etc.

Problematic Nutrients

Recalling that some strains may require more of a certain nutrient than others, we know that a balanced food might not have enough of that nutrient to allow the plant to grow without expressing a nutrient disorder. You may have to first identify the strain's 'problematic nutrient(s)' before finding a suitable feeding product. Mg is a common problematic nutrient, which means that many strains are more likely to experience a Mg nutrient disorder. In order to correct this you would have to use either pure Mg, a secondary nutrient feeding product or preferably a secondary nutrient product with higher Mg to Ca and S ratios.

Problematic nutrients are on the increase with stabilized plant breeding. As breeders develop strains for certain characteristics — flowering times, potency, yield, colors etc. — they sometimes accidentally stabilize other traits like nutrient requirements, smell or taste. Some breeders point out when their strains need more K or Mg, and this is worth taking into consideration when choosing your strain and feeding products. However be suspicious of breeders who claim that you should lower doses of a specific nutrient or range of nutrients. They could be telling you to do this in order to justify the floral and leaf color display that was published in the seed bank catalogue. Nutrient disorders can bring out nice colors in your plants, but you may be sacrificing yield and potency in favor of 'an image' by not allowing the plant to thrive in optimal conditions. Lack of K can bring out red hues all over your plant. With some strains this can even turn the bud purple. A few common CaMgS problems and treatments are described next.

MACRONUTRIENT DISORDERS: A ROUGH GUIDE

Most micronutrients are used by the cannabis plant in such small quantities that the role they play in plant functionality is quite limited. Also micronutrient disorders are extremely rare with cannabis plants unless you are using a completely neutral substrate with no added nutrients. Most loam soils already contain micronutrients so you do not need to add much, if any. Good growers, however, will always top up on low doses of micronutrients because they know that prevention is better than cure.

Macronutrients on the other hand are very important plant nutrients used widely by the plant throughout its grow. This guide will explain how these macronutrients work and how to spot macronutrient disorders in your garden.

Nitrogen (N)

Like most plants, cannabis uses N more than any other nutrient — especially during the vegetative growth stage of the life cycle. N directly helps the plant to create chlorophyll, which is used in photosynthesis for the production of plant energy. Without sufficient levels of N, cannabis plants turn a pale yellow-green, starting with the bottom leaves and gradually moving up to the top of the plant. Eventually the leaves wither and fall off. Lack of N also stunts plant growth.

Phosphorous (P)

Like most plants, cannabis uses P during photosynthesis to create chemical compounds essential to plant growth, especially floral development during the flowering phase of the life cycle. Lack of P causes plant veins to turn red and also stunts plant growth. Foods that are high in P are also called 'Bloom' foods.

Potassium (K)

K assists the plant's chemical synthesis and overall metabolism. Some chemical synthesis processes are used to help fight disease, so lack of potassium can make your plant vulnerable to plant diseases like mold, fungi and *wilt*. K also assists in seed and stem development. Without sufficient K, stems and branches become weak and break. Necrotic patches develop on leaf tips at the base of the plant and in blotchy patterns in the middle of those leaves. Red stems are a sign of a K problem, but red stems can be a genetic trait in some plants, especially in equatorial strains, and cold temperatures can cause stems to turn red as well. Be careful not to misdiagnose these symptoms as a K deficiency and risk overfeeding your plant.

Calcium (Ca)

Plant cells use and store Ca for cell development. Ca problems are rare and the symptoms are almost undetectable in cannabis, but if left untreated they will stunt growth and eventually cause the plant to wilt. If your plants display stunted growth yet do not display any symptoms associated with a another nutrient disorder then adjust the amount of Ca that you are adding to your plants in the feeding plan. To prevent secondary nutrient problems like our Ca problem here, which are hard to detect, you should top up on all of the secondary nutrients together.

Sulfur (S)

Like K, S assists the plant's chemical synthesis and metabolism. It is also used in the creation of amino acids and proteins. Without S, new growth is yellow and pale looking. The rest of the plant will also eventually yellow from lack of S. It is important to catch S and N deficiencies early, before they advance to the stage where it is difficult to detect the actual cause of the problem. N disorders run from the bottom of the plant upwards. S starts at new growth formations and spreads from there. A severe case of an S deficiency looks exactly like a severe case of an N deficiency, so check your plants regularly tO increase your chances of early detection.

Magnesium (Mg)

Chlorophyll is a group of magnesium containing green pigments that occur in plants, giving the characteristic green color to *foliage* and acting as absorbers of light for photosynthesis. Since Mg is central to chlorophyll production, the plant needs it to carry out photosynthesis. Plants with Mg problems exhibit both yellowing and leaf curl, especially leaves that curls upwards at the base of the plant. This is where the saying — 'The plant is praying for magnesium' comes from.

Mg problems are the most common secondary nutrient disorder you will come across. To correct this, feed your plant 1/3 of a tablespoon of Epsom salts per three gallons of water every three to four weeks. You should choose Epsom salts from your grow shop instead of Epsom salts from the drugstore because the grow shop version is designed for plant use (easier to break down in water). You also get a lot more Epsom salts for your money if you buy it in a grow shop. If your soil does not contain Mg, you will need to use a feeding product that contains Mg. You should be able to buy secondary feeding products from your local grow shop. They come either in liquid, powder or granular format. Avoid using granules because they take more time to break down in the soil. Granule type foods tend to be 'slow release' foods. 'Formulex' is a good secondary food product that can be used to correct Mg problems.

Micronutrient problems rarely occur unless there is a problem with lockout. Lockout is a chemical reaction that takes place with the nutrients in the soil and can occur if a large amount of one single nutrient is added or if salt gets into your mixture. Old nutrient formulas can also cause lockout. It is simply a chemical reaction similar to a precipitation, which results in the combining of nutrients to form new chemical compounds that the plant can not use. Lockout is hard to detect. If you have problems with a disorder that you can not seem to solve by adding more of the missing nutrient, then you need to consider that this nutrient is locked out. If lockout does occur you will need to flush your soil. Soil flushing is described later in this chapter.

Feeding

Feeding is the process of adding nutrients that the plant has removed back into your soil. We mentioned that you would need a maximum of four feeding solutions throughout your plants' growth. The first is to be used during vegetative growth, the second during flowering and the third and fourth only as needed. Plant food comes in all different forms — from solids, to liquids, to sprays, to powders, to granules. The most common form is liquid and this comes in either bottles or large containers.

You should only feed your plants when they need increased nutrition. Otherwise, you will risk burning them. What this means is that you need to be able to judge when cannabis plants need food. In the previous section we looked at certain nutrient formulas and feeding routines, for example one feeding every seven days at 1/4 strength of what it says on the label during vegetative growth.

Some cannabis strains will need N more than others. You can detect this if your plants start to yellow at the base in first few weeks of vegetative growth. If this happens, reduce your feeding schedule from seven days to five days, then three, and so on until you solve the yellowing. This will tell you how often you need to feed your plants at 1/4 strength. Instead of watering at 1/4 strength[*] more frequently, you could feed your plants a higher-strength nutrient mixture, but you increase the risk of burning your plants this way. Even though plant burn does not usually kill a plant if you solve the problem quickly, it can stunt and stress growth.

The amount of feed that you'll use is relative to your growing conditions and

---

[*] It usually takes about two to three days to observe a correction in a nutrient disorder. If there has not been a change in three days then you need to make ramifications to your diagnosis or treatment.

strain. You should never have to feed cannabis daily. In fact, the most nutrient-consuming cannabis strains should only need to be fed once every five days at 75% strength. Marijuana plants burn easily so *never mix your solution at 100 percent.* We will note some exceptions to this rule below, but they are very uncommon. In all other situations you should abide by the rule. If the instructions say to use 1 capful of feed per gallon of water, then aim for 1/4 strength by using one cap to every four gallons. If the instructions say to use one capful of feed per two liters of water and you know that your plants need lots of nutrients then go for 1/2 strength by using one cap to every four liters of water.

Try not to reduce the cap size in your feeding equation because 1/4 caps tend to be only enough to feed a plant or two. When you mix plant food you will want to be able to feed many of your cannabis plants as possible. Three-gallon watering cans are best for the job if you have six plants or more. It is possible to burn plants even at half strength, so take care when feeding and observe the behavior of your plants after feeding. If any of the leaf edges crumple up and appear dark green/brown and flaky, then you have probably burned your plants. The only way to solve plant burn is with a soil flush. We will discuss this procedure later in this Chapter.

There are some situations that call for mixing nutrient solutions at 100 percent strength but these are not common. They are:

1. *If you are using 'special' cannabis nutrients.* These are manufactured and sold in some European countries and can be legally imported into many other countries. You should still take security precautions when buying and storing these items, however, and make sure that it is not illegal to purchase or own them where you live. 'Special' cannabis nutrients are simply normal nutrients mixed at lower strengths so that they will not burn cannabis.

2. *If your solution contains nutrient values of less than 5 percent.* Doses of values lower than 5 percent on the bottle need to be mixed at higher ratios for some plants. An NPK value of 5:5:5 contains only 15 percent nutrients in the solution; the other 85 percent is usually just water. At 25 percent strength this nutrient solution will contain low nutrient values, so a more nutrient-hungry strain should be fed a higher-strength mixture. Some strains can use a 5:5:5 solution at 100 percent strength but this is not recommended because of potential plant burn.

3. *If your individual plants are extremely large and flowering.* Large, outdoor hybrid strains can consume lots of water and nutrients daily. In Australia,

there are hybrid Sativa strains that grow to near tree-like proportions. Even though growers take care to ensure that the soil around the plant is rich in nutrients they may need to feed these plants more often to improve bud growth during flowering with a strong bloom mix. A 100 percent solution may help boost the plant but only if the grower is certain that the mixture will be spread evenly around the base. By watering in a circle starting from the base of the plant and moving outwards, the grower can ensure that the strong solution has been distributed evenly to the area surrounding the plant. The soil around the plant will absorb the new minerals at 100 percent strength and the roots will find these as they grow outwards. This kind of 100 percent boost can be good for large plants.

As a final note to this section it would be wise to point out that you should never put food directly from the bottle into your plant's soil. This probably will kill your plant. Always mix it with water first or you could end up having to perform an emergency soil flush.

SOIL CONTROL

As your plant grows through its life cycle, it absorbs minerals from the soil and deposits waste material of its own. We have already stated that cannabis plants need a steady pH level of 7. The removal of nutrients and addition of waste material can cause soil pH levels to fluctuate.

pH

You should check the pH level of your soil at least once every week and one or two days after feeding. A pH test kit can be purchased from most grow shops. Be aware that the electronic test kits can be expensive. pH test kits are unfortunately the only way to test your mixture's pH. If you find that your soil's pH has shifted out of the 6 to 8 range you need to bring the level back to 7. Recall that below 7 is acidic and above 7 is alkaline. There are two ways to adjust the pH of the soil, and these are described below. You can also perform a soil flush. Soil flushing is not recommended except for in extreme circumstances, such as serious pH fluctuations or chemical burns, and is described in detail later in this chapter.

++ pH - Bringing Back to Neutral from Acidic

If your soil's pH is too acidic you will want to bring it back to a neutral 7. You can do this using lime (alkaline calcium oxide), a brittle white caustic solid obtained by heating limestone. Lime can be bought in small containers from any grow shop and added to your soil the next time you water your plant. Only add small amounts each time, testing the pH the next day to monitor the effects. You'll find that, over time, you will get to know your soil and what it needs. Advanced growers know by trial and error how much lime they need to use to push acidic soil back to a pH level of 7.

++ pH - Bringing Back to Neutral from Alkaline

If the pH of your soil is too alkaline then you will want to bring it back to a neutral 7 by adding small amounts of any of the following:

- Cottonseed meal
- Lemon peels
- Coffee grounds
- A high-acidity fertilizer

Always introduce small amounts of the substance, checking the pH level the next day and readjusting as necessary. Over time, you'll know what measures to use for different pot sizes and soil mixes.

++ pH up / pH down

Chemical pH products are growing in popularity among professional growers. They essentially act as a chemical agent for adjusting your soil pH and are available in most grow shops. They come in two forms: up and down. There is also a third type of pH solution called a buffer. The buffer solution is always a neutral 7 and is used to calibrate instruments so that they read correctly when you use them to test pH.

Both pH up and pH down come in liquid form. pH down contains nitric acid at roughly 38 percent strength and pH up contains potassium hydroxide at roughly 50 percent strength. Always check the label to make sure. The rest of the solution is usually just water. It is not a good idea to use your pH caps as measuring devices as this could result in foreign elements being introduced into the pH solution.

To adjust pH, read the instructions on the bottle carefully. It is wise to use a clean syringe for measuring how much of the pH up or down formula you need to use but a beaker or plastic measuring jug will do. Carefully add the recommended amount to water and mix well. Then, add this to your soil mixture and check your pH level with a reader. In general, 0.5 ml of pH up or pH down will move the solution by +/-0.1 pH per three gallons of mixture. A normal size syringe will usually drop out anywhere between 0.1 ml and 0.5 ml at a time.

FOR EXAMPLE:

Say you have a three-gallon pot system and your soil tests at a level of 5.6 pH. You need to move this up to a stable 7 so you need to go +1.4 pH by using pH up. Here's how to do it. Simply fill a watering can with three gallons of water and test it using a pH meter to get the reading of the water. If it is 7 then all is fine. If not then you need to balance the water to 7 before adding the +1.4 pH up. So if your water has a pH of 6 then you need to add 2.4 pH up (1.4 pH up + 1.0 pH up) to bring the soil mixture back to 7 after watering. 2.4 pH up roughly translates to about 12 ml of pH up. Use a pH reader to test the end results, which should be +8.4 pH. Simply add this pH-treated water to the soil, which has a pH of 5.6 and it should balance back to 7 again. Check your soil's pH a day or two after treatment to confirm this.

pH is important because low or high pH levels can cause nutrient lockout to occur. pH irregularities can also cause growth stunting, leaf spots and wilting. Always check the pH level of your soil before treating a nutrient problem. Another thing to note is that nutrient formulas have their own pH levels and you can use your pH reader to check a nutrient solution's pH level. You may need to balance the nutrient pH using the method of control we have outlined above. Serious pH irregularities occur in cannabis either when the pH drops below 5.5 in soil or goes above 8. The normal level of 7 induces optimal growth. It must also be noted at this point that the pH level and treatment of hydroponic solutions is very different to soil and is covered in chapter 9.

WATER CONTROL

Water your plant at least every second or third day, or better still, as needed. Never let the soil dry out completely for long periods of time. The following method works well with good-sized three-gallon pots:

- Day A - water
- Day B - let dry
- Day C - let dry
- Day D - check soil and water if needed

Your watering schedule will really depend on the size of your pots and soil type. If you pick up your pot when it's dry, then try to pick up the same pot when it has been watered, you will feel the difference in weight. This is one way to judge if your pots need watering.

You can detect signs of underwatering and overwatering simply by observing your plants' leaves. Watch your plants for two to three days after you have watered them. Do the fan leaves point outward to receive more light or do they wilt downward? Wilting leaves can be a sign of either underwatering or overwatering. Check your soil. Is it dry? If so, then add more water. You may find that you need to water every day because your lighting discharges a lot of heat and your soil is a quick-draining kind. If your soil is wet, then leave the soil to dry out until your leaves pick up again. You'll eventually establish a pattern for your plants' watering needs.

Be aware that overwatering will eventually kill your plants. If this happens, you can only let the soil dry out and hope for the best. Using a fan near the surface of the soil is the single best way to help solve an overwatering problem. Transplants are difficult to do with wet soil. If you think you need to perform a transplant because of overwatering then do so — but remember that the soil will be wet and break up easily in your hands. Try and do the transplant quickly and neatly over a short working distance.

AIR CONTROL

During the vegetative growth and flowering stages, cannabis plants love to get fresh air. Bearing in mind security — if you have a window in your grow leave it open for a while and let your grow room refresh itself every day. Also, during the dry periods in between watering, the roots like to breathe. The fresher the air, the better. During winter you may want to reduce the time that the windows are open as the cold may stunt growth. Just refresh the air in your room for 15 to 20 minutes during winter and close it again. If your grow is enclosed, without windows, then use fans to extract the old air outside and another fan intake to refresh the system.

A regular squirrel cage fan.

Odor Control

To say that we smell with our noses is like saying we taste with our lips. The nose channels air to our olfactory epithelium, a patch of cells which reside at the end of the nasal cavity. The olfactory epithelium senses the different compositions in the air and detects odorous molecules which gives us the effect of smell.

Cannabis plants continue to release odorous molecules into the air throughout their life. In vegetative growth the cannabis plant has a detectable odor which starts around the 1st week of vegetative growth and gradually increases until the end of the grow. This scent is very unique to the cannabis plant and can be described as a sharp, pleasingly pungent, freshly cut grass type of smell. In the flowering stages the plant tends to release numerous odorous molecules into the air in very large amounts. These scents are like the freshly cut grass type of smell coupled with fruity, forest, hash, skunk or chemical type odors. Cannabis naturally has a diverse range of smells and odors as the result of recombining its genetic material through natural selection and breeding (see Chapter 15).

You must deal with odorous molecules before they leave the grow room if you wish to prevent cannabis smells from traveling. Cannabis growers have found three ways to deal with this. *These are:*
- Ionizing   • Ozone Generating   • Activated Carbon Air Filtering

Ionizing

Ionizers are air purification systems that control - odors, smoke, mold, bacteria, chemical gases, mildew, stale air, pollen, dust and static electricity. Air ionization systems work by outputting negative ions into the area they are operated in. These negative ions are used to neutralize odor molecules that are in the air. The ions will attract the odorous molecules to them and when attached to the odorous molecule will deactivate the odor molecule by neutralization. Some ions will cause the odorous molecules to fall to the ground so that they will not remain airborne. The problem with ionizing is that these deactivated particles and negative ions tend to stick to surfaces such as the floor, pots, plant leaves, walls, lights, reflectors, ballasts and ducting. Some of the deactivated particles may be extracted by the outtake fan but your grow area will require cleaning every month if you use an Ionizer.

Ionizers are cheap to buy but are only suitable for smaller growing operations where up to six medium sized plants are concerned. Growers still use them but there are better options of odor control available to you.

Ozone Generating

Ozone is also known as activated oxygen. Activated oxygen contains three atoms rather than two which is what we normally breathe. Ozone is a very vigorous sterilizer. Ozone can be found in nature but we can also buy units that generate ozone. Ozone has a lifespan of about 30 minutes. When ozone (O3) comes in contact with odorous molecules, one of the ozone atoms detaches itself from the ozone and attaches itself to the odorous molecules. This oxidizes the cell walls of the odorous molecules which eventually destroys the odorous molecules leaving only oxygen behind.

Ozone does have some setbacks. Too much ozone is not good for plant health or human health although most ozone generators are specially adapted to render the health risks of ozone obsolete. The legal exposure limit for human beings is around 0.1ppm for a maximum of eight hours. Ozone generators that are used for horticultural purposes tend to only generate 0.05 ppm and a timed rate so that exposure is kept to a minimal amount.

Ozone generators are better at controlling cannabis odors than Ionizers.

Activated Carbon Air Filtering

Activating carbon is the safest most effective way of dealing with cannabis odors and is part of any professional grow room. Charcoal is carbon. When we treat charcoal with oxygen it opens up millions of pores in the carbon atoms. This type of treated charcoal is known as activated charcoal and is the main ingredient of our activated carbon filter. The activated charcoal is usually broken down into pellets so that it can be used with air filtering units.

Activated charcoal absorbs odorous molecules by chemical attraction. The activated charcoal is contained in a metal tube with filters screening the air that passes through.

The whole unit is called an activated carbon filter and is attached near your outtake vent. Not all activated carbon filters use charcoal. Some activated carbon is made from the husks of coconuts. Activated carbon filters need the carbon changed every couple of months. You will know when to change the carbon if it no longer filters out odorous molecules. Activated carbon can be found in most good filter supply stores. Make sure that you choose activated carbon pellets. There is another form of activated carbon called crushed activated carbon but this is not as effective as the version that comes in pellet form.

VENTILATION

Ventilation is a very important aspect of indoor environment control. Most cannabis flowers are sticky. Dust sticks to bud. So your ventilation system must not be allowed to blow dust into or around your grow room. This is simply done by keeping the grow room clean and making sure that all air intakes are equipped with screens. You will have to clean the screens every so often to maintain a clean air flow into your grow room.

You will also need to ventilate your grow room if it gets too hot for your plants. This is the primary reason why most growers need a ventilation system. The other reason is to prevent the humidity from increasing in the grow room, which can cause mold and other plant problems. Fresh air also contains gases (oxygen, nitrogen, carbon dioxide and traces of other gases) some of which are used up by the plants in the growing environment. This causes levels of these gases to fluctuate in the grow room. If a grow room does not have adequate ventilation then these gases will not be replaced and this causes problems with plant health. In order to provide optimal conditions for cultivating cannabis we must have a well ventilated grow space.

All good growers spend time getting their ventilation right before they start their grow. Here is a list of reasons to have a good ventilation system in your grow room.

1. To prevent mold.
2. To replenish various gases in the air.
3. To stabilize humidity.
4. To control air flow.
5. To boost yield using a slow release carbon dioxide system (covered at the end of this Chapter).

There are two main components in a ventilation system: the *passive intake* (air in) and the *vent* (air out). The vent should be located high up in your grow room because hot air rises. The vent should come equipped with a fan to push air out through the vent. Odor control devices (activated carbon filters, charcoal filters) are usually attached to or located near the vent.

When the fan has sucked all the air out of the room through the vent, it will create a vacuum. Air will need to get back into your grow room again so it will find any way in that it can. Holes in the walls, frame and roof are all vulnerable spots where air can be pulled in. Since we want our airflow to be under control we need to make sure that all false air intake spots are sealed first.

The passive intake (with a screen to prevent dust from getting in) should be installed low in the grow room so that, as air is brought in from outside, it passes through, around and over the plants. This air will help to cool the plants and the space between the lighting and the cannabis top colas before finally being extracted by the vent. Dust will also be forced out the vent. Passive intakes do not require a fan but some growers do use them to regulate how much air enters the room.

Nearly every cannabis grow room uses the above scenario for ventilation. Spend time designing your ventilation before you set up your grow room. The cost of setting a good system up is much lower than you think. Air-cooled hoods for HID lights need to be used in conjunction with a vent. Other ventilation methods are described in Chapter 8.

Fans

Fans can be placed quite close to mature marijuana plants and a slight breeze helps them to develop stronger stems and branches. Fans also circulate the air around your plants, simulating an outdoor environment. A fan's ability to 'move' air from one location to another is measured in cfm (cubic feet per minute). You should aim to replace the air in your grow room at least once a minute. If your room is hot then you may need to remove the air in your room as much as five times a minute. On average, growers use a fan with the capacity to circulate the room's air three times in one minute.

FOR EXAMPLE: If your grow room is 2 X 5 X 5 then it is 50 cubic feet in size. For this grow room you need a fan that ranges somewhere between 150 cfm (3 X 50 cfm) and 250 cfm (5 X 50 cfm). In this example, the 150 cfm fan can move all of the air out of the grow room 3 times per minute. The 250 cfm fan will do it five times a minute. The rate at which you want the air to be removed from your grow room depends on:

- How hot it gets inside the room.
- How cold the air outside is.
- If you are using C02.

You can find the 'cfm' written on the side of the fan. Squirrel cage type fans are highly recommended.

Sometimes a very good air extraction system causes areas of the grow room to receive less of the new air than others. If you want to ensure that all areas of the grow room receive adequate amounts of fresh air then use a regular domestic oscillating fan. Oscillating fans also help to build up thick stems and branches. The speed at which you set your fan depends on how much the plants move. Plants like movement but too much can make them uproot or fall over. Use common sense with these type of fans.

HUMIDITY

Cannabis plants grow best under conditions between 40 and 80 percent relative humidity *(rH)*. rH is the amount of water in the air. Introducing fresh air into the environment is the best way to control humidity. In short, if you have installed a good air circulation system then you should not have a problem with the humidity in your grow room. If your air has a high humidity level then you will need to purchase a dehumidifier. These expensive items are used to control rH in the room. They do this by simply cooling the air that travels through the unit causing it to condense and loose some of its water vapor.

Cannabis grows well at levels of between 40 percent and 80 percent rH. If you have a rH measuring kit you can judge for yourself how much fresh air you need in order to achieve the optimum 60 percent level. These measuring kits are also expensive to buy and usually have to be ordered in by your local grow store. Good cannabis growers try to avoid the cost of dehumidifiers and rH monitors by simply installing a good air circulation system from day one.

TEMPERATURE

Cannabis likes the same temperature that people do, so the best meter for temperature control is you. If you find it's too cold in your grow room, so will your plants. Under normal circumstances, room temperature is easily controlled by thermostat, but in your grow space, lighting will impact on temperature. You should aim for 75 degrees Fahrenheit, but slightly warmer temperatures do help plants to grow a bit more quickly.

Monitor your room's temperature with one or more thermometers. Hot air rises so you can expect that the temperature of the air above the thermometer will be hotter than the air under it. Using more than one thermometer, you get an idea of the temperature ranges in your room (at root level and canopy or light level).

You do not want to go above 85 degrees Fahrenheit. If you do, you will only heat stress* your plants and stunt growth. Going above 125 degrees Fahrenheit can kill cannabis but this depends on the strain. Some equatorial strains can still grow at 125 degrees Fahrenheit as their genetic make-up can withstand it. In order to cool the room, you will need to ventilate it either by opening a window or installing a ventilation system, as described above.

---

*Heat stress can be responsible for sexual dysfunctions. Avoid heat stressing your plants.

During the flowering phase of the life cycle you will alter the photoperiod to what is called 12/12. The procedure known as *changing the photo-period to 12/12'* is explained in detail in Chapter 7. 12/12 means that for 12 hours your grow room lights will be on and for the next 12 hours they will be switched off. Since bulb heat contributes to the grow room's temperature, the temperature will drop when the lights are out. During the dark periods of the flowering phase the temperature is allowed to drop down as far as 55 degrees Fahrenheit. You should prevent temperatures going lower than 55 degrees at night because this stunts growth. Below 30 and you can expect serious plant damage. If the temperature does drop below 55 during the dark period then you need to heat the grow room. The best way to do this is using an electric heater. For an average-size grow room, a small, portable heater that plugs into a domestic socket will do.

An automatic temperature switch.

TIMERS

Timers are important devices for controlling when lights, heaters, fans and any other electrical units in your grow should be switched on or off. Some lighting kits, ballasts and fans come with built-in timers. If you do not have a built-in timer you can buy one from any good home electrical store or grow shop. Timers simply act as a regulator between your power source and the device that needs the electricity. You plug your device into the timer and then you plug the timer into your electrical output. Some timers have a digital display and others have an analog display. Simply set your timer to turn on when you want the device to turn on and to turn off at the time you want your device to turn off.

Timers should not be overloaded. Current must pass through the timer unit so you may need to use multiple timers in your grow room. To understand your timer's limits consult the manual that comes with it.

CO_2 (CARBON DIOXIDE)

CO_2 is a gas that helps promote plant growth, especially floral growth. About 0.03 percent by volume of the Earth's atmosphere is made up of carbon dioxide. Carbon dioxide is natural and not harmful. Plants absorb carbon dioxide from the air and use it for photosynthesis. If the supply of carbon dioxide stops, so does the process of photosynthesis. Increasing the supply of carbon dioxide increases photosynthesis.

Millions of years ago there was much more carbon dioxide in the atmosphere. Somehow plants have still not lost their ability to process high doses of carbon dioxide which leads to lots of plant vigor at a faster speed of growth. The atmosphere on Earth today is different and has slowed down plant development — you could say that we have a planet full of underdeveloped plants!

Plants will use carbon dioxide in any growing environment. Using a simple air circulation system in your grow room will help replenish the carbon dioxide the plants have used. If you want to increase plant size, yield and vigor, and speed up growth you need to look closely at increasing carbon dioxide levels.

Carbon dioxide can triple yields. A one-ounce plant can quickly become a three-ounce plant but this depends largely on the plant's genetics. Every cannabis strain has a genetic threshold for bud production. It will not exceed that limit, even under optimal growing conditions. Introduction of supplementary carbon dioxide ensures that your plants will hit their optimal rate of growth. You do not need supplementary carbon dioxide to grow high-yielding plants but the noticeable effects on the speed and quantity of bud production with supplementary CO_2 places the gas in the same category of importance for high yields as 'plant genetics' and 'light source'.

Carbon dioxide 'generators' are expensive industrial units that burn fuel to produce carbon dioxide. Although you can buy different types of generators that use a range of diverse fuel sources, they are really only suitable for very large indoor or greenhouse growing operations. Most growers who use carbon dioxide in their grow room choose a 'timed release' system. This is simply a unit that releases a certain amount of compressed carbon dioxide from a tank at a timed rate of release.

Carbon dioxide tanks can be bought and refilled at any good welding supply store. It is best to use a welding supply store over any other type of store when you acquire carbon dioxide. If anyone asks — you are welding something. They are also the perfect place to refill your carbon dioxide canisters. Carbon dioxide can also be purchased from most 'fuel depots'. The tanks come in different shapes and sizes but you should aim for multiple 20-pound tanks or the 50-pound type if you have a lot of grow space. We will calculate exactly how much carbon dioxide to introduce into your growing environment in the next section. Twenty-pound tanks are easier to lift, move and fit into your grow room. Also, using multiple tanks allows you to refill on carbon dioxide while the other tank is releasing carbon dioxide into your grow room. Once you have a tank of carbon dioxide you need to purchase a tank regulator (an infrared sensor or combination flow meter will also do) and a timer. The tank regulator controls the quantity of carbon dioxide emitted and the timer controls when the gas is released.

Calculating How Much Carbon Dioxide You Need

How much carbon dioxide you need is quite straight forward but requires a bit of information about your grow room and ventilation system. Here are the steps you need to take:

1. Calculate the volume of your grow in cubic feet by multiplying the length x width x height of the room.
2. There is already carbon dioxide present in the room. It should be around 300 ppm (parts per million). The optimal level for cannabis is 1500 ppm. You will need to increase carbon dioxide levels by 1200 ppm.
3. Multiply the grow room in cubic feet by 0.0012 to find out how much carbon dioxide you need to supplement your room to 1500 ppm.

FOR EXAMPLE: $15 \times 17 \times 8 = 2040 \times 0.0012 = 2.5 \, c.f. = 1500 \, ppm$

1. A 10 x 10 x 10 room is 1000 cubic feet in size.
2. 1000 x 0.0012 = 1.2 cubic feet.
3. 1.2 cubic feet of carbon dioxide will be needed to bring this room up to 1500 ppm.

If you have an air-circulation system in your grow room you may wish to reduce the speed of your fan to prevent carbon dioxide from being vented too quickly (after all you are paying for it and you don't want to waste too much of it). If you reach 1500 ppm for carbon dioxide in your grow room you are allowed an increase of temperature to 95 degrees Fahrenheit because the increased carbon dioxide allows cannabis plants to grow in these temperatures without stressing them. If this does heat stress your plants then try to increase your ppm to 2000, which should be better for your plants in temperatures of 95 degrees Fahrenheit. If you find that slowing down the vent fan to keep carbon dioxide in the room is still causing your plants heat stress then you simply need to regulate how many times carbon dioxide is released into your system with every air change. The more often air is vented out, the more carbon dioxide you need to release. A hose can be used in conjunction with the regulator to ensure that the carbon dioxide escapes at a point that is furthest away from your vent. This ensures that as many plants as possible get access to the CO_2 before it finally is vented out.

Remember that heat stress stunts growth, voiding the benefits of any carbon dioxide supplement. Get your air circulation right before you introduce high levels of carbon dioxide into the grow environment. A good air circulation system should be flexible enough to allow for a slow carbon dioxide release system to work. It is just a matter of controlling the timing of the release, the amount to be released and how much air must be moved out of the grow room in order to keep it within a certain range of temperatures. During 12/12, carbon dioxide is turned off for the dark period, because without light there is little photosynthesis.

This is a mid-range climate controller that automatically manages the grow room's temperature and humidity levels. It also has the ability to directly control CO_2 systems in conjunction with these other tasks.

CLIMATE CONTROLLERS

These devices serve multifarious tasks in the grow room. Much like a timer they regulate the activity of the electrical device(s) they are connected too.

Climate controllers also go by the names of: environment controllers, climate monitors and climate sensors. They come in both analogue and digital formats. The more expensive the climate controller, the more functions it has and the more devices it can control. Climate controllers can be used to regulate the following systems in your grow room:

> LIGHTS
> VENTILATION AND EXTRACTION
> CO_2 DISBURSEMENT
> HUMIDITY
> PUMPS

The climate controller is usually fastened into your grow room wall. The devices that the unit is controlling plug into the separate slots of the climate controller. The controller itself is then plugged into your electrical mains and turned on.

Expensive climate controller are self-regulated and come with built-in sensors that detect when the controller should be activated for a specific task or a set of tasks. You set how it controls those tasks, with the setting of the controller.

By way of example an advanced climate controller can be setup to do the following:

> During the photoperiod the climate controller regulates the 12/12 pho-
> toperiod by turning the lights on for 12 hours and off for 12 hours. The
> controller monitors the heat in the room, which will vary when the lights
> are on and off. The heat sensors of the controller adjust the speed of the
> extraction fans to accommodate for the change in heat to meet your set-
> tings. If the temperature drops below your established temperature the
> controller turns on the heating device that you have attached to it to meet
> your fixed temperature or temperature range. At the same time the con-
> troller can also regulate CO_2 systems and Humidifiers in the grow room.

How much you want to spend on a controller depends on how many devices you want it to control and how much control you want over these devices. There are many controllers available to suite small to large tasks.

C.A.P, is a popular manufacturer of climate controllers and they have a product range varying from simply controllers for small grow rooms to full size greenhouse controllers. Consult your grow store for details on the type of the controller you are looking for. Basic controllers start at around $60.00 and expert controllers can cost up to $2000.00

60 Indica/Sativa hybrids in the final week before harvest.

SOIL FLUSHING

A soil flush is a last resort when all else has failed, as in the following scenario.

In this hypothetical situation, you are using a soil that holds a lot of water and you want to feed your plant. You take out the appropriate feeding bottle, add it straight to your plant and pour the water in after. *(This is never recommended. Always mix your plant food with water in a container, such as a jug or watering can, before administering it to your plant.)* As you move to pour the correct dose over the soil, your hand shakes and the bottle spills. The next thing you know, half of your raw feeding liquid has managed to find its way into the soil. You curse yourself for not following the instructions. What should you do? You pick up this book and turn to this page. You read about the soil flush and see that your plant still has a slim chance of survival. You know that all the raw chemicals could kill your plant and this is your last resort.

Here is how to flush your soil.
++ STEP A.

(1) Take the potted plant to a sink.

(2) Turn the plant on its side, making sure not to bend or break the stem.

(3) If you think the stem will break then find a long stick and place it in the soil, use thread to secure the plant to the stick at several points and secure the stick to the pot.

(4) Tilt the potted plant on its side so that the top of the pot with the soil is fac-ing at an angle toward the sink.

(5) Do this until all the liquid has poured out, noting the color of the liquid that runs out. Some nutrients will dye the water a pink, brown or yellow color. You may see a hue to this water coming out. When this changes color after the flush you know that all the nutrients are flushed out. If the nutri-ent does not dye the water you can still continue the flush. Just pour every-thing out.

++ STEP B.

If your pot is perforated continue. Otherwise, proceed to Step C.

(1) Pull your plant back up and sit it in the sink.

(2) Pour lots of water on top of the soil.

(3) Wait until the water flows out the bottom of the pot, observing the color of the flow as in step A.

(4) Repeat this process until the color of the water becomes clearer. The soil will get very muddy when you do this and some of the mud will pass out with the water. Try and keep hold of as much of as it as you can.)

(5) Once the water runs clear tilt your plant on its side again and wait for all the water to drain out.

(6) If your feeding solution doesn't have a color then flush water through the plant a number of times to ensure that all the nutrients are flushed out. This usually takes about seven flushes with a three-gallon pot. Remember that if you see color change then all your nutrients are flushed out and you do not need to flush anymore.

(7) Quickly take your plant to a warm, dry area and wait for the soil to dry out.

(8) Proceed to Step D.

++ STEP C.

(1) You can use a screwdriver to make holes in your pot if it is made of light-weight plastic. You can always use thick masking tape later to patch the holes up. If you do this, then follow Step B. If you can't do this, then you need to perform an emergency transplant.

(2) Prepare a new pot with soil, leaving a large gap in the middle where your plant will go.

(3) Take your plant and use a knife to cut around the edge of the soil as close to the rim of the pot and as deep as you can.

(4) Put your fingers in down around the inside of the rim and gently pull the plant and soil out of the pot. Try not to damage the roots.

(5) Hold the soil over the sink and place it down near the drain holding it together with your hands. If your root mass is big you may need help.

(6) Turn on the water and let it run slowly down over the soil.

(7) Keep holding the plant for a number of minutes until you see a change in the color of the water that's coming from the soil. Do not crush the soil just hold it. It will get muddy and will break up a bit, but this is to be expected.

(8) When the water changes, place the plant into the new pot.

(9) Fill up the spaces with new soil and use a stick to prop up your plant if needed.

(10) Quickly take your plant to a warm dry area and wait for the soil to dry out.

(11) Proceed to Step D.

++ STEP D.

(1) Every day measure the pH of the soil. If you have flushed your plant properly it should return to the near 7 mark (given that the water you use is a neutral pH of 7).

Sadly, few plants survive such an emergency soil flush. The soil flush is, in essence, overwatering your plant to the point of removing most of the minerals and ingredients in the soil. If your plant manages to pull through, you have done well. If your plant doesn't then you'll know better next time. A soil flush causes the plant a great deal of shock* and should only be attempted as a last resort if your plant

---

*Transplant shock causes plant stress. If your plant is sexually mature enough to flower (has calyx development) or is flowering, transplant shock can induce sexual dysfunctions to appear (the hermaphrodite condition). Even if your plant survives a transplant in the later stages of its growth it can cause problems down the line. Avoid transplanting after the 2nd week of vegetative growth if you can. It is during the 3rd week of growth that the plant's sex is usually determined and avoiding stress just before and after this point helps prevent sexual dysfunction. All strains are different in this respect. Some exhibit sexual dysfunction with only a little bit of stress. Others are more resistant and can endure quite a large amount of stress without exhibiting sexual dysfunction. The latter is especially true of strains that are recommended for the novice grower.

is dying and can't be cured by any other means. If your plant survives, it may have sustained some damage. If any of the leaves are burnt or look dead you can remove them by clipping them away. These damaged plants usually take about two weeks to return to full health.

This well maintained, well ventilated, HID soil setup yields over 400oz of bud every 70 days!

7 | PRE-FLOWERING AND FLOWERING

BY NOW YOU'VE MANAGED TO SET UP THE BASIC growing environment and experimented with modifying and controlling it to promote better, stronger plant growth. You will have observed your plants forming a number of nodes and a small leaf mass at the top, which you know is going to form the next set of leaves and branches. Your leaves should be flat and stretched out to receive as much light as possible across their surface area. If they are, then your plant is enjoying its environment. If not then maybe you should consider turning to the Problem Solver in Chapter 13 to see what has gone wrong.

You should also note that almost everyone makes mistakes the first time growing. Very few first-time growers get to this stage without experiencing at least one problem, so don't feel bad if you didn't get it right the first time. The trick to growing healthier, more potent plants is to keep growing (and reading this book).

During the vegetative growth stage your plants will begin to grow quickly and produce more leaves and new branches. The stem will also grow thicker. This is the point when your plants begin to really look like marijuana.

Then, one day you will notice that your plants appear to be doing more than just growing vertically and producing leaves. You take a closer look and there appears to be new leaf growth at most of the node regions between the stem and the branches. Your plant is now developed enough to receive more light energy and covert this energy into more side branch growth. These new growths produce more leaves, branches, and eventually flowers. This type of new growth at the stem's node regions is called lateral branching or secondary branching. This is really where the extra node regions begin to take shape.

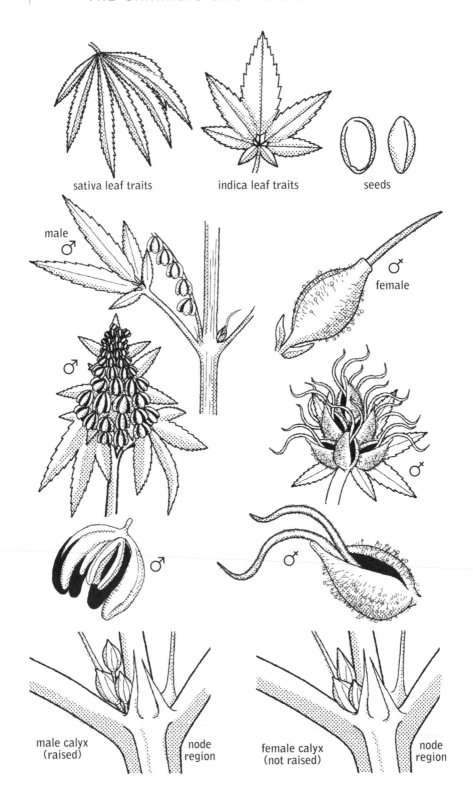

sativa leaf traits   indica leaf traits   seeds

male ♂

♂   ♀ female

♂   ♀

♂   ♂

male calyx   node   female calyx   node
(raised)   region   (not raised)   region

After a few more weeks of this secondary growth your plant is looking more bushy and certainly has more node regions. It is during this time that your plant has reached sexual maturity and is ready to show sex. How long this takes depends on the strain you are growing but after the seedling stage has finished you are looking at a time period of 4 to 8 weeks vegetative growth. With Sativa strains this can take much longer.

At a certain stage towards the end of vegetative growth the plant enters its pre-flowering phase and, as a grower, you need to tailor your grow space and gardening approach to this new stage in your plants' life cycle. The next section explains how to identify the pre-flowering stage.

PRE-FLOWERING AND EARLY SEXING

Recall that during pre-flowering, plants start to exhibit their sex. As a grower, you should be hoping for as many females as possible. Pre-flowering occurs at the node regions. Towards the end of vegetative growth you need to check your plant nodes for what is called calyx development. A clone will carry the exact same genetic makeup as the plant it came from, so if you know your clone's history you will already be able to predict it's sex.

CHECKING FOR CALYX DEVELOPMENT

Choose a plant. First of all examine the node regions of the plant where the branches meet the stem. You are looking for very small pod shaped organs here at these regions.* If you don't find any here then move outwards along each branch checking each node region until you come to the tip. If you do not find calyx development then your plant has not reached its pre-flowering phase yet. You need to wait for it. Calyx development will come in time.**

There are three early indicators of plant sex, but they are not 100 percent accurate.So remember, these methods can fail, but are often accurate predictors of your plants' sex.

First Early Sexing Method

If you've been growing the same strain and all the seeds were started at the same time, then you may notice that some plants are taller than others: the smaller plants tend to be female and the taller ones tend to be male. You can separate these plants into two sections in order to see how good your guesswork was when

---

* Do not confuse a calyx with initial secondary branch development which occurs in the first to second week of vegetative growth. If you are not sure, initial branch development or secondary growth produces two small leaves in a few days. These eventually extend into branches which form more leaves and node regions.

** Initial calyx development is not photoperiod responsive. You do not need to change your light photoperiod is order to find calyx development. Calyx development is a natural part of the plant's life cycle and occurs when the plant is mature enough to display sex.

you do definitively identify sex. The other thing to note is that male plants generally start to pre-flower before females. If you have taller plants that are producing new growths before the smaller ones then the taller plants are probably male.

Second Early Sexing Method

A good way to identify plant sex at an early date is to examine the calyx[*] with the aid of a very fine magnifying glass. If the calyx is raised on a small, short stem then it's probably a male. If the calyx isn't raised on a small short stem then it's probably a female.

Third Early Sexing Method

'Force-flowering' is probably the best early-sexing method. To force-flower a cannabis plant, simply take a cutting and place it in a cup of water or a cloning medium, such as rockwool. Expose the cutting to 12 hours of light followed by 12 hours of total darkness. The cutting should flower and display its sex — however the plant must be mature enough to present its sex. An immature plant will not show sex because initial calyx development is not photoperiod-related. Plants normally mature around the forth week of vegetative growth because sex is not genetically determined until the third week of growth. This also applies to 'feminized seeds,' which can, and often do, turn out to be male.[**] If your plants are exhibiting calyx development, then this is a suitable method of determining the plant's sex.

These methods are NOT 100 percent accurate. Later in this Chapter we will explain how to definitively identify the sex of your marijuana plant.

WHEN TO FLOWER?

Your plant will remain in the pre-flowering stage between one and two weeks. During this period, the new growth regions begin to change shape depending on the plants' sex. It is during this shape change that you can properly detect your plant's sex.

Pre-flowering is a sign that your plant is mature enough to start flowering. As a grower you have a simple choice to make: Do you want to flower now or do you want to continue vegetative growth? Here are a few issues to consider before you make a decision:

---

[*] If you have a light photoperiod of 24/0 then sexual expression may only be evident in the calyx shape. If you have a light photoperiod of 16/8 then chances are the calyx may display sex very quickly because there is a dark period involved. If you see pistils or tiny clear white hairs (pistils) growing out from the pods then the plant is a female. If the pods are very raised and growing in large numbers then it is probably a male.

[**] 'Feminized ' seeds can produce the following sexes if the growing environment is not well maintained: (1)Females, (2)Hermaphrodites, (3) Males. 'Feminized seeds' only increase the chances of getting females. 'Feminized seeds' are covered in detail in Chapter 15.

- Most cannabis plants can be kept alive for up to 12 years by simply keeping a light on the plant at all times. Even if the plant only receives light for a few hours a day it can still live for a long time. It all depends on how the plant is treated. These plants will grow to a certain height and then form into a bush. Eventually they will stop producing branches and will spend the rest of their lives growing new leaves to replace the old ones. By keeping the plant in vegetative growth longer, you allow it to reach its optimal size of vegetative growth and the plant will stop growing. Most growers flower before this, when they see calyx development, in order to speed up the growing process. For example: A plant that shows sex at the forth week of vegetative growth can be kept in vegetative growth for a few more weeks to allow the plant to generate more node regions (leading to more branch and leaf growth). When the plant is flowered, this extra stage of growth should help the plant to achieve optimal results however the grow time is extended by a few more weeks to obtain this.

- Bud production does not increase at the same rate as plant growth. Bud production depends on your growing environment, your strain's genetic makeup and the amount of nodes the plant has. All nodes are potential bud areas, but every strain has a genetic threshold for bud production.

- It is possible to get more bud with lots of plants that are flowered as soon as they're mature (which also keeps them shorter and smaller), than extending vegetative growth with less plants until they reach their maximum height and size. The time frame for the shorter option also produces more bud turnover per year.

Keeping these things in mind, you can either choose to flower now or choose to keep your plant growing until it reaches its size threshold before you start flowering. If you take the longer route, prepare to have the space for it, because in the flowering stage, some cannabis strains can more than double in height and width.

If you want your pre-flowers to flower you only have to do one thing: introduce the 12/12 light schedule.

THE ALL-IMPORTANT 12/12!
If you've never heard of 12/12, listen up. 12/12 is the key to producing high quantities of bud from cannabis plants.

Cannabis plants grow outdoors naturally between the months of April and October/November. This means that toward Sept/Nov* the plants will be flowering. During this time the days get shorter and the nights get longer. When this occurs, the plants are subjected to 12 hours of light and 12 hours of darkness.

When this 12/12 photoperiod occurs, the plant is naturally stimulated to flower. As long as 12/12 continues the flowers will grow larger and more plentiful. This is part of the cannabis plants' natural cycle. Naturally, as a grower, you want a large quantity of flowers, and you achieve this by introducing the 12/12 light cycle.

During pre-flowering you can either manually turn on your lights for 12 hours and turn off your light for 12 hours every day or you can use a timer to automate the process. Throughout the 12 hours of darkness you should keep your grow area as dark as possible. Even something as seemingly harmless as a small desk light at the other side of your room will cause your plant not to react properly to 12/12, resulting in continued vegetative growth. In fact, any light that penetrates the darkness could stop your plants from flowering properly. That means your grow room must be sealed to the point where it is completely lightproof.

If you want to learn how to do completely lightproof your space then I suggest that you read up on photography dark rooms, either on the Internet or in your local library. Photographers use common items that can be bought in most hardware shops to make their film-processing rooms lightproof. If you borrow ideas from their tried-and-true methods (basically a thick black screening around the doorframes or any open light points) then you will have a great space for flowering plants. You should be a long way towards achieving this already if you followed the advice on covering your grow room with Mylar. If you have prevented any light from leaking out, then you should also have prevented light from leaking in.

Problems with 12/12
If you switch to 12/12 before pre-flowers have shown, you may encounter the following problems:

1. Stress-related sex problems (hermaphrodites)
2. Abnormal bud growth

---

*Cannabis plants can be flowered as early as June but this depends on how well the weather was up until then. If the plants where started in March and have sexually matured by June then they may flower with as little as eight hours darkness. This is very strain dependant.

++ Stress-related Sex Problems (Hermaphrodites)

Stress-related sex problems *might* produce hermaphrodite plants. The stress of what's sometimes called early flowering triggers the plant into a situation where it thinks its chances of reproduction are slim to none. That situation induces a condition or act of self-pollination, in which the plant produces both male and female flowers on the same plant. The male flowers then pollinate the female flowers, which eventually produce seeds.

The reason for this is that the plant notices that the photoperiod is irregular[*] and should no longer be in the vegetative growth stage but in flowering. This shocks the plant into a last ditch effort to receive pollen because it feels that it's missed its chance to receive pollen already. In the wild, males release their pollen just around the time that females begin to flower.

This is what hermaphrodites look like. Notice that both male pollen pods and female pistils are present on the plant. Picture by Rasta Linus.

Hermies cause problems because they may carry the hermaphrodite trait with their offspring. Genetically the hermie condition is near impossible to reverse once started. Sometimes even plants from the hermaphrodite's offspring that did not display the hermaphrodite condition can still carry the hermie trait to future

[*] Variations in the photoperiod that cause hermies are mostly disturbances to the 12/12 photoperiod although early 24/0 or 18/6 photoperiod disturbances can also cause sexual dysfunction to appear later.

Another shot of the hermaphrodites condition. The male pods are clearly visible.
Picture by Rasta Linus.

This illustration clearly shows male calyx development within the female flower cluster.
Soon the male calyx will develop into male flowers and pollinate the females on the
same plant. This process is known as 'Selfing'.

offspring. If you ever see all-female seeds advertised by seed banks you have the right to know whether or not these seeds come from female plants that were stressed into producing male flowers. In general, growers try to avoid hermie plants because they spoil sinsemilla crops and breeding projects.

++ Abnormal Bud Growth

Abnormal bud growth is a side effect of the hermaphrodite condition. Because the plant produces male pollen sacks with female flowers you may notice that the bud looks different. Also, the quantity of female bud produced is decreased because of pollination.

Early-induced flowering* isn't the same thing as forcing your plants to flower. If you force flower a strain before it has pre-flowered it will flower at roughly the same time as a plant from the same strain that has been flowered after calyx development has occurred naturally. Force flowering simply acts by stressing the plant into a crisis condition.

You will get the best out of your plant by waiting until it starts pre-flowering before switching to 12/12.

Keep feeding and watering your plant as normal. Pay attention to the flowering areas as they begin to grow. At this stage you may want to switch to your flowering feeds. Soon you'll be able to see your plant's sex.

Pre-Flowering for the 24/0 and the 18/6 photoperiods

Both under the 24/0 photoperiod and the 18/6 photoperiod cannabis plants will undergo calyx development when mature enough to do so. In the case of the 18/6 photoperiod calyx development may appear more pronounced and even display its sex earlier than the 24/0 photoperiod.

It is easier to keep a plant in vegetative growth by using the 24/0 photoperiod because there are no dark periods. If you keep the plants under 18/6 the pre-flowering phase increase may cause a slow down in vegetative growth. Although pre-flowering under 18/6 does not cause flowering it certainly contributes to a decrease in vegetative activity. As soon as you go down to less than 14 hours of light the plant will normally start to flower. 12/12 is the best light regime for flowering and can be introduced as soon as calyx development appears.

---

* This hermaphrodite condition depends largely on the strain and how well the environment has been kept. Not all attempts at early-induced flowering will hermaphrodite the plant. If the light regime has not been consistent or was variable then early induced flowering may cause the plant to respond by exhibiting the hermaphrodite condition.

THE MALE/FEMALE THING OR HOW TO SEX YOUR PLANTS

You now have nurtured your plants and watched them grow in the hope that you'll get some high-yield females in the end. If you end up without any female plants out of all of your seeds then send the seed bank a letter explaining how 15 out of 15 seeds were male. If you're lucky and sincere in your writing, the seed bank may send you some free seeds or give you a discount on your next order. Seed banks or breeders aren't responsible for male/female ratios. It simply isn't under their control. Some people get 100 percent females while others get 100 percent males, but it is rare that such a thing will happen. To get five or more females in a pack of 15* is a good ratio.

A female at two weeks flowering.

---

*Not all seed banks provide their strains in packs of 15. The most common amounts sold by seed banks and breeders are packs of 10, 15 and 16. On rare occasions sometimes seed banks release 'mix bags' of 30. These lucky mix bags are unidentified seeds that got mixed up by the breeder. They are usually very cheap to buy because of this.

A male plant at one week after initial calyx development, by ChronicCouple.

A male plant at two weeks flowering. Most of the male flowers have already opened spreading pollen.

The two circles above indicate where the grower should look for initial calyx development. In this photograph two new shoots can be seen emerging from the nodes. Most novice growers mistake these shoots in their initial stages of growth as calyx development. Initial calyx development occurs at the same region though.

MALE FLOWERING

Males do not need a photoperiod to spread pollen. As soon as calyx development shows male flowers may appear within a few days under the 24/0, 18/6 or 12/12 photoperiods. Male flowers grow more vigorously and plentiful under the 12/12 photoperiod.

A male plant will continue to flower for the remainder of its flowering period developing new calyx formations and male flowers. It can take anywhere between 12 hours and one week from calyx development for male flowers to appear and shed their pollen. It is very important to separate the males from the females as early as possible if you are growing a sinsemilla crop. In general males usually appear before females.

Pollen can easily be collected as described in Chapter 15. You can also gather falling pollen using a white sheet of paper placed in between the plant stem on the top of the pot. All fans must be turned off if you want to collect pollen this way. Fans will only blow pollen around your grow room.

Female plants can be pollinated at any time but are best pollinated between 15 and 30 days into their flowering period. Plants that are pollinated less than three weeks before harvest may result in immature seeds although plants pollinated two weeks before harvest have been known to produce seeds mature enough for germination.

FLOWERING

If all has gone well and you've cared for your plants, they will now enter the flowering stage of the life cycle. You will remove the males and should have a number of females to work with. This is going to be the most important time you'll spend taking care of your plants.

The male plant produces pollen sacks, which, when ripe, burst and scatter pollen to the female plants. The female plant produces white hairs at the internodes and top cola (head) of the plant during flowering. These hairs (pistils) begin to curl slightly and grow longer and thicker. The top cola should carry the most pistils. These pistils are sticky to touch (don't touch them too much as they also contain the sought-after THC), and become covered in resin during the flowering period. The reason for their stickiness is that the pistils are used by the female to catch falling pollen. If the female plant isn't pollinated she'll try to grow more sticky areas. Hence the results of a sinsemilla crop...bigger and better buds.

During the strict 12/12 cycle, a female plant will fill out more. More leaves, more branches and more flowers develop until eventually, plants reach a peak period of flowering. Your plant will start to almost take the shape of a Christmas tree. The lower fan leaves will be stretched to the maximum in order to receive the most light. Running upward in a cone shape the plant will exhibit strong floral and leaf development.

During the peak period of flowering, the female pistils on the flower's tips will swell. When the swelling occurs, the pistils will begin to change in color. They'll generally change from a white to an orange tint or from a red to a brown tint. All strains are different but in general it's a white to red or a red to brown color change. It's best to use the breeder's recommended flowering times for harvest guidelines. When your plants do this you're ready to harvest and sample your favorite herb. Each strain has its own flowering times and each strain may also have a different color tint when they reach a flowering peak.

A female floral cluster developing at a node region.

Most strains have trichome development on the pistils and their surrounding leaves.

8 | ADVANCED INDOOR SOIL-BASED GROW METHODS

NEW, ADVANCED WAYS OF IMPROVING YOUR CANNABIS plants' yield have emerged over the past several years and some methods have become quite popular. The three most common types of advanced indoor growing are SOG, ScrOG and cabinet growing. SOG and ScrOG are ways of growing serious numbers of cannabis top colas. Cabinet growing is a method of stealthily growing several plants in the corner of any room without drawing too much attention to your grow. Although these methods don't have to be soil-based (you can adapt a hydroponics setup to use these methods as well) soil is the most widely used medium in these setups, and so will be the focus of this chapter.

The idea behind these advanced indoor grow methods is that, in most cases, the cola is going to produce the most bud so why not try to get that part of the plant to grow really big by creating an environment that concentrates on the top part of the plant? After all, the bottom branches of indoor cannabis plants don't catch much of the light cast from your HIDs. Enter SOG, which stands for Sea of Green and the two other advanced indoor grow methods we will discuss in this chapter.

PREPARING THE 'SPECIAL CLONE MOTHER'
Before we discuss these popular advanced grow methods we will touch on cloning because this is an important part of advanced cultivation. Before you select that 'special' plant that you wish to replicate numerous times via cloning you must first of all grow out a test crop from seed. During the third and forth week of vegetative growth you take cuttings from all the test plants and label each one. How to take cuttings and grow them is discussed in Chapter 11.

You must not flower any of these cuttings. If any of cuttings get too big to manage then reproduce them by taking further cuttings from each one and labeling them. Continue to grow the test plants and flower them by manipulating the photoperiod. At this point you can remove the males and the corresponding male clones because we are only looking for a special female. At the end of the test plants' flowering period you should be able to identify the 'special' mother plant that has done better than all the others. The corresponding cutting that was taken from this 'special' plant is then allowed to grow to its full size. The other cuttings are simply discarded because you will not be using them. In order to ensure that you find a good 'special clone mother' you should try and grow more than twenty plants. Good breeders will test grow as many as 100 or even 1000 plants to find a truly exceptional specimen.

The reason for taking the cuttings before flowering is so that you will not have a bunch of flowering cuttings, which need to be reverted to vegetative growth.* That would be too time-consuming.** If the clone has flowers on it then it can be flowered right away by manipulating the photoperiod. The result is much like a piece of bud on a small stick. Clones carry the same age as the parent plant they where taken from. Not only that but they are sexually mature enough to flower if taken from a flowering plant. If they only had a week to go before flowering then you will have to wait a week before you can flower them. You can flower two-inch clones if they were taken from a plant during the flowering cycle. They will finish when their flowering time is over but the quantity is reduced because the clone was not allowed to grow more node regions during vegetative growth. *In short, clones are best if taken from the mother before flowering begins.*

A cutting that is taken in the vegetative state allows the grower more control over the plant. That is why you should take lots of cuttings from different plants during the vegetative stage of growth and then later select the clone(s) that came from the 'special clone mother'. You might want to allow the 'special clone mother' to fully flower at the end of the test grow to confirm the plant's potency. The corresponding clone(s), on the other hand, will not have flowered yet because you will have kept the clone(s) in a constant state of vegetative growth under a 24-hour light cycle. It is your job, as the grower, to then take multiple cuttings and grow these multiple clones into a room full of highly potent, 'special females'!

You should also keep at least one cutting from this original clone mother elsewhere and in the vegetative growth stage so that you can continue to take cut-

---

*Reverting to vegetative growth or 're-veging' is covered in detail in Chapter 11.
**Clones usually take up to three weeks to root properly but some root in two weeks. This is covered in Chapter 11. You should root your clone before trying to flower them if you want to see the 'bud on small stick' effect.

tings. This clone that is put aside becomes the new 'clone mother' and is the source for all our future clones of this special plant.

The disadvantages of selecting for that special clone is that it takes time to grow the test crop and you need two grow spaces to house your plants. Once you have finished harvesting, you must grow the special clone for three weeks before you take multiple cuttings from her. How many cuttings you take depends on how many clones you want to grow to full maturity next time around. Sometimes you might have to go another round in order to generate enough clones. Clones also share the exact same problems — be it pest resistance, nutrient requirements or genetic disorders. If a problem affects one clone then it will generally affect all the rest just as quickly. The advantage of using clones is that you can have a room full of identical copies of that special plant you really liked. You will not need to prune the plants to keep them in formation. It is possible to produce twice the harvest size of the test grow based on the selection of a clone that yielded more than others did.

For clarity we will list each process step by step.
1. Grow a large test crop.
2. Take cuttings from each plant and label everything.
3. Do not flower the cuttings.
4. Continue to grow the test crop.
5. Remove the males during flowering and their corresponding clones.
6. Select the best female at the end of flowering and her corresponding clone.
7. Grow the new clone mother but do not flower her.
8. Take multiple cuttings from the new clone mother when she has developed lots of branches. You can use pruning techniques to increase branch numbers.
9. Use these clones as your next source of genetics for your following grow.
10. Keep at least one clone aside and do not flower it. It will be the next clone mother.

Growers like to sometimes swap or buy clones because it prevents them for having to grow a test crop and select a special female. Although this method is certainly less time-consuming it means that you will have to communicate with other growers and this is a security risk. Sometimes medical cannabis clubs offer clones for sale to medical users.

Although any of the advanced growing methods can be done from seed you will not get all the benefits unless you use clones.

SOG

A SOG setup can be any size but must maintain the same basic shape and follow certain SOG rules. In SOG grows you're looking at one plant per square foot or even one plant per 0.1 square feet. Very short Indica plants can be grown in as little space as 0.1 square feet. Most Indica varieties can be grown in less that 1.0 square feet but in general most growers end up using 0.5 square feet per plant. Pure Sativa strains generally do not need to go much more than 1.5 square feet in SOG. This should give you a good idea of how many clones you will need for your grow area.

Next, you need to select pots for the setup. SOG calls for tube-shaped pots or pots of greater depth than width. You can make these yourself or buy these pots in a store. The objective here is to pack as many pots full of plants as you can into the SOG grow area so that it becomes a big cluster of pots with clones. This is the basic rule of any SOG grow. Pack everything in as densely as you can. The clones are planted all at once, after which time no new plants are introduced into the SOG grow room. When they have reached the desired height (keep it small), they should be flowered. It usually takes about one to two weeks of vegetative growth before the clones are ready to be flowered.* Because the clones have been taken from a mother plant, they are effectively adult plants carrying the age of the mother plant with them and don't need to spend much time in the vegetative growth stage of the life cycle. Since you took them from a plant that was nearly flowering they'll start to flower shortly after you introduce the 12/12 light cycle.

The end result will be a full, dense canopy of bud, hence the name Sea Of Green. Because you're using clones, you only have to grow them for the remainder of their flowering times. You can expect to turn out a large quantity of bud every couple of months (a short period of vegetative growth with a full period of flowering).

SOG essentially uses clone plantlets to increase the rate of bud production in a growing operation. It is especially useful where grow height is a problem because the plantlets will never reach their optimal size. SOG plants are always much shorter than plants grown from seedlings and they are flowered as quickly as possible in the SOG environment. You can not do this with seedlings because young cannabis plants are not sexually mature enough to be flowered like this. In fact sexual orientation is not even genetically determined until the third of fourth week of vegetative growth. This same rule applies to feminized seeds that can become males under certain conditions.

---

*Remember to add for a rooting time of two to three weeks before you begin vegetative growth.

SCROG

ScrOG is like a SOG grow except that fewer plants are used in conjunction with a screen to fill the grow area with heavy top colas — hence its name, ScrOG or Screen of Green.

The screen is simply a large wire mesh placed between your light and the plants. Again, clones from a female plant are used, but we allow at least one square foot per flowering plant in the ScrOG method. The plants aren't flowered until they have covered the entire mesh with green. As the plants grow up through the wire mesh they're trained and worked around the netting to form a very even canopy. The top colas and side branches are all trained under the screen.

ScrOG by A Merry Caner

Another basic ScrOG grow, by Rattdog

There are many variations of the above two methods, yet they all utilize the same principles. SOGs and ScrOGs were originally developed to get the most out of poor quality fluorescent lights. The grower would line the roof of the shelf or box with fluorescent tubes to try and get the most out of their grow. Today's growers, using good HID bulbs, have taken these setups to a new level: pushing their buds to the limit. Some people even grow top colas that are the size of large corncobs or soda bottles!

ScrOG Growing
by RealHigh

RealHigh is a ScrOG lover and has been growing ScrOG style for some years. He has added a bit to the ScrOG method through his experience with the process. This should help you understand more about the ScrOG method and what people have learned with this new technique.

My setup is like a SOG grow, but a screen is used to train the plant to grow horizontally, creating a canopy of buds beneath the light. The screen is simply made from chicken wire or nylon poultry fencing, or you can use hooks and 20 lb. fishing line to make the net.

This picture shows a ScrOG variation. It is a small ScrOG setup for a cabinet grow. This picture also contains a home-made octagonal vented hood for a 250-watt HPS light. Picture by Foz.

The screen is installed at a fixed height above the plant medium. For Indica varieties the screen does not need to be much more than 8 inches above the pots. Indica Sativa hybrids need about 12 inches while Sativa plants tend to have longer internodes so you may have to use a screen that is about 18 inches above the pots. If your strain is a pure Sativa variety, like Haze or Thai, you may have to raise your screen to around 24 inches. This space allows the base of the plant a certain amount of vertical growth before branching occurs on the clone. The clone should start to branch just under the screen but if it does not do not worry because you are going to be training them anyway. The light should be suspended by adjustable chains so that it can be raised if necessary.

ScrOG growing doesn't require as many plants as SOG (allow at least one square foot per flowering plant), but takes anywhere from one to three weeks longer per grow because we will be in the vegetative growth stage longer than a SOG grow to allow the plants to fill out.

The plants are trained to grow horizontally under the screen until they're two weeks into the flowering cycle, at which point you let the tops grow vertically through the screen. You should always train the main growing tops from the outside of the screen moving inwards so that the colas are focused as closely as possible on the light dispersed from the bulb. You will not be able to get all of them centered under the light, but you should aim for this shape. As the tops grow vertically, push the large fan leaves down under the screen, allowing the light to get to all the developing bud sites.

If leaf growth is excessive, you can first cut fan leaves in half making a shorter leaf and allowing light to get to the bud site. Leaving half the leaf on the plant still allows it to make energy for the plant to grow. Taking a whole fan leaf away in one go can stunt growth. In about a week, you can take off the rest of the leaf. Some people don't remove the leaf at all, but I do it to help with air movement, reduce the chance of mold or fungus and to allow more light to penetrate the bud sites. Just remember to remove a little at a time if you do remove leaf mass.

At this point flowers are forming and growing vertically, creating a carpet of bud above the screen. Now we go below the screen and remove all the lateral branches and stray bud sites. The canopy has thickened enough that light is blocked from reaching this lower growth. It's only diverting your plants' energy away from the buds. You can remove all branches that haven't made it to the screen and the stray bud sites but you may experience stunting. Although you want the plant to concentrate all of its grow energy on the developing flowers above the canopy, removing too much leaf mass and branching can prevent additional flowering.

The three main differences between a SOG and ScrOG grow are the number of plants grown, the use of a screen and the slightly longer grow cycle of the ScrOG. Both methods can be done under the same light and in soil or with hydroponics. There are many variations of the ScrOG grow — including V-ScrOG, Stadium ScrOG, Flat ScrOG and Cylinder ScrOG — but they are all based on the same principles. They work essentially the same way but use different shapes.

One of the best strains available for your ScrOG garden is C99. You will find *that a pure Indica or Indica dominant cross will produce the best in a ScrOG grow. A good ScrOG grow will average two ounces of bud per square foot of screen, but you can't expect this the first few grows, because it takes proper timing and the correct strain to accomplish this.*

ScrOG was originally designed for grow areas limited in height and lit by fluorescents. Today's growers are using HID lights for growing ScrOG. They've taken it to the next level with these lights and are generating far greater results. Today's grower is always trying something new to improve the production of their favorite plant.

So there we have RealHigh explaining how he has worked with the ScrOG system. As you can see, he's added more to the basic ScrOG grow. With experience, practice and experimentation, you too can create your own customized grow.

++ Some Notes on SOG and ScrOG Growing

Even though MH and HPS lights can be used in conjunction with ScrOG and SOG grows, most ScrOG and SOG growers will use HPS because of the short vegetative period before flowering. Sometimes growers use smaller wattage HPS lights like the 250W and 400W series to keep the cost of electricity down and bud production within an acceptable range. In fact, ScrOG grows are so dense that smaller lights are sometimes more cost-effective than lights in the 600 to 1000W range, but again this depends on your strain and level of experience. If you get it right you can effectively direct 95% of available light onto your bud. The end result is like a canopy of pure bud with the light belting down on top of it all for 12 hours a day.

Some ScrOG growers like to tie the center of the screen down to avoid it being pushed up by the center of the bud production, which should be the most vigorous since it is directly under the light. If the plants were to push the screen up it would affect the overall results because the light would not be able to reach all the bud areas. The pushing effect could also cause stems and branches to break.

You should not leave your plants growing in vegetative growth for too long because this causes more leaf matter to develop than bud which will make our SOG or ScrOG grow less effective. Also watch out that you do not crush or pinch the stems as this will cause branches to develop at those areas or close to them. Branch development means that plant energy is being used in leaf and branch promotion rather than bud production.

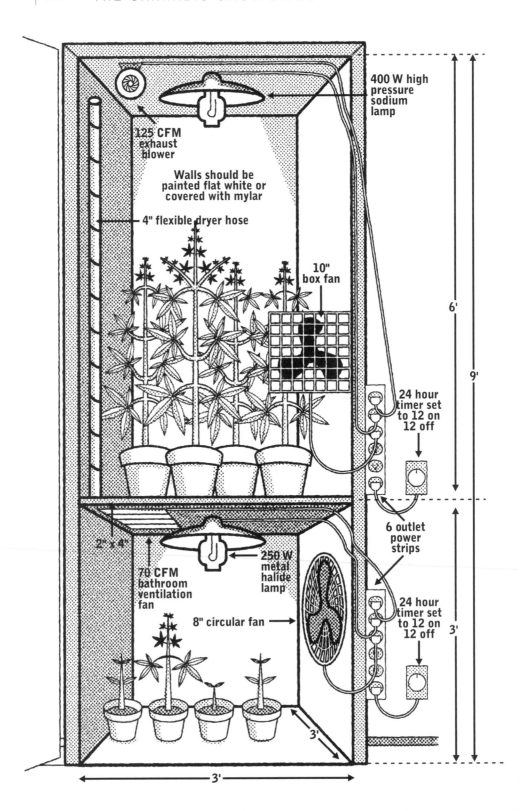

400 W high pressure sodium lamp

125 CFM exhaust blower

Walls should be painted flat white or covered with mylar

4" flexible dryer hose

10" box fan

24 hour timer set to 12 on 12 off

6'

9'

6 outlet power strips

2" x 4"

70 CFM bathroom ventilation fan

250 W metal halide lamp

8" circular fan

24 hour timer set to 12 on 12 off

3'

3'

3'

You can experiment with different shapes of ScrOG to see how it effects your overall yield. Some ScrOG growers even advocate a dome shaped screen to match the curvature of light dispersal patterns — however it must also be said that the differences between shapes in the final yields is not always significant and the overall effect is more exciting looking than anything else.

CABINET GROWING

Although cabinet growing is not truly an advanced method of cannabis cultivation it certainly is a very popular one because of its ease of use, containment, stealth and harvest results. A cabinet can be anything from a small closet, an old refrigerator, a box or a simple cupboard. The grow area is usually small and can accommodate one to twelve plants at a time. The idea behind a cabinet grow is to keep a cycle of plants growing at all times. There are three things a cabinet grower needs to get started. They are:

1. Cabinet
2. Lighting
3. Air vent with fan

Most people simply set up their lights so they are adjustable by using versatile chains or a spring-type cord. A large hole is made in the cabinet to allow air to enter while another hole is made to allow air to escape. A fan is placed in one of the holes to extract the hot air being generated by the heat from the bulb. This vent and fan would be near the top of the cabinet close to the light. Hot air rises and should be extracted from the top of the cabinet. The intake hole is on the opposite side of the grow area and can have a fan inside. This fan is generally moving quicker than the extractor fan to allow a fresh supply of air to circulate before leaving the grow room.

Your cabinet can be air-cooled in a few ways. The most common way is to mount a 4-inch dryer flange on the hood and link from the hood flange to the exhaust fan flange with a 4-inch dryer hose. A fan can be mounted on the hood also.

The walls are painted flat white or Mylar is hung for reflective purposes. The plants are usually placed in separate pots and spend their entire life cycle within the cabinet environment. Clones are taken and placed on a shelf in the cabinet. Some people have made small compartments in their cabinets for clones and germination. Such a compartment can be any size, but is usually kept small enough to just keep the clones alive. This small compartment will probably have one or two fluorescent lights for the clones. It would be best to keep the compartment at the top of the grow chamber near the exhaust fan. You don't need an intake fan for these clones unless it is a big setup. A simple hole in the side will allow the plants to breathe.

After harvest, the clones are put into the grow cabinet and the process is repeated in a perpetual grow cycle; the legal term is a marijuana factory. In this kind of setup, you can harvest bud every 30 days with the right strains.

A simple cabinet grow, by X3n0

PERPETUAL GROW CYCLES

The objective of the perpetual grow cycle is to keep most of your plants flowering at all times. This means that you'll have an equal amount of plants in the vegetative growth and flowering stages at any given time. In essence, half of the grow is in its vegetative growth stage and the other half is in its flowering stage of the life cycle.*

CUSTOMIZING ADVANCED SETUPS

As you can guess all of the advanced grow methods mentioned in this chapter can be customized. Many cannabis cultivators have turned entire rooms into ScrOG or SOG grows. For those who are happy with four ounces of dried bud every month a small SOG or cabinet grow is the best choice. For those who want a bigger yield that lasts all year a large ScrOG grow may be considered. When conditions are at their optimum potential, ScrOG growers can produce up to 30 or even 50 ounces of marijuana every two months in a medium sized room. For 30 ounces you would need roughly 30 square feet of space. That is a 5 x 6 foot room with one plant per square foot.

An expert's indoor grow room might also include the following advanced features:

- Several vertically suspended HIDs lights
- Roof, walls and floor covered in reflective material (flat white paint or Mylar) and completely lightproof
- All lighting fixtures would meet at a junction box on the wall
- Ballasts would also be attached to the wall
- Plants placed in large containers
- Multiple air ducts and extraction fans would remove the hot air and replace it with fresh air.
- Activated Carbon Filters installed to minimize cannabis odor
- CO_2 generator to maximize yield
- Electrical generator to power equipment

If you are like the growers who contributed to this book, you will be continually experimenting to make the best use of your grow space. The room will become an intense hobby area and a most rewarding one too. In time you may even begin to learn more about plant genetics and start to develop some strains from your own breed and stock, perhaps even entering competitions or producing some of the finest seeds available on the market. For an in-depth look at breeding and genetics, turn to Chapter 15.

---

* Remember that flowering plants require a strict light photoperiod of 12/12 and plants in vegetative growth require a light photoperiod of 24/0 or 18/6. For this reason plants used in a 'Perpetual Grow' operation must be kept in separate grow rooms or partitioned off from one another.

9 | HYDROPONICS

THE GROWER AND THE GROWING MEDIUM

You now know that plants need a base material, called the medium, that holds nutrients and minerals, drains well and allows air to get to the roots. As you begin to experiment with soil types and mixtures, you may want to investigate the use of alternative mediums to soil, such as rockwool, clay pebbles and other artificial grow mediums.

In the early days of experimenting with artificial grow mediums growers discovered that the roots didn't always respond well to the 'soil-less' medium. Then,

Rockwool cubes are excellent for cloning.

someone had the bright idea of creating a small unit to hold water and nutrients separate from the plant and medium. The roots then accessed the water after they grew down through the medium. Plants respond quite well to the use of a soil-less medium in conjunction with this new design, which became the basic model for all hydroponic systems.

Hydroponics is a very successful way of growing marijuana if you're looking for large bud quantities or bud all year long. Hydroponics is the technique of growing plants without soil in beds of sand, gravel or artificial mediums that are flooded with a nutrient solution.

Hydroponics is a highly popular cannabis cultivation technique, however new growers should note that it does require a certain degree of maintenance and expertise. If a hydroponic system is not well maintained the whole unit can fail and kill your plants very quickly. This is the biggest problem that the hydroponic grower has to contend with. On the other hand, the results can be simply incredible!

Hydroponics, when done correctly, can produce a flowering plant in only 3/4 of the normal time it would take with a soil grow. That's right! Hydroponics can grow bigger and better buds in 3/4 the time it takes to grow the same strain in soil.

HYDROPONIC SYSTEMS

A simple hydroponic system consists of a pot, a reservoir, a grow medium, a pump and a complete set of nutrients. The system is set up in two layers: the top layer holds the grow medium and the bottom layer holds the water with added nutrients. The plant is grown in the medium where it will develop a stem and a set of roots. The roots will grow through the medium and down into the nutrient solution. Water and nutrients are pumped into the lower portion of the tank through a reservoir at timed intervals. The plants drink the solution and expose their roots to the air. If this is timed correctly and the growing solution is maintained properly, the plants will flourish. This is because the plant can devote the energy it would normally spend using its roots to search for water, air and nutrients, towards upper growth. That said, hydroponic systems produce massive root clusters. One can easily pick up a three-gallon bucket full of root growth from a single plant. This is because roots thrive in hydroponic systems.

There are many different hydroponic systems that can be easily made by hand or are available commercially as complete kits. Those that are most commonly used are briefly described below.

A manual NFT system.

Nutrient Film Technique (NFT)

NFT systems are usually bought as all-in-one hydroponic tray systems. In other words, the reservoir that holds the pumps and nutrient solution is contained in the same system although the grower can separate it if they wish. NTF systems are generally very flat and long but some are sloping in their design to allow the nutrients to run towards and through the plant roots and medium. The unused nutrients are recycled to create a constant flow of nutrients to the roots and back into the reservoir.

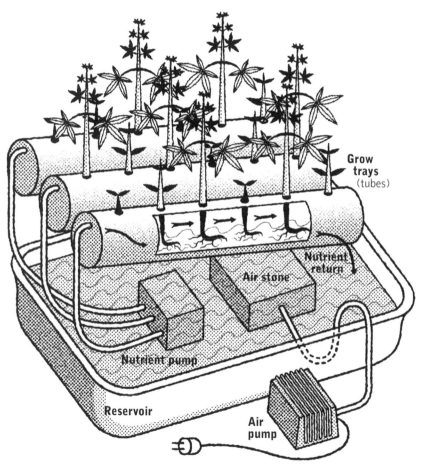

In an NFT system the plants sit on a rockwool slab that is cut to meet the NFT tray's length and width. Most NFT systems come with a lid that divides the space between the medium and solution to allow root growth for you. You should use this as a guide for how thick your rockwool slab should be.

Some NFT systems do not use a rockwool slab. Instead, the trays have holes in the lid where 'net pots' should sit. A net pot is a plastic pot with lots of holes in the sides and a base that allows roots to grow out from the gaps and down into the nutrient solution. 'Clay pebbles' are the most popular medium used by growers in conjunction with these pots because they are very good at supporting cannabis stems and tend not to escape through the net pots into the nutrient solution like vermiculite or perlite does.

Flood & Drain/Ebb & Flow

The flood & drain, also known as ebb & flow, system is another all-in-one system that is easily distinguished from other types of hydroponic systems by its greater depth. The grow medium is located above the reservoir, which delivers the nutrients and water to the roots at a set time and at a fixed rate. This means that throughout the day the plant will go through spells of dryness as the nutrients flow down through the roots and back into the reservoir again. The rate of flood and drain is measured so that the nutrient solution does not overflow the apparatus. An overflow hole in the system also helps to control flow, by allowing the nutrients to spill back into the nutrient reservoir.

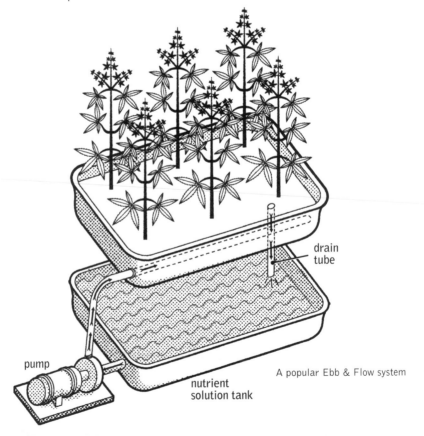

drain tube

pump

nutrient solution tank

A popular Ebb & Flow system

The nutrient solution is pumped into the medium and is slowly drained back into the reservoir again. The whole unit recycles the nutrient solution at timed intervals. These systems are generally flat to ensure that the nutrients find their way to all the plants. If it where slopped there would be an increased chance of some of the plants not receiving any nutrients at all.

Some systems have a separate reservoir, which sits under the system. A hose connects the reservoir to the system and a pump is used to push the nutrients from the reservoir and into the system, where it will flow back down into reservoir again. This setup requires less pumping than an NFT system: in some cases, pumping nutrients to the plants only two or three times a day.

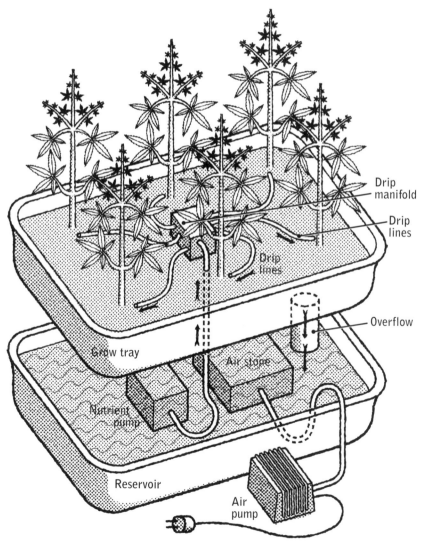

Drip Irrigation

Drip irrigation works much like the ebb & flow method, except that the nutrients are moved to and from the plants much more slowly via a dripper. In most setups, each plant is located in a separate chamber within the system. The nutrients are fed to the medium through a small dripper, which regulates the nutrient flow to and from the reservoir.

Most drip irrigation systems include separate compartments for plants to ensure that each plant receives nutrients. Some drip irrigation systems do not have separate chambers and, instead, plants are placed together in the same tray. In this kind of setup you must ensure that the nutrient solution reaches the base of the plants, where it can be distributed evenly to all of the plants in the tray. In drip irrigation systems, plants receive ample amounts of air and nutrients together, causing them to flourish in a well-maintained growing environment.

Aeroponics

Aeroponics is a branch of hydroponics that has steadily been developing into a field of its own. These systems are generally expensive and are used by profes-

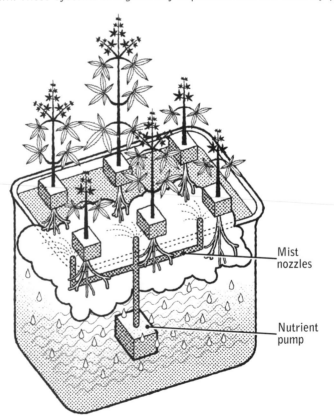

Mist nozzles

Nutrient pump

sional growers. The unit itself is easily recognizable by its unique design, which uses tubes. The plants are grown in a medium that is placed into slots along a lengthy tube. The tubes can run anywhere from 1 to 20 meters in length. Inside the tube are nozzles that mist the roots of each plant with grow nutrients at regular intervals. The reservoir, which contains nutrients, is kept outside of the tube in a tank. The nutrients are pumped from the tank to the nozzles and then the remaining solution that drips from the plants is drained into another tank that is normally checked before being reused again.

Wick

The Wick System is one of the easiest hydroponic systems to make because it relies on a simple wick (or multiple wicks) to absorb nutrients from a reservoir and deliver them into the growing medium. In a Wick System, the nutrient solution is held in a reservoir (a nutrient solution container) above which another container (the grow container) is placed. The grow container holds rockwool, or another type of soil-less substrate, and the plants.

Building the system is simple. Before you add the substrate and plants, make several holes in the bottom of the grow container. Push the wicks down through the holes into the nutrient solution below. Something as simple as cotton strips from an old T-shirt can be used as wicks. The tops of the wicks are secured in place in the grow container to guarantee that the nutrients absorbed are evenly distributed to all areas of the substrate. This ensures that your plants have access to adequate nutrients and water.

Less sophisticated than other hydroponic systems, the Wick System does not offer growers much control over the rate of feeding. In a Wick System, capillary action causes the nutrient solution to travel upwards along the wick. The problem with capillary action is that the amount of time it takes for the nutrients to travel up the wick and into your medium may be much less than the time it takes for your plants to use up those nutrients. To control nutrient delivery to your plants, you need to either add wicks to or remove wicks from your system. If you use too many wicks you risk overwatering or overfeeding your plants. If you find that you need to add more nutrients and water quickly then you should hand water the medium from above. Wick System growers often have to hand water to compensate for slow capillary action of the wicks.

Gravity

The Gravity System is another hydroponic system that is easy to make. Aptly named, it relies on gravitational forces to deliver nutrient solution into your substrate and feed your plants. Gravity Systems are either sloped or horizontal.

In a sloped system, the nutrients are held in a reservoir above the grow container and are allowed to flow from the reservoir to the grow container, where they will naturally flow downwards through the substrate to the plant roots. The solution is then delivered to another reservoir on the other end of the grow container. When the nutrients have completely run out of the original reservoir it is swapped around with one full of nutrient solution and the process is repeated again as needed.

The horizontal system works in much the same way except that there is only one reservoir that is moved manually from an upward position (where nutrients drain out) to a downward position (where the nutrients are captured) after it is emptied into the grow container.

In both types of Gravity System, the reservoirs and containers should each be equipped with a tap so that the nutrients are allowed a certain amount of time in the substrate before being released back into the reservoir again. Some advanced gravity systems uses pumps to feed nutrients from the catching reservoir back into the original reservoir again.

Automatic Hydroponic Pots and Manual Hydroponic Pots

These are pots that are used for growing one plant at a time. In each pot, a pump delivers the nutrients (or they are manually fed by hand) into the bottom of the pot until the nutrients reach the roots. The roots then drink as much as they can until they're dry. Once the roots are exposed, the pot is fed again with more nutrient solution. These units are good for the grower who wishes to grow one or more big, bushy cannabis plants in a simple stand-alone unit — however they do require lots of supervision to ensure that they do not dry out for too long.

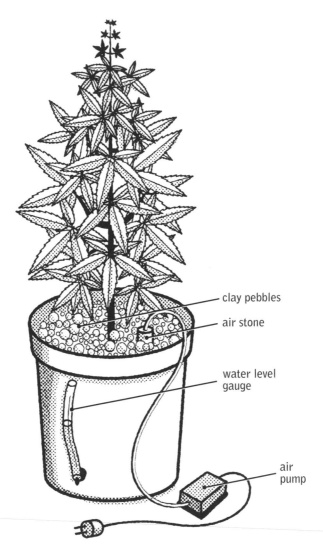

clay pebbles

air stone

water level
gauge

air
pump

An automatic pot system

SETTING UP THE HYDROPONIC ENVIRONMENT
Hydroponic Nutrients

Nutrients are the most important part of your hydroponic setup. Nutrient solutions come in a number of different forms. It is vital to check that the solution you use is the best for your type of plant and setup. Some solutions should only be used with soil as they contain the wrong elements for hydroponic use. There are soil-based supplements/fertilizers and then there are hydroponic nutrients.

Most hydroponic nutrient solutions are complete nutrient solutions, meaning that they provide every element and compound needed for proper plant growth. Because of this, hydroponic nutrients can be pricey. Always spend your money on the correct nutrients because shortcuts can be expensive in more ways than one: they could lead to total devastation of your crop. In a hydroponic system especially, plants are entirely dependent on you, the grower, for nutrients and an imbalance in the system can quickly kill all of your plants.

Hydroponic nutrients come in single and multiple packs, described below.

++ Single Packs

If all the required nutrients are contained in a single pack, there is a chance that the elements will combine and precipitate in the pack. This can cause the solution to become unbalanced, making it useless to you and your plants. Keeping this in mind, get a complete nutrient solution that is contained in several bottles called twin or triple packs.

One brand, called Formulex®, has managed to hold all the elements in a single pack using certain chemicals to prevent precipitation. This pack is very good for starting clones or seeds in a rockwool SBS tray and can be used in soil grows as well.

++ Twin/Triple Packs

For best results, the hydroponic grower should consider a twin or even a triple pack. Basically, in these multi-packs, the chemicals are separated in order to prevent precipitation. Optimum, Power Gro, Ionic, Earth Juice and General Hydroponics (G.H.) Flora Series are the most common multi-part nutrient solutions. The most popular one for cannabis cultivation is the G.H.

Triple pack nutrients

Flora Series, a three-part system with Gro, Micro and Bloom components. An experienced grower can adjust these nutrients to get optimum performance from their plants. These packs have instructions on the bottles as to how to mix the nutrients in water at different strengths, according to the grower's needs.

The Hydroponic Growing Medium

There are many hydroponic mediums to choose from. Rockwool is probably the most popular, is easy to work with and comes in either slabs or cubes. The cubes vary in size from one to six inches cubed. The slabs can be cut to suit the shape of your pot or container.

++ Rockwool

Many growers like to use the cubes for seed germination and for rooting cuttings. This seems to be the easiest method. Many growers claim that rockwool should be pre-soaked for 24 hours in water with a pH level of 5.6 (7.0 for soil grows), in order to stabilize the pH level of the rockwool.

This is a picture of rockwool in various forms. You can see slabs and cubes in this picture. Grow Dan is a popular brand of rockwool.

++ Expanded Clay Pellets

Expanded clay pellets are also called 'grow rocks' and come in a variety of different sizes. They are an ecologically sustainable medium, usually manufactured into round shapes by baking clay in a rotary kiln at very high temperatures (at these temperatures clay will pop like popcorn becoming porous). They are also inert, pH-neutral and contain no nutrients. They are

good for use in hydroponic systems, as they add needed support to the cannabis plants' stems. Clay pellets are full of tiny air pockets, which make them light. Most clay pellets will float.

Clay pellets can also be reused. Just mix 10ml of Hydrogen Peroxide with 1 gallon of water and let them steep in the mix for a few minutes before drying them out. After a few hours they should be ready for reuse. Expanded clay pellets tend to be a bit more expensive that most other soil-less substrates but the fact that they can be reused makes this extra expense worthwhile. They can be used on their own as a growing medium in a hydroponic system but are quick draining and so they should be mixed with another substrate when used with soil or soil-less based growing techniques.

++ Oasis Cubes

Oasis® cubes also come in several formats, including Horticubes® and Rootcubes®. They are like rockwool cubes but are made from different materials. Prior to use, Oasis cubes should be completely saturated with water. If you use a tray to soak them, you can drain away the excess water by tilting the tray over on its side, leaving about an eighth of an inch of water in the tray. Feel the weight of the tray — it should feel heavy. Oasis holds a lot of water! Like rockwool, growers can expect a high success rate using Oasis cubes. Oasis should never be allowed to completely dry out.

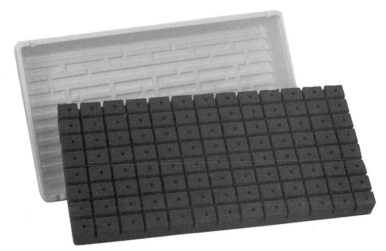

++ Coconut Fiber

Coconut fiber provides added protection from root diseases and fungus infestation. It also contains natural rooting hormones. Coconut fiber comes dry and compressed usually in block format. It must be re-hydrated to a texture similar to that of wet ground coffee. When re-hydrated, most of the compressed blocks expand to roughly nine times their original size. Coconut fiber can also be purchased in different thickness and lengths of mats (1/2 inch thick and 24 to 36 inch widths). These mats are very suitable for hydroponic systems as they can be placed directly into the tray without requiring much shaping. Coconut fiber also retains moisture, which helps to prevent the roots from drying out between watering cycles.

++ Soil-less Mixes

Soil-less mixes are pre-packaged bags of combinations of soil-less substrates. The soil-less substrates and ratios used are usually printed on the bag. They can include the following: vermiculite, screened peat, peat, perlite, composted bark, fine silica sand, quartz, construction grade sand and coconut fibers. Most growers prefer to prepare their own soil-less mixes because it is cheaper and offers them more control.

++ Perlite

Perlite is the name for a naturally occurring silicon-based rock. Perlite is distinguished from other rocks by its ability to expand to up to twenty times its original size when heated. This increase is due to water present in the raw rock. When heated, the rock pops like popcorn into large pieces of nutrient- and water-retaining puffy perlite. Perlite is a form of natural glass and is graded as chemically inert. It usually has a neutral pH of 7.

ANALYSIS OF PERLITE *	
ELEMENT	%
Aluminum	7.2
Bound water	3.0
Calcium	0.6
Iron	0.6
Magnesium	0.2
Oxygen	47.5
Potassium	3.5
Silicon	33.8
Sodium	3.4
Trace elements	0.2
TOTAL	100.0
*Some elements subject to change.	

++ Vermiculite
Vermiculite is the name given to 'hydrated laminar magnesium-aluminum-iron-silicate'. When heated, vermiculite expands into worm-like pieces (the name ver-miculite comes from the Latin 'vermiculare' which means to breed worms). These pieces can expand up to thirty times their own size. This makes vermicu-lite a good water- and nutrient-retaining material for horticultural use.

ANALYSIS OF VERMICULITE %*	
ELEMENT	%
Silicon	30.6
Aluminum	14.4
Magnesium	19.7
Calcium	4.3
Potassium	5.1
Iron	9.9
Titanium	3.2
Water	11.8
Trace elements	1.0
TOTAL	100.0
*Some elements subject to change.	

PREPARING NUTRIENT SOLUTIONS

Always follow the instructions on the products and dilute to the strength that best suits your strain. All you need is a container in which to mix the nutrient solution and the nutrients themselves. Each of the packs should have A, B and C written on them and this method of tagging is used to calculate the mixture instruction on the label. A usually represents the primary nutrients, B the secondary nutri-ents and C the micronutrients. In some cases, A represents the vegetative food, B the flowering food and C either the secondary nutrients or a secondary and micronutrient mixture. Check your pack for specific details.

In most cases the mixture is about 3.5 ml of each (A, B and C) per liter of water. This is called a 100 percent strength mixture if you follow the instructions on the pack.

Hydroponic pH

After you have mixed your nutrient solution you'll want to take a pH reading of it. Just as in soil growing, you may need to adjust your pH level; however *you do not adjust pH to the same levels.* For hydroponics, you will need a pH up and pH down adjusting solution. These are relatively inexpensive and can be added to your solution to balance the pH level. *Cannabis plants in a soil system like a pH of 7, but in hydroponic systems they like a pH of 5.2 to 6.3. You'll discover it is easier to maintain a pH range than a set level.* Check your hydroponic pH level as often as you can, as the pH level can change very quickly in hydroponic systems.

pH up and pH down products for hydroponic use.

Algae

Algae is part of a large group of non-**vascular**, mainly aquatic cryptogams capable of photosynthesis. Always keep your container away from exposure to direct light, as algae will grow if you do not. Most hydroponic kits are manufactured to be lightproof* to eliminate this problem. If you built your own system, like the bubbler described later in this chapter, then you will want to keep your solution sealed from the light using thick black tape to cover the lid and the entire reservoir. This will help prevent algae from growing in your system. A thick, black garbage bag also works well to keep the light out and algae from forming.

If you notice algae growth then you will need to clean your system. Wash the unit and replace the nutrient solution with a fresh mix. Throw out all old algae-infested nutrients. Also try to find the source of the light leak and patch it up.

Grow and Bloom

Some of the double nutrient packs come in two different sets: grow and bloom. The grow solution is used during the plants' vegetative growth stage and the bloom is used during the flowering stage. The bloom formulas contain more phos-

*Mylar is an excellent material to patch light leaks because of its high reflectivity.

phorus and potassium and less nitrogen. Other packs have a complete all-in-ɔ. function, but beware; they may lack important nutrients or minerals.

A Word about Nutrient Strengths

When nutrients are mixed at full strength, cannabis has a tendency to suffer from chemical burn. It's suggested that when using any hydroponic formulations with cannabis you do so in moderation for your first grow. Many cannabis growers have bought these products anticipating the production of great big buds only to get great big plant burns.

In fact, even medium-strength formulas have the power to burn your plants. Consult the information on the packs, but in general 3.5 ml of A, B and C per liter is called 100 percent strength. The same amount mixed with two liters or of water is 50 percent strength. Marijuana can grow very well with nutrient solutions of between 30 and 50 percent. It's best to start off with 30 percent strength and then increase as needed. You'll be surprised at how rich a bud content you'll produce with a nutrient strength of only 30 percent.

The most common problem associated with hydroponics is plant burns. I have rarely heard of anyone underfeeding plants in a hydro system. I have heard plenty of reports about overfeeding plants in hydro systems. Over time you'll get to know your strain and what it likes. The better you know your strain the better you'll be able to control the feeding amounts.

CONTROLLING THE HYDROPONIC ENVIRONMENT
Monitoring Recycle Systems

Depending on the setup you're using, you may find it beneficial to recycle your water and nutrient solution. As the plants extract nutrients and minerals from the solution it will be depleted of its resources over time. For this reason we must understand how to monitor nutrients so that we know when to recycle and when to replace the solution. Monitoring systems are a bit expensive. If you have a ppm reader, also known as a total dissolved solids (TDS) meter, you can understand how much of your nutrients have been used and how much more you need to add to reach the optimal nutrient level. All reservoirs will become unbalanced and need replenishing. As a general rule, an initial amount is used to fill the reservoir. As the plants use up the solution, top up the reservoir to maintain a constant, appropriate level. If you start with 10 gallons of solution then you need to top up to that total of 10 gallons every few days.

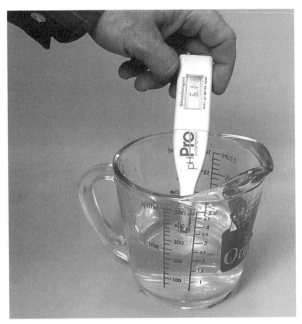

A ppm reader (TDS meter)

If you don't have a ppm reader you can still grow a good crop using hydropon-ics, but it takes practice to get it right. If a hydroponic grower doesn't have a ppm reader they tend to replace the reservoir more often instead of topping it up. That way the grower is certain that the new solution contains everything the plants need. If you have a ppm reader, you only need to top off the reservoir as needed. These readers can be expensive, but over time they'll help save money on the cost of pricey hydroponic nutrients.

Hard Water Problems

Hard water is the most common problem found in domestic water supplies. Water is classified as 'hard' if it contains minerals other than H_2O in amounts above 1 GPG (grain per gallon). Soft water contains minerals other than H_2O in amounts below 1 GPG. Very hard water reaches levels above 7 GPG.

If you observe scales forming in your reservoir or what looks like kettle rust then you haven't been maintaining your pH level in the correct range. Minerals will build up into grains in the solution causing it to become 'hard'. Your local water company can provide you with a readout on your water. You can also buy nutrient products to use with hard water. If scaling persists just drain and clean your reservoir and mix a new batch of nutrients to the correct pH level. Some growers use a reverse **osmosis** water-filtering system to clean their tap water, producing distilled water that has a stable pH level of 7.0.

When to Add More Nutrients

Beginners should rely on a ppm meter, but a veteran grower learns to read the plant. The plant will reveal if it is has too much, too little or just enough nutrients. It takes a few grows to learn to read the plant and this is part of growing experience. The plant may have siphoned all the nutrients or just some of them. Some nutrients are taken up by the plant and stored until it needs more. A top up can be done if you don't want to change the reservoir completely.

If you don't have a ppm meter to calculate nutrient levels accurately, simply record your nutrient mix ratio from day one. Let's say you used 3.5 ml of A, B and C in a one-liter container. If the plant has used 1/2 liter, all you need is to make another liter of 3.5-ml mix in another container and add 1/2 of that to the reservoir. This is a simple way of doing it, but you're left with 1/2 liter of solution. By doing your math and making a mixing chart, you can mix different amounts as needed. Every now and again you will need to mix a fresh batch of nutrient because topping up becomes increasingly inaccurate over a period of time.

AFFORDABLE HYDROPONICS

Growing using hydroponics is not rocket science. It's a simple process that varies slightly depending on what kind of setup you choose. Most of the nutrient mixes are explained on the packs. If you follow the instructions and remember that cannabis only needs 30 to 50 percent strength nutrients then you'll do just fine.

Over the years, many cannabis cultivators have experimented by building their own growing contraptions. There are more than 100 different types of systems that can be handmade at home. Out of these 100, about 15 are ideal for cannabis. One of the most famous and simplest systems is DWC (deep water culture), also known as the bubbler. This system is very cheap to assemble and yet still provides excellent growth rates. There's nothing like it for the price and it can be quite a rewarding way to grow.

A bubbler, by Strawdog

The Bubbler

The bubbler is simply an all-in-one nutrient and plant holding container with a lid and a pump, but it produces extraordinary results! Using the bubbler method, you can produce optimal growing conditions for top yielding strains, as long as it is maintained and managed well, by you, the grower.

++ The Bubble Bucket

1. Get a container that can hold roughly 3 gallons of nutrients per plant. For a double bubbler use a container that can hold 6 gallons. For a single plant you can use a 3 gallon bucket. Make sure that the container comes with a lid.
2. Wrap the entire unit and lid with black gaffer tape. This will keep light out of the unit and prevent alga from forming in the nutrient solution.
3. Get some 6-inch net pots.
4. Cut circular holes in the lid, enough to allow the entire net pot to rest fully down into the lid. The rim of the net pot should be enough to keep it from slipping into the container totally.
5. Cut a hole in the bottom of the container. Insert a small valve in here and use some waterproof sealing around the sides. A good glue will work too. Make sure that the valve can accommodate the pump's air tube without leaking.
6. Insert the pump's air tube into the valve.
7. Attach an air stone to the air tube inside the container. Let it rest on the bottom somewhere around the middle of the container.
8. Attach the air tube to your pump.
9. Fill the container with your nutrient solution just so that it covers about an inch of the bottom of the net pot.
10. Get your growing medium together – rockwool, clay pebbles, and place these into the net pots.
11. Transplant your rooted clone to the net pot.
12. Fill up the remaining area of the net pots with more clay pebbles to support the clones.
13. Turn on your air pump 24-hours a day. That's all there is to it!

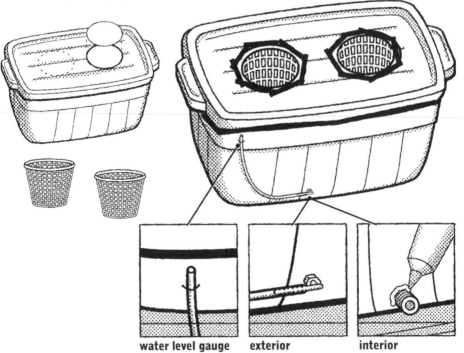

water level gauge   exterior   interior

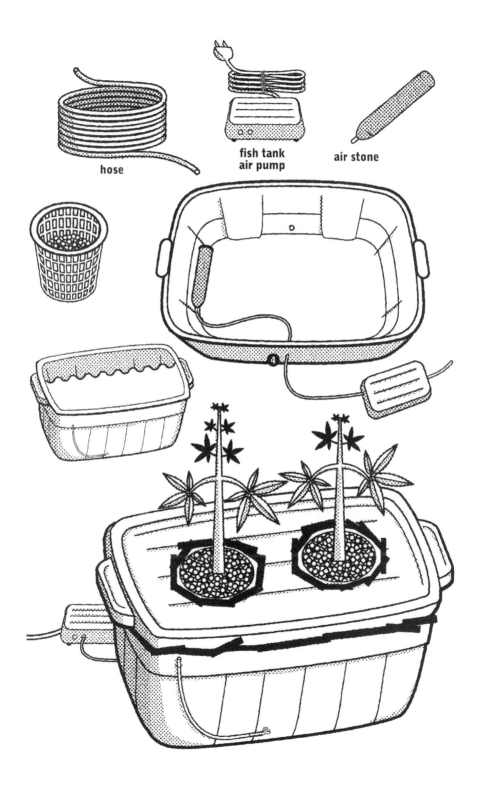

hose

fish tank
air pump

air stone

The pump will send air through the tube to the air stone and this releases air into the water. The air "bubbles" the solution causing it to splash at the surface wetting the bottom of the net pot.

The clone will be able initially live from the nutrients and water that is in the clay pebbles.
As the roots grow down they will experience water bubbles coming into contact with them. They will gradually grow through the net pots and down into the nutrient solution where they will drink until the unit is dry or the roots no longer touch the nutrient solution. Check the bubbler every day to see how much your plant has absorbed.

Let your roots get air periodically by letting a root zone form. To do this, simply let the solution level drop a few inches below the net pot. Do not constantly top up your reservoir, it is sometimes better to let the water level drop one gallon per 3 gallons and then just replace the missing gallons. Once a good root mass has developed your plants will exhibit unprecedented growth!

You can also keep a spare container of the same size handy for when you want to completely change your nutrient mixture. Simply swap the lid over with the plants and root mass into the new bucket. You can do this by lifting the whole plant and root mass out by pulling on the lid with both hands. Just lift the plant and roots out by the lid and put it into the other container. Empty out the nutrients from the old one and replace it with new nutrients. This is a great and cheap hydroponics system that comes highly recommended.

10 | OUTDOOR GROWING

MANY OF THE ELEMENTS THAT YOU NEED to complete your outdoor or guerrilla grow site are described in the indoor growing chapters of this book. If you skipped through Chapters 5 and 6, be sure to go back and scan through them — paying particular attention to information about germination, feeding and cloning — as they will give you ideas about what your cannabis plants need to thrive.

Many cannabis enthusiasts claim that the best cannabis they ever smoked was grown outdoors. If you live in a climate that is warm enough for tomatoes to grow outdoors, then you have the perfect climate to grow good weed outdoors. If your climate is very warm and if you have a long summer then you may be able to grow high-yielding Sativa varieties like the Australian bush, Haze and high yielding skunk hybrid strains. Although these strains have long flowering periods, they also have the ability to yield more than two pounds of bud per plant when grown to full maturity outdoors.

As an outdoor grower, you may either choose your own backyard or a guerrilla grow in the woods or a field as the site for your patch. When you have found an area that suits your needs (refer to Chapter 4), you can start to prepare your plot. Be aware that seeds planted in untreated ground will have a low germination rate. To avoid this problem, most outdoor cannabis growers begin their plants indoors, germinating seedlings indoors and growing them in plastic pots. By cutting away the base of the pots and holding the soil in place using a piece of cardboard secured with strong tape, pots can be transported to the grow patch and planted. This method offers the advantage of cloning all females for transplanting to the outdoor patch — for the ideal all-female, sinsemilla, high-yield outdoor crop.

The months of March and April are very good times to start your plants outdoors because they should mature and begin to flower by August or September — when the daylight hours start to decrease. So, you should plan to find your grow spot and start your garden by April. If you are using clones you will probably want to wait to transplant them until just before the flowering season, since clones only need to grow for a week or two before flowering. Pure Indica or Indica hybrid strains can be planted in May or June because they have shorter vegetative and flowering times than Sativa strains.

Try to remove as many weeds as possible while preparing your grow patch and don't leave heaps of earth around for people to notice. Carry the earth away in bags if you have to. You can then simply sow your seeds or plant your seedlings or cuttings.

If you must work with seeds outdoors, don't bury them too deep: 1/2-inch to 1-inch below the soil's surface is fine. If you are working with seedlings or cuttings, dig small holes and place the plants and 'bottomless' pots described above directly into the holes, removing the piece of cardboard before doing so. Ensure that the pot is completely below ground and not visible to passersby. The roots will grow down through the hole in the bottom of the pot and into the surrounding soil.

You may choose to add prefab, store-bought soil to the patch. Look for a soil with a higher N than P and K value. Adding soil is a good idea because it the store-bought kind does not contain living masses, such as weeds. Even though you may have weeded and treated your outdoor soil patch, it could still contain seeds or spores from weeds and other plants. You'll most certainly have to weed your outdoor area nearly every week during the initial growth stages.

After you have sown your seeds or planted your clones, simply sprinkle them with water. That's all you need to do. You don't need to adjust the soil pH yet or feed the soil. What you've done should be fine for starting seedlings or clones.

If nature does not provide water for your plants then you need to draw water and feed your plants when needed. There are a few irrigation techniques you can use to bring water to your plants however these may reveal your grow site to others. By simply digging a partial trench around your plants you can force the roots to grow in a certain direction. You can also channel running water from a stream to your plants by digging a water route. Water always runs downhill so you need to take this into consideration when investigating different schemes of irrigation. All of these irrigation methods may compromise your security and this is why 'hand watering' is still the single best way to water your outdoor plants.

Polymer crystals have water-retaining properties and can be used in conjunction with your soil mix so that the plant has some access to water during the dry spells. Simply fill a plastic bottle with water and the crystals and allow them to expand overnight so that they absorb as much water as possible before you mix them in with your soil. Polymer crystals will retain and then release the water at a very slow rate, which is why outdoor growers like to mix polymer crystals in with their soil.

When growing outdoors you need to keep your plants healthy and free from unwanted predators that may find your top cola and leaves to be quite tasty. In the second week of vegetative growth, you may even want to spray the area with some pesticide. Pests and predators are discussed in detail in Chapter 12.

OUTDOOR SOIL

If you have not yet read about soil in Chapter 5 you should do so now before read-ing on to understand exactly what kind of soil and nutrients your cannabis strain prefers and how to maintain the right balance throughout your grow. Frequently, an outdoor grow patch is selected because it looks like it is already sustaining some form of life such as weeds, grass, trees and bushes. This usually indicates that the soil is probably a loam type, meaning that it has some sands, silts, clays and humus in it. In some cases the soil may be missing some of these components or have a very high percentage of one of them.

Check the soil in your outdoor patch. Sift through it to determine if it is primari-ly a sand, silt, clay, loam or humus type. As you dig down you will find that the composition of the soil changes. Generally, the top few inches of 'surface' soil will contain humus and some living matter. The next layer below this, the 'topsoil', is the one that the roots will grow down into. Try to determine whether this topsoil needs more loam. If you need more you should consider adding more soil to your grow area. If you have chosen well, your grow patch will not need additional soil supplements and by simply turning the soil you should be able to achieve very effective results.

If you want to dig your own patch go down a minimum of 1.5 feet to a maximum of 3 feet. You should be able to remove a large amount of ground's natural composition. Most growers would do this if there appeared to be too much clay in the topsoil. Clay on its own, as you know from reading chapter 5, is not good for cannabis roots but is good when mixed with sand, silt and humus to form a loam. If you have sand, silt and humus you can mix it with the soil you have dug up. Do this by using a shovel to break the clay in with the sand, silt and humus.

The problem with digging up a patch is keeping it looking natural. If you are using vermiculite, perlite or other colorful soil-less substrates, be sure to keep them well below the surface. A good sprinkling of a coconut-based grow medium over the surface makes your patch look more like part of the surroundings. Coconut fibers also add nutrients to your soil. If you mix coconut fibers in with the soil you will also provide the roots with additional room to breathe and grow. Coconut substrates are very popular with outdoor growers and can be obtained from grow shops.

The next section focuses on the specific challenges that outdoor growers face in caring for their plants from the beginning of the vegetative growth stage to the end of flowering.

CARING FOR OUTDOOR PLANTS
Weeding
The best way to weed is by hand. Don't attempt to add weed killer to your grow area unless you know a great deal about the weed killer you're using and how it reacts with cannabis. Some weed killers claim they'll protect your plant and only kill the surrounding weeds, yet are not very agreeable to marijuana plants. If you want to test weed killers then it's suggested that you create a small patch with one clone to see how the clone reacts to the weed killer. Also, remember that people could be ingesting or inhaling this cannabis so use a food plant friendly weed killer. To begin with, we recommend that you do your weeding by hand.

When you've weeded a grow area, your plant will grow much better without having to compete for nutrients and light. Generally, you'll have to weed the patch every week for the first 2 to 3 weeks and then once every month throughout the plants' grow cycle. Some grow areas may be weed-free in March but, come June, the area may seem like it hasn't been weeded at all because of the speed of weed growth. Whenever you visit your plants make sure you pull up a few weeds to keep them under control.

If you feel your area is very dense with weeds you may want to consider a ground cover. A ground cover is placed on the ground and cut to allow the marijuana plants to grow through it. Covers can be anything from plastic garbage bags to sheets of paper. Of course, this is not conducive to stealth growing, but it does keep the weeds from receiving light.

Most growers who wish to clear a large area for a bigger grow do so the year before. Around autumn growers can clear the area of any leaves, branches and dead matter with much more ease than in springtime or summer when weeds and new plant growth can get in the way or hide potentially good growing areas.

There is absolutely no reason why anyone should ever fell a tree in order to grow an outdoors plot of cannabis plants, unless the tree is already dead.

A very bushy Mostly Sativa plant with lots of node regions promises plenty of bud for harvest time.

Watering

This is nature's job, most of the time. If you find that your crop is experiencing a warm spell or drought during the summer you may wish to carry some water to your grow area. If you have to trek over long distances then it's recommended you fill a backpack with plastic bottles of water. Some garden growers use sprinkler systems during dry spells. This is great but can attract unwanted attention to your patch.

How much water your plants need depends on the size of the plants. Larger plants can require a minimum of a gallon of water per day. Natural loam soil is able to hold water for anywhere from four to six weeks before becoming extremely dry under the sun. Deep pockets of water may be held underground. The best way to judge whether your plants need water or not is through a simple visual inspection. If they're wilting badly, they need water. If you want to ensure that your plants have a constant water source then factor this into your choice of outdoor location and use water-retaining polymer crystals.

Clones flowering outdoors in hydroponics.

If you want to check for an underground water source, simply dig a small hole about a foot deep next to your grow patch taking care not to hit any major roots. Put your hand down inside the hole. Does it feel dry or is it cool and moist? If it's cool and moist then the soil has stored some water below the surface that your plants can drink without any problems.

Nutrients can be added to the soil at any time during the plants' life cycle. Switching to a P feed during the flowering weeks will help promote bud growth. Outdoor soil treatment is much like indoor soil treatment, except for the weeding. For further information on feeding throughout the plants' life cycle refer to Chapters 5 and 6.

If you have good sunlight and enough water then your plants will grow throughout the full cycle quite well. At the end of the flowering season you'll be ready to harvest your plant and reap your bounty.

The more you experiment, the more tricks you'll invent for yourself to get the most out of your yields. Some of the best cannabis growers use very exotic and original methods. A number of people have even tried outdoor hydroponics to get their plants to grow bigger and better.

Air Pruning

Depending on the soil's composition it should retain a certain amount of air between watering. The presence of too much air can necessitate 'air pruning'. If you dig a trench around an outdoor plant, the roots will not grow into the trench. Instead they will sense that there is too much air and not enough nutrients or water to continue their development in this area of the medium. That is why roots do not grow above the surface of the soil, nor do they grow out of the bottom of your pots and onto the work surface or floor.[10b] Air pruning by creating trenches around your plant will eventually cause the roots to grow in the direction of your choice and can be used by outdoor growers who wish to guide their plants towards a natural source of water or nutrients.

Outdoor Flowering and the Photoperiod

Towards the end of summer the photoperiod will naturally change outdoors. The cannabis plant automatically controls its own flowering by calculating the alteration in the number of hours of daylight and the uninterrupted darkness at night.

The plant hormone phytochrome is responsible for regulating when flowering

---

10b. Sometimes roots can grow out through the bottom pot pores if there is a vacuum created between the pot and the dish/tray. Pots with small raised bases help prevent this from happening.

should commence. Normally, in summer there is more daylight than darkness. As the year progresses, there is gradually less daylight and more darkness. Phytochrome reacts to this change and reaches a critical level, which triggers flowering in the plant. However the plant must be mature enough for flowering to begin. If the plant is not mature enough, the photoperiod will have no effect on the plants flowering capabilities.

The photoperiod differs slightly from strain to strain because of the uneven amounts of light and darkness available at different latitudes around the world. Some plants only need eight hours of darkness to trigger flowering and others need more, but most mature plants will be begin flowering when the photoperiod changes to 12/12. Do not confuse the latitude you are growing in with the plant's own natural photoperiod. The plant's natural photoperiod regime is genetic and is part of its lineage. The seed bank you acquire your plants from should indicate if their strain requires special adjustments to the photoperiod, especially if it is an outdoor strain. All mature cannabis plants will eventually flower when the photoperiod changes.

The bottom line for outdoor growers it to estimate when the photoperiod naturally changes so that they do not miss the start of the flowering period due to late outdoor cultivation. It is far better to let a plant vegetate longer than to flower late. If you are behind schedule you may find that the weather is no longer suitable for cannabis cultivation. Early spring is always the time when growers should be thinking about planting their outdoor crop.

Lambsbread is an original landrace cannabis sativa strain from Jamaica. Bob Marley would describe these long outdoor buds as some the best herb he ever smoked.

11 | CARING FOR MATURE MARIJUANA PLANTS

TOWARDS THE END OF THE FLOWERING STAGE, your cannabis plants will fill out and take on a Christmas tree shape. From vegetative growth to the end of flowering, the cannabis plant develops in three main sections: the top cola, mid-section and the base. The top cola will develop a large amount of bud. The mid-section contains stems along with old and new leaves and should fill with buds growing between the nodes. Although these buds will generally be smaller in size to those found at the main cola, they should be just as potent. Growers who find that bud taken from the mid-section is less potent have likely not developed their plants to full maturity. Towards the base of your plant, you will find large fan leaves and a small amount of bud. Growers should learn to treat each section differently to get the most out of their plants.

The bottom fan leaves are generally not smoked or ingested. If your plant is growing under an artificial light source and the fan leaves are not receiving much light, you may be tempted to cut them away. *This is not a good idea.* Fan leaves produce sugar that is used in bud production. Cutting away the fan leaves may cause bud growth to stunt, resulting in a smaller harvest. The only time to remove fan leaves is when a plant is either dying, badly burnt or the fan leaf is covering a large bud mass. Light is probably the most important factor in bud development and if the fan leaf is preventing light from reaching a bud you will want to remove or tie it back. Refer to the ScrOG section in Chapter 8 for information on clipping fan leaves.

You should always remove dead leaves from your plant and throw them away. Never leave dead matter on your soil as a fertilizer, as it tends to attract unwant-

This pruned mostly Indica plant is frosted up with trichomes.

ed pests while it decomposes. Place dead matter in a compost heap where it will eventually turn to humus.

This chapter covers several important aspects of caring for mature plants, including: thinning, pruning, light bending, training, topping, bushing, increasing yield and *cloning*. Using these plant care methods you can directly manipulate your plants to give them a better chance to achieve optimal growth.

THINNING

Thinning is the action of manipulating plant height and numbers either via cutting the plant at the stem or removing plants from the grow altogether. Naturally plants compete for light and plants that grow taller than the rest can easily prevent light from reaching other plants in the group. This is especially noticeable with unstable strains and new hybrids in which some of the population may grow more vigorously than others. The action of thinning your crop either by cutting or total removal creates a more even canopy and allows light to penetrate every top cola without some plants getting in the way of the other plants' light requirements.

Thinning generally applies to outdoor growers, but some indoor setups such as ScrOG and SOG may also need to be thinned.

As a cannabis grower you should aim to produce plants of relatively uniform growth. When all of your plants are approximately the same height, you can more easily achieve optimal lighting conditions. If one plant grows more vigorously than the others, you risk ending up with light gaps. For instance:

- Distance from Plant A to light is 3 feet
- Distance from Plant B to light is 1.5 feet
- Distance from Plant C to light is 8 inches

Obviously you will be wasting light, not to mention space, on this setup. The reason for uneven growth is simply that some plants tend to be more vigorous than others.[*] If this happens, the more vigorous plants will cause the smaller ones to receive less light. We use a process called thinning to control these vigorous plants.

Clones, taken from the same mother, should not need to be thinned because they will all possess the same genetic makeup. The only time that clones will not grow in a uniform manner is if light dispersal is uneven. Obviously the clones that

---

[*] F1 hybrids and non-uniform plants tend to exhibit more of this vigor than stable strains and IBL lines.

receive more light have a better rate of photosynthesis and will grow more vigorously. If all the clones are treated in the same way, they should grow uniformly.

If you discover a vigorous plant, either cut it down to the same level as the others or remove it from the grow altogether. *Do not throw away the cuttings from thinning. You can clone these cuttings into new plants!*

You may be tempted to thin the other way round, leaving the taller plants and removing the smaller ones. Recall that in cannabis growing, if you have started from seed, the taller plants are generally male and the smaller ones are female. For this reason do not give in to the temptation of removing plants before you actually identify their sex.

Thinning your grow makes it look nicer, tidier and helps to improve your overall yield by preventing potentially good plants from being covered by weaker ones that are growing much taller. Remember that height and size have nothing to do with potency. Some plants with very long internodes tend to grow very tall, covering other plants and diverting most of their energy into vertical growth rather than bud production. This kind of competitive growth will only lead to less than optimal results.

By the time you have finished your thinning you should have a uniform grow area with some clones that you can use to grow more bud.

LIGHT BENDING
Light bending occurs when a plant grows at an angle toward the light. You may have noticed plants on the perimeter of your grow area bending toward the light to try and get their share. If your plants bend too much they will eventually grow toward or even into another plant and block other plants from the light. Also, during flowering the buds will become heavy and may cause plants to fall over.

A simple way to avoid light bending in an indoor grow environment, is to simply switch your plants around. If a plant leans too much in one direction, then move it toward the middle of the grow space or turn the plant around. It only takes a day or two for the plant to straighten. If your plants can't be easily moved, as is the case with hydroponic setups and outdoor gardens, then you may have to tie your plants so they don't bend.

If you are growing outdoors and have a major problem with light bending you may have to cut away surrounding foliage to allow more light to reach your plants. If this is not possible, try using thread and small stakes, such as bamboo, to keep your plants upright. Remember: if your plants are bending they are trying to tell you that they need more direct light.

PRUNING FOR YIELD

Pruning is the action of manipulating the number of node regions (potential bud sites) that your plant creates and has nothing to do with the thinning process. Cutting a plant at the stem will automatically result in 'topping'. For this reason, plants that are thinned via cutting will end up growing more than one top cola. Topping is discussed in the next section. This section covers pruning to increase yield.

By using stakes you can also control and separate branch growth after pruning.

This plant has generated more than eight new node regions after pruning.

Prune cuts are made using clippers held at a 45-degree angle to the shoot being cut. For every stem or branch that you prune, the cut area will develop two more branches. This process is natural: just look at any tree to see how the stem divides into branches which sub-divide into more branches which divide into new shoots and leaves. Marijuana plants grow branches out from the stem. Any filling out occurs when new leaves and branches develop at the node regions. Some of these branches may develop new shoots, but these are somewhat smaller and thinner and don't support as much bud growth. If you prune your plant you can make it more like the example of the tree.

Recall that Indica plants tend to be smaller than Sativas. If you learn to prune your plant properly you can produce small bushy Sativa plants that grow in tiny spaces. Without pruning, a Sativa plant can stretch to five feet or more.

Keep in mind that there is a limit to how much you can prune a marijuana plant. If you prune the stem, it will split in two. You can prune both of these new stems and end up with four stems. You can try to prune each of these four stems to create eight stems, but results will depend on the strain and its genetically predetermined branching limit. You might be able to prune some of the lateral branches, but again, if the plant has reached its threshold it will not produce more branches. All strains are different in this respect.

The results of pruning, by Chrisesq

TOPPING

Some marijuana growers will take a pair of clippers to the top of their plant just above the last branch formation during the third or fourth week of vegetative growth. The top is removed by shearing it away at the stem. What happens next is that the main stem splits off in two or more directions, creating a V-shape at the top of your plant. The end result after flowering is two or more top colas instead of one. Now, two top colas instead of one does sound appealing and some growers have even managed to force a plant to grow more than six top colas using this method. Unfortunately this topping method of pruning doesn't always lead to better results.

Depending on the strain and the growing environment, the 'topped' plant may produce two small top colas instead of two big ones. Also, each strain has a threshold for bud production that cannot be improved upon because it is a genetically predetermined factor. On the other hand, some plants when fully grown without topping do not reach their threshold. The strain Blueberry is a good example of this. If you grow Blueberry without topping you won't achieve maximum bud production from that plant, but if you top the Blueberry, you will. Other strains aren't so flexible and the two top colas will simply share the same volume of bud that a single cola would have produced on the same strain.

The two top colas are growing on the same plant as a result of topping.
As you can see both colas share the same volume of bud.

It's advised that you keep in mind that pruning for yield using the topping method is strain-dependent and experiment carefully with this pruning method. Do this with 2 out of 10 plants in every grow. You'll find in time that during this vegetative prune you will be able to shape your plant. Plants are generally pruned three to four weeks into their vegetative cycle, but can be pruned sooner or later or more than once.

Pruning during flowering is not advised as the plant will be forced to divert its energy from bud production into branch and leaf production. This results in a slower rate of bud growth. For optimal growth finish your pruning well before flowering.

FIM Technique

There is a topping method known as the FIM technique. If you push the leaves apart at the very top of the plant you should see a small bud (not flowering bud but an actually leaf bud). Use a pair of nail clippers to pinch off about 3/4 of the bud. This should result in more than two top colas being developed. In a single FIM clipping you can produce up to eight new top colas.

The origins of this technique are humorous. As the story goes, FIM was discovered accidentally when a grower messed up a topping exercise. FIM stands for: "Fuck I Missed".

Super Cropping Technique

Another method of topping is called 'Super Cropping'. By taking a branch between your forefinger and thumb you can gently crush the branch, causing it to develop multiple branches above the crushed area. You must crush it on the correct side or risk breaking the branch. Just squeeze lightly until you feel the branch give, then let go. If it gives easily then you have crushed it on the correct side. If it is hard to crush and the branch splits then you have chosen the wrong side. Practice makes perfect with Super Cropping.

Super Cropping should be carried out during the second or third week of vegetative growth and does stunt the plant. You should also note that plants that are Super Cropped can remain in the vegetative growth stage for twice as long as normal but the end result is a very bushy plant with multiple node regions that should all produce bud. Many growers have thrown Super Cropped plants away because they believed that the plants were not flowering in time. If you Super Crop your plants make sure that you have the patience to wait until the process is finished which — usually about four to six more weeks of vegetative growth.

HOW TO MAKE CANNABIS BUSHES

Some people prefer their plants small and wide. Fortunately for them, making cannabis bushes is a simple process. During the third week of vegetative growth prune half the plant's branches. Cannabis plants need at least 50 percent of their leaves in order to continue growing without experiencing fatal stunting problems. If you prune off more than 50 percent of their leaves, you may end up killing your plants.* Do not prune only one side of the plant; prune both sides to achieve the 50 percent. You may also prune the main top cola if you want to split it into two or more parts.

If the prune cuts you previously made grow new branches and leaves, you may wait until the fourth or fifth week of vegetative growth and prune again, leaving 50 percent growth.

During the seventh week of vegetative growth you'll notice that your plant has started to grow outward more than upward. Let's say you have a plant with eight shoots. That means it is four nodes high. You prune the plant and end up with 16 shoots, but the plant is still only four nodes high. Now this does not mean that you can keep doubling shoots forever. Pruning merely pushes the plant to grow all of its shoots early. If you keep pruning a plant that is four nodes high until the eighth week of vegetative growth, the greatest number of shoots you will get will be about 32. Most marijuana plants will not grow much beyond this factor, but again this is strain-dependent.

Now each new shoot has a junction point or a node that it grew from and each node should produce bud during the flowering stages. It is possible to create a marijuana plant that droops over the sides, completely concealing its own pot. With the right strain, it is also possible to have a single plant spread over an entire 6 x 6 foot space using this method. Creating cannabis bushes usually requires a few additional weeks of vegetative growth.

TRAINING

Training was covered in Chapter 8 in our discussion about advanced SOG and ScrOG setups. Training simply means tying down your plant's main stem so that it grows in an S-shaped pattern. You can also train your plants to bend into other shapes but the S-shape is the most common. Training is mainly used to prevent plants from reaching their natural vertical height without pruning, although you can also prune trained plants without a problem.

---

*Most cannabis plants rarely fail if they have lost 50% of their leaves somewhere after the seedling phase of growth but it will stunt them. Most strains will fail if no leaves are left on the plant.

Training does not stop your plants from growing to their natural height but instead promotes horizontal instead of vertical growth. You can also prune trained plants if you want but most growers just rely on the training to achieving optimal results. Training is accomplished by bending the plant over, attaching a piece of thread to the stem and securing the thread to either another part of the stem or another plant or object. By tightening the thread bit-by-bit, day-by-day, you can successfully bend your plants without causing them undo stress.

Fishing line works very well in cannabis plant training. Some of the threading may be located very close to your lighting and heat can cause some threads to snap or even burn. Fishing line works best because it is one of the most durable and heat-resistant filaments you can buy. Make sure not to tie your line too tightly around the stem or you could end up cutting into it and causing plant stress, topping it or even killing it. People have managed to grow plants of all sorts of shapes using this method — from corkscrews to full circles. Some growers even like to grow their plants horizontally during the vegetative growth stage with just a single 90-degree bend at the base of the plant. When done correctly with the right strain, training can lead to excellent overall bud production.*

If a stem breaks during training, simply hold it in place using a stake/stick and bind it with cheesecloth or a porous cloth bandage wrap. There are many types of plant waxes that you can buy from gardening stores to help close the wound. If you do not have a wax, applying honey to the wound also helps. Honey has healing properties that help rejuvenate plant wounds but must be carefully examined every day for fungi development on the honey-treated area. If you do find fungi development simply refer to Chapter 12 on how to solve this problem. Watch for any new growth at the break area and trim these away, because they will try to break away the upper part of the stem, effectively topping your plant. It is not uncommon to find roots trying to grow out from a damaged area although the high percentage of air outside of the break zone will prevent the roots from growing much more.

CLONING

Cloning is a simple method of replicating your plants. In most cases a clone is taken from a mother plant and grown into a new plant that contains the exact same genetic code as its mother plant.

In a selection of 30 seeds you may find a nice mother plant that you wish to keep. You can sustain and keep using her genetic profile indefinitely through cloning.

---

*Fishing line is also great for keeping those top colas upright. If you find that a top cola is bending over from the weight (and you will after using this book!) simply train it upright by using fishing line.

Any cannabis plant can be cloned once it's been grown to a certain height and has developed a number of node regions.* The best place to take a cutting for cloning is above a node that has at least two nodes above it. The smallest cuttings on average are three inches in length. Once the cutting has been taken it is placed in the growing medium and should form new roots over the next one to three weeks.

One hundred and twenty clones rooted in rockwool!

Cloning straight to soil can have a low success rate and is very dependent on the type pf soil that you are using. Use the wrong soil and the clone will fail quickly. The best soil for cloning is a standard loam type with an even NPK ratio. Avoid using seedling or cutting soils as most of these have added hormones and nutrients that are not suitable for cannabis or cannabis cuttings.

Cloning in water also has a low success rate because the roots need air to breath once they have developed. If they remain submerged, the cuttings will eventually die. In water cloning, the cutting needs to be transferred to another medium, such as soil, rockwool or a hydroponics system. This means that the clone will have to

* The exception to this rule is Ruderalis and other strains that have autoflowering properties. These strains can only be continued with seed and can not be reverted back to vegetative growth.

move through a number of mediums before finally being transplanted to the main growing environment. Multiple transplants can lead to stress and the overall success rate can decrease because of this.

Some advanced growers like to use an aero cloning kit that acts like a miniature aeroponics systems for the propagation of clones. These systems can be expensive, however, and tend to require a lot of practice before getting cuttings to successfully root in the system.

The best medium for cloning is rockwool cubes or Oasis foam bricks. In order to increase your success rate with cloning you may wish to purchase a rooting solution, which can be bought from most grow shops.

Make sure you that use a clean instrument, or better yet a sterile instrument, when you make your cut. Try to take a piece of stem of no more than three inches between the cut zone and the next node level. The longer this section is, the more difficulty the cutting will have in the uptake of water and nutrients it needs to grow and produce roots. Take the cutting and dip the cut area into the rooting solution before placing it into the medium. Make sure that you close any holes where the cutting may have punctured the medium to prevent air from reaching the cut zone, which can stunt root growth. Do this by simply filling in any gaps with little pieces of the medium. Clones don't need much light to root. Try to avoid using the bigger grow bulbs for cloning as this can be a waste of electricity and bulb life. A simple window with some outdoor light is all you will need for the clone to root. Many people use fluorescent lights for clones.

When the clone takes root in the rockwool you will see the roots jut out from the sides of the cube. It is best to keep the cube size small so that you can observe the roots' progress. A two-inch squared cube is ideal for rooting cuttings. Any bigger and it will take longer for the roots to grow outside of the cube. When they do the clone should be transferred to its new grow medium: soil, hydroponics or aeroponics. This is the most successful way of producing clones. The great thing about cloning is that you can create hundreds of female plants from a single mother. Clones also flower more quickly and you know what you are getting in the end because you have already seen, smoked and grown the plant that the clone was taken from. For information about how to obtain the best results with clones, turn to the section on SOG and ScrOG growing.

Two labeled trays of fresh clones. After a few days of rooting the clones will look more vigorous.

Although you can take clones at any time during the plant's life it is best to do so during the vegetative stage of growth. Clones carry the same age as the parent plant. Some clones used by seed-bank breeders are actually more than a decade old. They have been propagated for years and years by constantly taking cuttings from clones and then taking further cuttings from these cuttings. If you take a cutting a week before the plant is mature enough to display sex then the cutting should only need a week after rooting before it is able to flower. If you take a cutting during flowering the clone should be able to flower right away after it has rooted. If you want to revert a cutting from flowering to vegetative growth simply keep the cutting under 24 hours of light and clip away any calyx or flower formations that appear. After a short time under constant light, the cutting will revert to vegetative growth; however any manipulation of the photoperiod will throw the plant back into flowering almost instantly.

Clones that are taken from a plant during vegetative growth are much easier to control than clones that are taken from a flowering plant. That is why we generally take clones during the third or forth week of vegetative growth.

Growers can use cloning hormones or rooting hormones, which come in two main formats: powders and gels. Powder hormones are generally used for cloning in soil. The powder is tapped into a small hole in the soil and the cutting is placed into this hole. A small amount of the powder is then added to surface of the soil so that, with successive watering, the powder will seep down into the soil and promote root growth. Rooting gels are much better because they act as a seal, preventing air from reaching the cut zone. In addition, gels are not water soluble, whereas powders tend to be. This means that gels have a longer lifespan than powders.

A proper rooting hormone should contain the vitamin B1 (Thiamine). As an experiment, cut some roots from a test plant and place half of the 'dead' roots into a solution of water and the other half into a solution of water and vitamin B1. The roots in water with added thiamine will continue to grow for quite some time, while the roots in the plain water solution will die.

The time it takes to root a clone depends on the strain and the cloning method used. Some strains, like Blueberry, are notoriously hard to clone. Others are much easier. On average it takes about a week and half for a clone to develop a root mass suitable for transplantation. Do not be surprised if you find that it takes a set of clones more than three weeks to develop a root mass. The best way to tell whether or not your clones are rooting properly is to clone in batches from the same strain. If some of the clones do not develop a root mass after the others have, chances are that these clones have failed to root. Take one of the clones without any obvious root mass from the medium and pull it up to check for roots. If none have developed then the cutting has failed to root and should be discarded.

You should never let your cloning medium dry out. Keep it damp (not soaking wet) and check for fungi development regularly. Cloning environments containing damp mediums like rockwool are ideal breeding grounds for fungi. If you find that fungi is attacking your clones, consult chapter 12 for details on how to eradicate it from your grow space.

Another method of cloning, called air *layering*, is described next by Strawdog.

How to Air Layer a Clone

Items Needed:

- Plant
- Match sticks or toothpicks
- Tape
- Razor blade (preferably sterile)
- Rooting hormone (Clonex)
- Tweezers
- Plastic wrap
- Scissors

1) Sterilize all your cutting tools before using them
2) Find a branch that is at least 1/8 inch thick with a minimum of two nodes
3) Use the razor blade to split the branch vertically/lengthwise. Cut at least 1/4 into the branch to meet the *phloem.*
4) Use tweezers to open the slit; do not break the branch completely
5) Apply rooting hormone to the open wound. Tape a matchstick parallel to the stem for support
6) Pack the open wound carefully with any grow medium, or use a rockwool cube to cover the area (just split the cube down one side and slide over the branch)
7) Wrap the area with the small plastic bag. The effect should be a funnel-shaped plastic wrap enclosure
8) Pack the bag with grow medium before sealing with tape
9) Use a pin to create holes around bag so that you can water the medium
10) Use an eyedropper to keep the medium wet every day

After two weeks, your cutting will have developed roots and you can cut away the branch below the roots. Now you have a clone with roots ready for growth. You can choose to remove the plastic bag if you feel that it is too tight to allow all the roots to pass through it and transplant the clone to its new growing environment.

This method is especially good for growers who wish to transplant a cutting with roots directly to a hydroponic or aeroponic system. It effectively allows you to skip at least one transplanting step, reducing the risk of shock to your clones. The fact that you can grow roots without using a medium (do not use rockwool if this is what you want to do) makes it an extremely effective cloning method for aeroponic systems.

Bonsai Clones

Bonsai clones are easy to make. The objective is to produce a small bushy clone with multiple branches so that lots of cuttings can be taken from it.

Simply prepare a cutting using your preferred method and prune the clone using the 'how to make cannabis bushes' technique. The end result is a clone with multiple branches and node regions that can give you a constant supply of cuttings.

Keep the bonsai short, about 1.5 feet in height, and you can store it in a very small place. Diminutive bonsai mother plants can be used to generate at least a hundred clones per year.

In countries where cannabis clones are legal, there is quite a market for them. Medical users especially like to buy clones from experienced growers because they know that the grower has worked on multiple strains to find a 'special' mother that suits the medical users needs.

SINSEMILLA HERMAPHRODITES

It is not uncommon for some strains to generate a few hermaphrodites in the final weeks of flowering. This is quite a familiar condition with sinsemilla crops as some plants, in a last ditch effort to continue their line via seeds, will generate a few male flowers to try to self-pollinate. In most cases the pollen produced is not viable, but as a precaution you should clip them away. Simply check your sinsemilla for small yellow banana shapes in the bud during the final weeks of flowering and clip them away.

INCREASING YIELD

Yield, the amount of bud your plant will produce at the end of its grow, is what marijuana cultivation is all about. The more you grow the more you'll learn about what your plants need. The two most fundamental factors in high-yield growth are strains (good genetics) and lighting. Optimal lighting along with good strains will lead to great yields and bud-rich plants. Of course, high yields may not mean highly potent bud. Remember, potency depends on both the strain and how well your plant is grown.

Many growers have found that some of the grow bloomers and advanced-feeding products actually produce greater amounts of bud, but reduce potency and produce a different taste. Learning which feeding products are best requires a degree of experimentation on your part, but experimentation is what growing is all about. *To discover new methods of growing, the marijuana cultivator must experiment and through failure learn more.*

I should caution you that, although marijuana has no physically additive properties, you may become addicted to growing! I know plenty of growers who gave up smoking pot and yet continue to actively develop new strains and discover new ways to increase yield. Cannabis cultivation is a very addictive hobby.

REVERTING TO VEGETATIVE GROWTH

This is also called Re-veging, regeneration or rejuvenation and can be done anywhere between the start of flowering and the end of the plant's peak bloom when it is ready for harvest. This does not work with strains that have autoflowering properties like Ruderalis.

The first thing you need to do in order to revert a plant back to vegetative growth is to quit the flowering photoperiod of 12/12 and change this to a vegetative photoperiod of 24/0 or 18/6. The 24/0 photoperiod is certainly better because it reverts your plant to vegetative growth quicker.

The next thing you should do is to remove all of the plant's flowers and calyx development by clipping them away from the plant at their base. When your plant is bare of its flowers and calyx development you can then choose to reduce the height of your plant to a stage where it resembled its vegetative growth. After a few weeks your plant will revert to vegetative growth and will no longer flower until the 12/12 photoperiod is initiated again.

When you are satisfied that your plant has reached a satisfactory level of node production change the photoperiod to 12/12 and your plant will flower again.

Reverting to vegetative growth is a way to harvest more flowers from the same plant again, however it does have the following disadvantages:

- Reverting to vegetative growth can take up to four weeks to occur properly. This time could have been spent by simply cloning the original plant and growing these clones out instead. Cloning is usually much quicker than rejuvenation.
- Plants that are rejuvenated tend to not produce the same quantities of bud that they did during their peak bloom although it is not impossible for them to do so.

- The growing medium will contain higher levels of P than N and K. This needs to be changed to higher or equal amounts of N to P and K. This can be hard to do without flushing your soil or performing a transplant. Both of these can cause stress which may lead to sexual dysfunctions appearing in the flowering stage a rejuvenated plant.
- Rejuvenated plants go through a certain amount of stress because of the photoperiod change and this can induce sexual dysfunction.
- Stress from cutting the plant during regeneration may also induce sexual dysfunction.

Some other grow books have suggested that rejuvenation compromises the genetic integrity of the plant. This is false.

A good example is if you take an IBL strain (covered in Chapter 15) which is stable for all of its traits and pollinate the females with a male from the same strain you will produce a batch of offspring. Keep some of the male pollen used in this exercise and rejuvenate one of the females. After you rejuvenate her use the male pollen again on her to create another batch of offspring.[*]

If rejuvenation compromises the genetic integrity of the plant then these two sets of offspring will show variations. Do the normal offspring exhibit variations when evaluated against the rejuvenated female's offspring? No, they do not. Thus rejuvenation does not compromise the genetic integrity of the plant.[**]

INCREASING YOUR CHANCES OF FEMALES

A well maintained grow room with plants growing in optimal conditions will naturally produce more females than males. There are some other things you can do to increase your odds of improving your male to female ratio. These are as follows:

- High nitrogen levels in vegetative growth have shown to produce more females than males. This might be a good to reason to use feeds with a higher N to P and K ratio rather than foods with an equal N to P and K ratio. Remember though that plant burn will only lead to stress and this will produce more males and hermaphrodites than females.

---

[*] It does not matter if you regenerate a female that has been seeded or is sinsemilla. The results with be the same.

[**] The compromising of the genetic integrity of a rejuvenated plant usually occurs when the plant has reached an age where cellular breakdown occurs causing death. If seeds are made from this dying plant then it is possible that D.N.A repair malfunction, because of cellular breakdown due to age, may be passed onto these offspring. In this case the genetic integrity of the plant has been compromised. Also cuttings taken from this dying plant may also express the same problems or are mutated.

- High potassium levels in vegetative growth and flowering tends to produce more males than females. Keeping your potassium levels down is another good reason to choose a food with a higher N than P and K ratio where the P and K ratios are even, or where the K ratio is kept lower than P. Remember though that lack of K can cause plant stress due to this nutrient deficiency and this can cause more males and hermaphrodites to appear than females.
- Cannabis plants grow best under conditions of between 40 and 80 percent relative humidity (rH). In the higher rH range of between 70 and 80 your female to male ratio may increase.
- Cannabis plants grow best at 75 degrees Fahrenheit. If you do not allow the temperatures to increase beyond this you will improve your chances at getting more females than males. If the environment is supplemented with CO_2 the temperature may be allowed to increase as far as 95 degrees Fahrenheit.
- Using MH lights in vegetative growth will improve your female to male ratio.

END OF THE GROW

This concludes the propagation portion of this book. At this stage you should have a fair idea of the following:

- The history of cannabis
- How it is used
- The life cycle of the marijuana plant
- THC and potency
- Different species and strains
- Security issues
- Types of seeds and where to get them
- How to germinate seeds
- Setting up your grow space
- Indoor/outdoor/guerrilla growing
- Hydroponics and advanced grow techniques

With this amount of information you should feel ready to tackle any challenges with your grow. Right? Wrong. You still need to be able to answer the question: what do I do if something goes wrong? The next two chapters focus on how to solve problems with your grow. After that, we'll discuss what happens after the grow: from harvesting your bud to making hashish. We will also cover breeding.

12 | PREDATORS, PESTS AND PLANT FUNGI

PLANT PESTS WILL ALWAYS BE A PROBLEM for cannabis growers and should never be ignored. An infestation or infection can kill all of your plants very quickly. Minor pest attacks can stunt plant development, which can prevent them from achieving optimal growth or even cause the hermaphrodite condition to appear in your sinsemilla crop.

Of course, some strains can cope with pest attack better than others and some experts will tell you that a little pest attack only serves to 'harden' the plants up a bit. Although stress brought on by pest attack can cause the plant to produce its fruits and foliage more vigorously, there is a fine line between hardening a plant up and causing the hermaphrodite condition to appear along with impaired growth.

You should also keep in mind that, outdoors, pests have to contend with the forces of nature and predators, but pests will thrive in clean, healthy indoor environments and spread quickly. As a result, you can expect pest attacks to be more frequent and damaging indoors than outdoors. Indoors, any pests must be dealt with immediately.

DOMESTIC PETS

It must be said that, for an outdoor garden, a cat is the number one defense system against most small predators, but a cat can bring unwanted pests into an indoor grow room! Cats also like to play with indoor plants so be very careful with your plants and pets. Cats, especially kittens, like to use the base of cannabis plants as a litter box. Puppies and young dogs also like to play with cannabis plants (including biting their stems). Keep domestic pets out of your indoor grow room.

PESTICIDES, HERBICIDES AND FUNGICIDES

Pesticides are substances for destroying pests. Herbicides are products that destroy weeds and plants. *Fungicides* are used to kill fungi. New growers should not attempt to use herbicide, as the risk of harming your plants is too great. Solutions to specific pest and fungi problems are covered below in detail.

ATTENTION! READ THIS:

Use only repellents and pesticides that are clearly marked for *Food Product Use* on the label. If a repellent or pesticide is not safe for food product use then *do not use it on your plants!* You could be smoking or cooking with your plants later and you don't want to end up in a hospital because of poisoned bud. If a pesticide is safe for food product use then it will be safe to use on your bud. Read the product instructions clearly and carefully. Do not take short cuts. Follow the instructions on the label carefully.

Pesticides

Pesticides come in a variety of different formats. These include: pellets, sprays, powders and gases. Pellet-type pesticides usually come in boxes or tubs. The pellets usually range from 2 mm to 10 mm in length and are eaten by pests such as slugs, snails and larvae. Sprays come in liquid form or as a fine powder that you need to mix with water. Most liquid pest sprays come with a nozzle attached to the bottle so they can be used directly without mixing or transfer to another spray can. Powder pesticides that are not to be used as a spray are simply added to soil around the base of the plant, but not directly onto the plant itself. These powder pesticides are useful for removing low-level area pests like slugs and snails. Gas pesticides are also known as 'pest bombs'. These types of pesticides are used to fumigate indoor areas to eradicate pests. Dead pests can then be removed from the room.

++ Why Cannabis Resin and Soapy Pesticides Don't Mix

Soaking a flowering female with a soapy pesticide is not a good idea for several reasons.

First, any liquid applied to the bud in large amounts will remove some of the trichomes simply because of the way in which it must be applied and not because of the solution coming into contact with the THC-containing resin glands. In fact,

THC is not water-soluble as we will explain in more detail when we cover hashish making and resin extraction in Chapter 17. Repeated application of soapy pesticides as directed will only remove more trichomes.

Secondly, soaps add additional water weight to the flowering plant, causing stems and branches to bend. This added weight and film of soapy water on the leaves and stems can stunt growth by slowing photosynthesis until the plant is dry again.

Thirdly, turning on indoor lights before plants are dry creates a risk of burning as the pesticide chemicals can change composition due to heat. The result is much like white powdery blotches on the leaves with indications of burning.

Try to avoid using soapy pesticides or any pesticides on a flowering cannabis plant by solving pest problems back in the vegetative stage of the cannabis life cycle before any bud or resin is produced.

PEST INDEX

This index is by no means exhaustive. The pests described in this section were selected because they are the most common and are responsible for most cannabis-related pest attacks.

New growers should bear in mind that pest attack symptoms can look exactly like those caused nutrient disorders, overwatering, underwatering, overfeeding, pH fluctuation or heat stress. In fact, the 'bite mark' damage commonly associated pest attack does not always occur. This is because instead of eating the plant some pests will suck on the plant leaves, flowers, branches and stems.

In some pest attack cases the plant's leaves simply change color or curl. Leaf color changes or distortions like leaf curl are often associated with nutrient disorders or overfeeding, so before you make a nutrient disorder diagnosis you should examine your plants carefully for signs of pests. It is good practice to get in the habit of doing this anyway every time you check your plants.

The main difference between a pest attack and a non-pest related disorder is the presence of the pests themselves. Since pest damage is highly variable you cannot rely on the damage alone to identify the pest. You need to find the pest, identify it and eradicate it. A magnifying aid is an extremely useful instrument for pest identification.*

---

* Using small amounts of sticky pest tape around your grow will help you to detect if any pests have entered the grow room. Remember though that sticky pest tape can still catch friendly pests.

In indoor spaces especially, acting quickly is critical. Try to commit the signs of infestation described in this section to memory, as this will help you to identify them quickly if you come across a pest attack in your grow. Remember though that not all insects are bad for your garden. Some experts make the mistake of listing pests that actually do not harm cannabis. Some of these insects instead prey on pests that you may want to get rid of. We will also list these 'friendly' pests so that you can get to know them.

Ants
Ants are small insects from the family Formicidae. They are usually wingless except during mating season. Ants are colony pests, are well known for their cooperativeness and industriousness and can destroy cannabis plants quickly. Ants eat cannabis leaves and carry portions of the plant back to the colony for food storage and construction. Ants are easy to spot because of their size, speed of movement and numbers. Along with leaf discoloration an ant-attacked plant may exhibit bite marks on the edges of the leaves. Ants also farm aphids, another type of pest that growers will want to eradicate. Ants can be removed using boric acid or any popular colony killer pesticide.

Aphids
Aphids are small soft-bodied insects of the family Aphididae. Aphids are the single most common pest attackers experienced by cannabis growers both indoors and out. They mainly live on plant juices by sucking sap from stems, branches and leaves. They are about 1/8 of an inch long and can be any color but yellow/green is most common. Some aphids have wings.

Aphids tend to secrete frothy or foamy waste material, called honeydew, around their feeding areas on the plant and are most likely to be found attacking new growth or the underside of leaves near a node region, but they can be anywhere. Aphids are generally surrounded by their young and they reproduce at an extremely rapid rate and spread quickly. In addition, some aphids transmit viral diseases. This pest must be eradicated from your grow as soon a possible.

Aphids are small and do not move very quickly so growers need to take extra care when checking their crops for aphids. Aphid attack looks a bit like underwatering resulting in leaf wilt. You may also find some plant stunting and exhibiting signs of leaf curl during an aphid attack.

Ants also farm aphids by gathering the honeydew they excrete, and so you must

First fill the container with the new medium.

In this case, a soil mix.

The transplanted clone in its rockwool cube is then placed in the soil mix.

Extra soil mix is added to cover the rockwool cube.

The soil is then patted down, leaving about an inch of space between the top of the container and the soil mix.

Here is the plant two weeks later, growing vigorously. It is important to label our plants, including the variety and transplanted date.

This outdoor plant is watered through irrigation tubes drawing water from a nearby lake.

Clones are best watered by hand and, if using Oasis cubes they should be pre-soaked in a water-nutrient solution.

This hydroponic system uses drip irrigation. The young clones grow in a medium of expanded clay pebbles.

This clone nursery setup uses a wick system. At the back of the grow room you can see a large cluster of plants in a kiddy pool.

This is a hi-tech Ebb & Flow hydroponic system. There is plenty of space to handle recirculating the water and, like the most effective systems, it is well organized and clear of clutter.

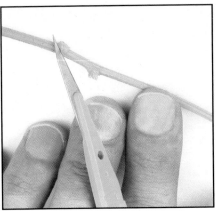

When cutting clones, it is important to use a sharp blade, like a scalpel, to get a clean cut.

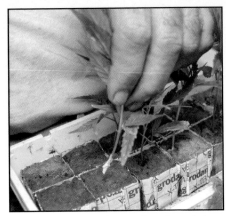

The clones should then be dipped in a cloning solution, before being added to the medium, in this case rockwool.

Here you see healthy root development on a new clone.

A male plant that has seeded, vital for new plants, but not something you want to find in your garden.

A fresh tray of new clones, ready to be transplanted to larger pots.

Seeds germinating, with the fresh shoots breaking through the shells.

The initial start of female pistils growing at a node region.

This is what every grower is looking for, when they decide which plants to keep in their garden.

A close-up of the trichomes, which contain the all-important THC.

This pistil can clearly be seen growing out from the calyx. During flowering even the calyx can produce trichomes. Trichome numbers differ from strain to strain.

Pruning and staking your plants is an important part of maximizing use of space and overall yield.

This small garden makes use of pruning and staking to ensure that each plant provides the maximum yield.

This garden uses clones, transplanted into grow bags with a soil mix. Here the plants are about four weeks old.

Twelve weeks later and you can see how space has been maximized using stakes to ensure the best possible growth from the garden as a whole.

Some famous B.C. bud growing in its natural habitat.

Some kind Australian Sativa growing outside of Nimbin.

A backyard grow, which takes advantage of neighbors who turn a blind eye.

A simple balcony grow in Amsterdam, where the authorities have a better understanding.

These giant fields of cannabis were the result of the Swiss government's loosening of the laws. One can only hope that in the future we see the same sights across America's heartland.

Trichome Technologies, voted "Best Growroom" in the 25-year history of *High Times* magazine.

This elaborate hydropinic setup is simply amazing in its size, organization, and efficiency.

Here, the plants are a couple of weeks from full maturation.

NLx6, THC: 22.5% Back-crossed six times, it is one of the most stable and consistent varieties produced by Trichome Technologies.

Ultra Violet, THC: 16.1% Exotic and desirable, this variety is world famous for its dark color and one-of-a-kind aroma. Pure Indica. Trichome Technologies

Washington, THC: 22.6% Named after one of the first pro-marijuana activists for his dedication to hemp production. Trichome Technologies

Kryptonite, THC: 16.9% This Indica-Sativa hybrid boasts a fruity, tropical flavor and excellent yield, both indoor and out. Trichome Technologies

Even simple net screens can increase overall marijuana bud densities. This ScrOG variation is very suitable for training non-uniform hybrids so that the top colas receive optimal amounts of light.

This light mover allows two 1KW HID bulbs to cover one hundred square feet of marijuana.

Pruning and topping for production is strain dependent. In the background the same strain generates more bud without pruning or topping. Experimenting with strains is important.

Bubblehash has become one of the most popular ways to process cannabis. You need 2 buckets, either 1 or 5 gallon, electric whisk, ice, water, and of course Bubble Bags.

Use up to 50 grams of dry trim or 100 grams of wet trim for the 1 gallon size. For the 5 gallon size, use up to 150 grams of dry trim or up to 300 grams of wet trim.

Place your trim leaf in the bucket with the Bubble Bags already in place.

Fill the bucket to a few inches from the top with water and then add a bag of ice.

Agitate for 15 to 30 minutes with an electric whisk.

Begin the filtering process, by lifting out the first bag and letting the water and good stuff drain through to the next bag. Then continue the process through the ever decreasing filter bags.

Bubble Bag kits come in series of 3, 4, 6 and 7 bags and each bag provides smokeable hash.

The more bags that your trim is processed through the better the quality of your hash. You can learn more about Bubble Bags at http://bubblebag.com.

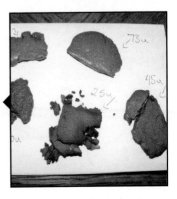

The Sativa influence is easy to see in these long dense buds. Chronic from Serious Seeds.

Some top colas get so heavy they need to be tied up. Kali Mist from Serious Seeds.

Inside of the grow rooms at Serious Seeds. Although a small seed company, Serious Seeds has a reputation for high-quality, stable, and consistent varieties, including the AK-47 and White Russian, which have both won awards at the Cannabis Cup.

One of Greenhouse Seeds' breeding rooms. Among the excellent varieties produced by Greenhouse are Super Silver Haze, White Widow and Great White Shark, to name just a few.

Indica Plants at the famous Hash Museum in Amsterdam. The museum covers every aspect of the drug including hash, marijuana, and other associated substances.

Once the plant is dried out, the manicuring can begin.

After the plants are harvested, they should be suspended upside down in a cool, dark room.

It is important to use sharp scissors or shears, and to cut away the excess leaves.

You are left with a mound of fresh bud and, as a bonus, the cut leaves can be used to make marijuana butter for your cooking and baking needs.

remove any ants before you try to treat an aphid problem. Aphids can be removed from your grow using any pyrethrum-based insecticide. Spraying your plants with pyrethrum-based insecticide before flowering will help prevent future aphid attacks but a full spraying tends to cause a certain amount of plant stress and growth stunting. If you want to keep aphids out of your grow room, then you should spray down the grow room with a pyrethrum-based insecticide before introducing the plants to the environment, making sure that you cover the corners and door frame.

To treat a mild aphid problem try to only spray the infected areas of the plant. An aphid attack on flowering plants can be a problem because spraying can damage the bud and separate your trichome glands from the cannabis flowers. Try to solve aphid problems before flowering at all costs. Chances are that if you have prevented an aphid attack before flowering then you should not get one during flowering unless aphid contaminated items are brought into the grow room.

A soapy pesticide like Safer's Soap can also be used to deter aphids. A mixture of dishwashing detergent in hot water can be used to clean down the grow room and pots of any unwanted aphids by suffocating them. As stated in the introduction to this section, soap and detergents should not be used during the flowering period. Ladybugs are a natural predator of aphids and can be used to control them.

Cutworms, Caterpillars and Larvae

Insects that are in their early stages of development are problem pests because they are insatiable and will eat anything green that they can get their tiny mouths around. Their appetite is surreal when you actually discover how much a caterpillar can consume in a single day. One caterpillar can reduce an ounce cola to stem and stalk in less than four days. These pests pose a huge threat to your crop and must be stopped right away. Caterpillars especially like to eat young seedlings and new growth. They are also known to leave holes in leaf but other pests can do this too.

The only sure way to get rid of cutworms, caterpillar and larvae is to use a cutworm, caterpillar or larvae repellent. Usually the same product will affect all three pests. Cutworms can also be hand picked from your grow. At night they sleep in a 'C' shape in the soil or under the cover of something else like a piece of wood.

Deer

Deer are so curious that even electric fences won't stop them over time. Deer will eat leaves, stems, flowers and branches. Damaged areas are usually large including complete topping of the main cola from the stem. There are much kinder ways to keep deer away from your crop. You need to get a hold of predator urine from hunting shops. Find out which urine works best with deer to keep them away without attracting other plant-eating animals. Simply spray the urine on your patch and this will help keep the deer away. This method has a very high success rate at keeping deer from your grow.

Gnats
Gnats are insects with long, thin fragile legs from the family Culicidae. Gnats can eat leaves but mostly suck sap from the phloem. The damage from a Gnat attack is similar to that of an aphid attack and can be treated in the same way: using a pyrethrum-based insecticide. Gnats cause less damage than aphids but need to be treated quickly nonetheless.

Grasshoppers
Generally harmless to cannabis unless they are found in large numbers, grasshoppers are insects from the Acrididae family with legs designed for jumping long distances. The males make a high pitch clicking sound.

There is a particular species of grasshoppers often called 'locusts' that form in large migratory swarms and are highly destructive to nearly every kind of vegetation. Locust attacks are so severe that they can strip a plant down to its stem and branches within a few hours. During a locust attack the grower can only take cuttings from his or her plant and continue the strain elsewhere. Locusts will even eat pesticide-laden plants when traveling in large numbers so pesticides are rarely effective against these types of attacks.

Grasshoppers are treated as tourists in small numbers. They stay around only for a short period of time and move on. Grasshoppers are best hand picked from your plants if you wish to control them. Birds also eat grasshoppers.

Groundhogs
Groundhogs are a burrowing colonial rodent of the genus Marmota. They eat the shoots and leaves of the cannabis plant. Dry chlorine helps keep groundhogs away from your plants. If you find any groundhog holes near your grow area, apply the dry chlorine around the hole.

Mealy Bugs
Mealy bugs are insects from the Pseudococcidae family. They are often described

by growers as 'hard aphids' because of a waxy powder that makes their backs look shell-like under a microscope. They attack plant tissue and suck sap from the phloem. Mealy bugs are treated in the same way as aphid attacks: using a pyrethrum-based insecticide.

Rabbits
Rabbits are burrowing plant-eating mammals of the Leporidae family. They can be recognized by their long ears and short fluffy tails. Rabbits are voracious eaters and can reduce a crop to nothing in a couple of days. They will continue to feed from the same patch until they're done or the patch is destroyed. The best way to keep rabbits from your grow is to use predator urine. Rabbits also shy away from cats and dogs.

Scale
Scale is closely related to the aphid and comes in several different forms. Scales are born mobile but will eventually solidify (at any plant location but mostly on the branch and stem) and insert a small hollow tube into the plant to tap into the juices. They also spread mold. Scale can be hand picked from your plants with ease because, when they solidify, they stay on that area of the plant. Ants farm scale so ants need to be removed from your grow room before you treat a scale problem. Scale can also be scrubbed from the branches, using a scouring pad. Dormant oil sprays, a form of organic pest control, also kill scale. You should be able to obtain dormant oil from any good grow store.

Slugs and Snails
These pests are molluscs of the class Gastropoda and characteristically have a flattened ventral bottom that they use for movement. They eat the leaves and stem and will kill cannabis seedlings. Slugs and snails are best hand picked from your grow area. Another way to remove them is to make a circle of table salt about four feet away from the base of your plants. Then make another circle a foot in from that. Salt is deadly to snails and slugs and will keep them out. Slugs and snails can also be repelled or killed by using slug and snail pest pellets.

Spider Mites
Always keep a bottle of pesticide that kills spider mites on hand because marijuana plants are extremely vulnerable to mite attacks. Spider mites can reduce your plants to garbage within a couple of days so you should *never bring a plant inside that has been outside.*

Spider mites are tiny, about half the size of this period. Spider mites cannot be seen without a magnifying aid but are normally spotted because they gather in large numbers to form clusters on areas of your plant. Spider mites feed off plant juices and leaf wilt is a common symptom of a mite attack. If the attack continues the plant will eventually die. Spider mites also spin webbing on the effected areas of the plant.

Specialized spider mite pesticides like Avid will curb attacks. Sulfur also deters spider mites. During vegetative growth spider mites can be exterminated using soaps. Sticky pest trap tape is not effective against them. After aphids, spider mites are the second most common pest attackers experienced by cannabis growers both indoors and out.

Termites
Termites are a type of Isoptera and live in colonies. Termites are very destructive, even in small numbers. They have the ability to chew through wood rapidly and can chop a plant at the base of its stem within a few days. Termites don't like water. If you overwater the soil around your plant they will leave but you will be left with an overwatering problem.

There are commercial products available that kill termites but most of these are not for plant use or human consumption. Termites can be killed by finding their nest and flushing it with water. Try to find the source of the termites rather than treating your plants.

Thrips
Thrips are a member of the Thysanoptera family and are minute dark-colored insects with slim bodies that have wings in adult form. They usually attack the flowering parts of the cannabis plant and suck juices from the leaves. Thrips infestations usually cause the cannabis flowers to fall apart and look silvery in patches. Thrips are not typically around for long because their natural predators are beetles, ladybirds, lacewing and mites. Thrip infestations can be treated with any good thrip pesticide or pyrethrum. Thrips also do not like garlic.

Whitefly
Whitefly are from the Aleyrodidae family and are usually about 4 mm in size, although there are more than 200 species of this insect vary in shape, size and color. One particular species even likes to spend its entire life within greenhouses — hence its name 'Greenhouse Whitefly'.

Whitefly normally have waxy white wings and use these to fly over short distances. If you shake your plant you should be able to hear them before you see them. They make a buzzing sound when moving in small groups. The whitefly can be deadly to your crop and can reduce your plant to trash in days. They feed on plant juices and secrete a honeydew, which has the natural ability to develop a dark mold on the secreted areas. This mold will also affect your plants' health if left untreated.

Safer's Soap™ helps to kill whitefly and can be bought in most grow shops. Other soaps and sprays will also kill whitefly. The whitefly's natural predators are spiders, ladybirds and beetles. Pest tape can also be quite effective against whitefly. Whitefly are the third most common pest attackers experienced by cannabis growers both indoors and out.

Woodchucks and Other Small Rodents
Woodchucks will nibble your stems and collapse the plant. The way to solve this is by either using predator urine (see also deer and groundhogs) or building a very small mesh fence around the base of your outdoor plants. This will keep the woodchucks from eating your stems and branches. Use more than one layer of mesh and make sure that you keep it tight. Planting marigolds near your grow will also help keep the woodchucks away.

PEST PREDATORS
There are many predators of pests that, at first glance, may appear to be plant pests but will not actually damage your crop. You should keep these 'friendly' pests around, since they are nature's way of eliminating many of the pests listed above. Beneficial pests can even be bred or bought so that you have a constant supply of these pest killers.

Ladybeetles or 'ladybirds' as some call them, will breed on their own if they have a constant supply of aphids and other insects to feed on. Many places now stock pest predators. Contact your local agricultural supply store to find out where predatory pests might be available. There are companies out there that provide this service and will even send some predator pests by mail order.

Beetles
Ground beetles are usually black, brown or have a bluish tint along with wings and solid covers that surround the wings on their backs. Beetles usually work best at ground level eradicating most types of snails, slugs, cutworms and other insect pests. They are usually found in soil or hiding under debris like rocks and wood.

Braconid Wasps

Braconid wasps are from the hymenopterous family of insects. Their eggs actually act as a *parasite* on unwanted pests like aphids, scale, cutworms and other kinds of larvae. In most instances this occurs shortly after the wasp has injected several of the pests with its own eggs. Injected cutworms will eventually develop several microscopic cocoon-like pods on their back and sides. The braconid wasp larvae sucks the insect dry as it develops inside these cocoons.

Bugs

Certain types of what gardeners refer to as 'true' bugs will curb unwanted pests. 'True' bugs will actually suck all the bodily fluids out of their victims. The assassin bug (red underside), big-eyed bugs (has big eyes), pirate bugs (checkered black and white or gray and brown) and damsel bugs (long and large front legs and are gray, brown or tan in color) are the most common true bugs you will find although there are many more. Pirate bugs are especially effective against spider mites and thrips. Bugs are usually more than half and inch in size and will move relatively quickly around your plant.

Earthworms

It is worth mentioning earthworms here even though they are not pest predators. Earthworms help to aerate your soil along with depositing nitrogen, calcium, phosphorus and potassium in the soil. One organic type of feeding product is called 'Worm Casting' and is mostly made from earthworm waste material. If you farm earthworms you can create your very own organic fertilizer.

Lacewings

Lacewings will eat aphids and spider mites. They are usually green with large semi-transparent wings that extend well past the length of their bodies. The have two long and thin protruding antenna from their heads, grow to about 2.5 cm and can be approached and handled without much difficulty.

Ladybird Beetles

Ladybirds or 'ladybugs' are amazing predator pests because they eat a lot of other insects that are damaging to cannabis. They eat aphids, mealy bugs, scales and spider mites. Ladybirds must eat aphids and other insects in order to lay eggs. The more they eat, the more eggs they lay. As a result, the amount of new ladybirds born is directly proportionate to the amount of pests they consume. One female ladybird can consume up to 4,000 aphids in a lifetime and lay 2,000 eggs as a result of this. Ladybirds are the cannabis grower's pest predator of choice.

Spiders

Unfortunately a common garden-variety spider is not enough to prevent a pest attack from occurring in your crop. You need them in large numbers to prevent any damage and even then spiders are very slow in their work. They also tend to spin webs in places where you do not want them and are not very controllable — however one type of spider that flies is of enormous benefit to your grow and is easy to control. That spider is the common 'daddy long legs' and will consume nearly any insect in your grow room. Because this spider flies, it is not restricted to building webs in awkward places nor is it likely to cover your bud with spindle fibers like other spiders do. Also, those with arachnophobia don't seem to mind this type of spider as much because they are not very vicious looking and are easy to spot.

RECOVERING FROM A PEST INVASION

Sometimes the pests win. No matter how much you might spray to control or kill them, they keep coming back to your grow area. To solve this you may have to create a clean room or simply find another patch, which means a total and complete cull of your harvest — you don't want to re-introduce any pests or diseases into your new crop.

If you are growing indoors, first set up another grow room of smaller size, just enough to support some cuttings and clones. Take cuttings from the plants you have and move the cuttings to that room. You'll use the cuttings again eventually in your clean grow room if you want to continue those strains. Next, take all the grow equipment excluding the electrical equipment to the bathroom. Clean down all of the equipment with bleach. Fill a tub with water and bleach and allow the grow equipment to rest there for a day. Do not wash electrical equipment. Instead clean it down with a cloth.

In the grow room, first start with the walls. Clean the walls down with bleach if possible. You may have to paint them after. If you use Mylar — replace it after. Do not reuse Mylar after a pest infestation as some pests can find ways to attach themselves to it. Don't neglect the corners and clean out any holes, extraction holes, fittings, pipes, etc. Then clean around the rim of the room. If your floor can be lifted up then you can also do this to get at the corners a bit better.

After this cleaning has been done you can consider smoking the room. Various pest-killing smoke bombs can be bought in most grow stores. Follow the instructions carefully and smoke bomb the room. This will guarantee the demise of any bugs, eggs or larvae, but remember eggs can remain safe from these sprays. That is why the labels recommend a reapplication 7 to 10 days after the initial treatment. Once this is completed, clean the room as you did the first time. Repeat the process if needed. The more you clean it, the better it will be.

Now you should have a clean room, free of pests. Electrical items should be dusted before returning them to the grow room. Dry your other grow equipment, which was bleached, and return this to the grow room as well.

Next, your cuttings need to be checked for bugs. You will not move any plants back into the grow room until you have taken cuttings from these cuttings. Grow the cuttings out for a week or two and check them every day for bugs. If you find any then you may have to use a pesticide on the cuttings. When you're sure your cuttings are clean, take new cuttings and place them in a growing medium. Take these to your grow room and watch their progress, being wary of any signs of pests and bugs. If you've done this correctly you should have eliminated all pests in your grow room.

Spider mites and other small pests can lay their eggs in cuttings and can be missed when you look for pests, because they aren't as obvious. The pesticides should have killed them but some pests, like powder bugs, lay their eggs inside the stem and seem to always come back. If you can't get rid of bugs like these then you may have to toss your plants away and get new ones. For breeders this can be a difficult task. A long-term project can be terminated by a few bugs wreaking havoc in the grow room. Breeders should pay strict attention to maintaining a clean grow room at all times. Remember: Never take anything that has been outside into your grow room.

FUNGI

Fungi are types of bacteria, organisms and disease, which actually live by extracting nutrients from the plant. Fungi include molds, mushrooms, toadstools and rusts, and are usually made up of lichens, which lack chlorophyll and grow as they obtain more nutrients from the plant. Mold is a type of fungi that grows in high humidity. Most molds can be stopped by simply allowing fresh air into the grow room. Fungi can be eradicated using fungicides.

Fungus Botrytis
This is the most common variety of fungus found on cannabis plants. It is also called gray mold, gray *blight* or Botrytis blight. It begins its life as a white powder-like growth, which eventually turns gray as it spreads.

Fungus Botrytis forms spores that dislodge and are spread to neighboring plants. The spores can stay dormant for quite some time, so growers should treat all the plants in the surrounding area for Fungus Botrytis. This is because the fungus has a high tendency to stealth spread itself without notice in spore format. Spores do not need living matter to stay alive. They can lay dormant almost anywhere.

If you can solve a Fungus Botrytis problem quickly then you may prevent spores from being produced and this is why growers need to keep a close eye on their plants. Fungi are very hard to clean by hand. Rotted areas must be clipped away instead.

Fungus Botrytis will grow wherever it comes in contact with plant nutrients. This means that the fungus is more likely to be found developing on necrotic plant tissue or other damaged areas of the plant where the nutrients are more readily accessible. From here it spreads to other areas of the plant causing its feeding patches to *rot*. Cut areas after pruning and cloning are especially susceptible to Fungus Botrytis.

High humidity will cause fungi to spread more rapidly so lower humidity levels if needed. In some cases, lowering the humidity is all that is needed to prevent the fungi from spreading. Mold should also be treated the same way. If lowering the humidity does not solve fungi or mold problems then you need to apply a fungicide on the infected areas. Fungicides can be used on the infected areas to remove the fungus — preventing further plant rot. Spores tend to fall downwards so remove the top layer of soil from your infected plant and throw this away. After harvest, a previously infected grow area should be cleaned down to prevent further fungi growth during your next crop.

Root Rot

Root rot is a waterborne disease that attacks the plant roots. There are several varieties of root rot but all are treated the same way. Rot can cause a crop to fail rapidly. The symptoms are almost like those of a nutrient disorder, overwatering or underwatering. Wilting is a very common symptom of root rot.

Poor water drainage promotes root rot. Water and soil that is not suitably aerated (either by the growing method or by the soil's natural composition) promote root rot. Dead roots from a previous crop can also cause root rot. Root rot can easily be prevented by selecting suitable soil types and aerating water if needed.

Root rot prevents the plant from accessing water and nutrients by attaching itself to the roots and smothering the plant of its requirements. Root rot also causes pH to rise. In hydroponic systems the root tips may look burnt although some feeding products can dye the plant roots as well. In the advanced stages of root rot the roots appear to be covered in a brown slime that looks like dead algae. Eventually the base of the plant will rot away causing the plant to topple. Once a root is dead it remains dead. The plant can grow new roots but not regenerate old ones. This causes plant stress and the effect is very similar to transplant shock.

There are products on the market that can be used to eradicate root rot and are usually referred to as 'root shields'. In its advanced stages root rot is very hard to stop. In severe cases it cannot be and the plant needs to be cloned to continue its line. In order to recover from root rot you should increase aeration of the medium if possible while applying the root rot fungicide. If you lower pH below 6.0 you should prevent the rot from spreading. It is wiser to cull a number of plants then to allow the rot to spread to other areas of the soil, especially outdoors.

Overwatering promotes root rot. Better drainage systems, keeping your grow items clean and hydrogen peroxide will all help to prevent root rot. Vitamin B1 (thiamine) will help promote root growth.

Powdery Mildew

Powdery *mildew* is a common fungus that can rapidly infect a crop. Like Fungus Botrytis and mold it can be prevented using good ventilation and low humidity levels.

Powdery mildew starts its life, grows and produces spores much like Fungus Botrytis, except that powdery mildew does not turn gray but stays a fluffy white color. Powdery mildew is easier to wipe off than Fungus Botrytis but tends to spread more quickly than Fungus Botrytis, causing the plant's leaves to be covered in a white film. This inhibits photosynthesis and leads to stunted growth. Powdery Mildew also rots bud.

Powdery mildew can be curbed using the same techniques used in the treatment of Fungus Botrytis.

13 | PROBLEM SOLVER

GOT A PROBLEM WITH YOUR GROW and you want to know how to sort it out — this Chapter is all about providing you with solutions.

CHEMICAL BURNS

Plants suffer from chemical burns due to overfeeding. A plant with a chemical burn can be likened to a half-smoked joint. At the tip of the joint you have a shriveled gray ash. In the middle you see the burn creeping towards new paper, leaving a burn pattern behind it. At the end, there is the part you have not smoked yet. A plant chemical burn looks similar, and the leaf will tend to curl down and inwards into a claw shape at the tips.

The plant has a vascular system that takes in water and food and distributes these elements first to the bottom fan leaves, then upwards to the rest of the plant. This process takes time, as you know from Chapter 5. You will notice that the damage from chemical burns also starts on the tips of the fan leaves, then slowly moves towards the center and up the plant, leaving behind crispy matter that flakes away between your fingers. This is a chemical burn.

The main cause of a chemical burn is overfeeding that can occur if you use soil that contains high ratios of nutrients, if you use strong feeding mixtures or if you feed your plants too often.

To rectify chemical burns consult Chapter 6. If you cannot find a solution to what appears to be a chemical burn then check your medium's pH level. pH problems can sometimes resemble chemical burns or even nutrient deficiencies.

NUTRIENT DEFICIENCIES

A nutrient deficiency looks like a cell collapse (the natural appearance of the firm leaves lose some or all of their stiffness), usually along with some form of discoloration and or wilting. The affected part may wither and die, but it should not look like chemical burn. That is the major difference between a chemical burn and a nutrient problem. In time, you should be able to easily tell the difference yourself. If you suspect a nutrient deficiency be sure to check your pH. *If your pH is not right, then solve the pH problem before you attempt anything else.* If you feel that the problem is pH related then consult chapter 6 for solutions to this problem.

10 Steps to Saving Your Grow

Here is a quick step-by-step approach to troubleshooting problems with your grow.

STEP 1: Examine your plant, looking first for the presence of insects or disease. When you have completed this search, eliminate any pests or disease using the advice in Chapter 12.

Also note the type of attack to make sure that your bug problem isn't really a nutrient problem. The two can be confused. Are there any black dots on them, which would indicate bugs? Do your leaves look discolored, dry and limp as if something has been sucking their fluids from them? This could be a nutrient disorder but pest attack can do this as well.

Nutrient problems damage the plant on a more consistent level than pest attacks, meaning that the damaged areas are not as sporadic as a pest attack. Nutrient disorders tend to be more linear — either affecting the bottom leaves moving upwards, or the top leaves moving downwards. The disorder should be somewhat regular unless the pest attack has managed to occur over the entire plant. This is why it is important for you, the grower, to check on your plants regularly so that you can identify problems sooner rather than later. This is essential to do because a problem left untreated is a problem that becomes increasingly more difficult to identify.

In short, pest damage is sporadic, random and often concentrated on a single area of the plants before moving onto another. Nutrient disorders are more regular and affect the plant in a linear movement running either from bottom to top or top to bottom.

STEP 2: If your plant is in the vegetative growth stage and the leaves are turning yellow at the base and this is moving slowly up the plant without upwards leaf curl then you need more nitrogen (N). If your plant is in the flowering stage and shows signs of stunted or slow growth, yellow leaves and it looks to be dying then you also need more N. Nitrogen problems also cause the stems to become soft and the leaves become a pale green color. Normally nitrogen problems occur with older leaf growth first. Severe nitrogen problems result in stunted growth and eventually plant death.

If your plant is in the flowering stage and looks red or dark green/yellow then you need to treat it with more phosphorus (P). Phosphorus deficiencies also result in stunted root development. Stems can become either very rigid or very weak depending on the strain.

If these measures do not help, proceed to Step 3.
STEP 3: If your plant's leaves are curling up, twisting and turning yellow then check to see if your light is burning them or if the grow chamber has enough air circulation. This is usually the result of heat stress. Consult chapter 6 for information on how to solve heat stress related problems.

If these are not the cause of the problem then you need to consider adding more magnesium (Mg) to your medium. Epsom salts are good for this. Prepare a mixture of 1/4 to 1/3 tablespoon of Epsom salts to three gallons of water and water your plant with this mixture.

Magnesium problems generally start with old leaves first and show signs of yellowing between the veins of the leaf moving outwards. The leaves curl upwards, hence the term 'praying for magnesium'. Necrosis is the eventual result of Mg problems. Although a plant can still grow to full maturity with Mg deficiency it certainly results in below average results.

If you still experience problems, go to Step 4.
STEP 4: If the tips of the leaves turn brown and curl slightly then you have a potassium (K) problem. Solve this by adding more K to your plants.

Potassium problems also result in red/purple stems although this can be a genetic trait in the plant or due to a cold growing environment. To solve a cold growing environment problem turn to chapter 6 for advice.

Potassium problems normally affect new growth first, before moving on to the older leaves. A potassium deficiency will also eventually affect the stems causing them to become either soft or brittle depending on the strain. In severe cases the plant will eventually die.

If this does not solve your problem, move onto Step 5.

STEP 5: Does your plant look wilted? Are the leaves drooping or curling down? This could be root rot or a watering problem, which sometimes can cause nutrient-like deficiencies to appear on the plant. For information on how to solve root rot problems turn to chapter 12 for guidance.

If this doesn't work check your soil. If your soil is very damp or very dry then turn to chapter 5 for information on soils and then turn to chapter 6 for watering information, related watering problems and solutions to those problems.

If this does not solve you problem go to Step 6.

STEP 6: If the veins are green but the leaves are yellow, this indicates an iron problem (Fe). Iron problems generally occur at new growth regions, which eventually turn necrotic and die. Add more iron to solve this problem. Although iron is not essential to plant growth you will certainly end up with less than average results if it is lacking. Iron problems do not tend to cause leaf curl at the start but as the necrosis spreads leaves may curl.

If this does not solve your problem then move on to Step 7.

STEP 7: If the leaves are yellowing at the veins but the tips are fine and are not curling or twisting, you have a manganese (Mn) problem. Manganese problems can be solved by adding more Mn to your plants. If the problem persists, necrosis will set in and the leaves may curl. Plants do not need manganese to grow to full maturity but a lack of Mn will result in less than average results.

Move on to Step 8 if your problem still persists.

STEP 8: If you still have not solved your problem then add a secondary and micronutrient formula to your soil. This should help solve problems like Ca, S, Cu, B, Zn, Mo deficiencies, which are hard to detect and their respective symptoms are often different from strain to strain. By mixing a secondary and micronutrient formula you should be able solve these problems.

If this still has not solved the problem then turn to Step 9.

STEP 9: Still haven't solved it? Then flush your soil using the information provided in chapter 6 and find another type of plant food that has all of these: N, P, K, Ca, Mg and S. Purchase Epsom salts and get a small canister of micronutrients, such as iron, boron, chlorine, manganese, copper, zinc, and molybdenum. Try using a nutrient mixture that we've already mentioned in chapter 6.

If you don't want to flush your soil or transplant to another growing environment then proceed to Step 10.

STEP 10: Your plant may be experiencing nutrient lockout. There are a number of factors that can cause this problem. If you followed Step 9 properly then you shouldn't have this problem, but we'll explain it anyway. Lockout occurs when the plant cannot access a nutrient or a group of nutrients. This could be caused by the absence of nutrients (a deficiency) or by a chemical reaction in the medium/solution, which either causes a toxic substance to block the roots or a chemical reaction to take place, creating a new substance that changes the chemical properties of the other nutrients. As you can see this is a very broad subject matter. pH problems can lockout nutrients. The wrong soil type can also cause nutrient lockout. Under the right conditions, even water can lockout nutrients. But these lockout causes occur rarely, and more than likely something other than what the cannabis plant needs has been added to the solution to cause this reaction.

When in doubt, transplant into fresh soil or a fresh hydroponic solution. Certain feeding products might contain active ingredients that do not work well with cannabis. Lockout can only be solved by flushing or a transplant. With hydroponics you will have to change your nutrients. Out of date liquid feeding products can precipitate, causing nutrient lockout. Salt is another compound that can cause nutrient lockout. Follow Step 9 to solve these problems.

Your plant may be pot-bound or root-bound—it may simply have outgrown its pot. When the entire root mass grows to its maximum capacity, this can cause the plant stress and a variety of other problems that may resemble a nutrient problem. The only cure for this is to transplant the plant to a bigger pot. Follow the transplant method described in Chapter 9.

NO CURE FOR BAD GENETICS

When all else fails, you may have to face the fact that you are dealing with "a bad seed." There is a lot of garbage in the market. Problems associated with bad genetics include *mutations*, warping, flowering problems and poor germination rates that will often cause nutrient symptoms to appear even though your nutrient problem doesn't exist. The only viable solution is to obtain new genetics —

preferably from a different breeder. Make sure that you let the originator of the seeds know about your problem. Seed banks sometimes do pull a line from the market because of consistent problems like germination rates or weak, unpredictable genetics. They only way they can find out about such things is to get feedback from you the client.

14 | HARVESTING AND CURING YOUR BUD

HARVESTING IS THE ACT OF REAPING YOUR REWARDS and is without doubt the most fun you'll have in your garden. Assuming that you have followed the guidelines for flowering times the breeder set forth and that your grow was successful, you should be in a position to harvest an extremely high-yield from your crop.

First of all, you should know that harvesting is smelly and dirty work. It stinks up the place extremely quickly, so keep this in mind. Also, resin rubs off on nearly everything. Your fingers will be covered in a mass of resin and this will stain everything from metal to plastic, clothes, furniture, paper, books, equipment and even other pieces of bud. Resin is sticky stuff that is very hard to wash off. It must be scrubbed off using a metal-type cleaning pad. Keep this in mind when you are harvesting your crop.

At the end of the flowering stage, examine your bud to see if it is ripe and ready for harvest. Here are some indicators to help you identify that it's harvest time; however, please note that not all of these indicators will appear on every strain.

- 50 percent to 70 percent of the pistils change color
- Plants stop producing crystals
- Plants stop producing resin
- The fan leaves and lower leaves have turned yellow and are starting to drop off
- The smell has reached a peak
- Bud mass has not increased in the past few days

Another good way to determine when to harvest is to create multiple tasters of the same bud. You can do this by harvesting plants from the same strain at different times. If you do not have enough plants to do this you can take selections of bud from a single plant. These samples can be tested to gauge the optimal harvest time for the strain. The next time you grow this strain you will know exactly when to harvest. It must be said however that breeders' flowering times are generally pretty accurate. The experience of growing a strain more than once will also undoubtedly result in a more accurate timing of your harvest.

THE HARVEST

There is really only one way to harvest marijuana—anything else is just a variation on this theme. It should be noted that there are slight differences between harvesting an Indica and a Sativa plant.

Growers will sometimes flush their plants of nutrients a week or two before harvest.*

If you are growing multiple strains, you should have a method of labeling which strains are which before you harvest. Otherwise, you will end up harvesting your bud into one big pile. This means that your entire labeling process from seedling stage to harvest will have been in vain. Keep your buds separate if you want to know your bud strain type when it is time to sample the results of your hard work.

Some highly potent manicured colas.

---

* The lack of nutrients prevents the plants from making chlorophyll. Although this reduces overall bud quantities due to stress it does help the bud to cure easier and quicker because there is very little chlorophyll left in the plants before the harvest. Chlorophyll contains magnesium. It is magnesium that gives the harsh throat burning taste to badly cured bud.

Quick Bud Samples

Some growers just can't resist a tester but remember that these testers do not in any way reflect the final quality of well cured bud. Just take a fresh bud sample and put it on a dish. Place the dish in a microwave on medium heat for about two minutes. Check the bud to see if it feels dry and brittle. If it doesn't, heat it a bit more. Once it feels dry and brittle it can be smoked. The smoke will be harsh and the microwave heat will destroy a good portion of the cannabinoids in the bud but you should get something from your sample.

Another way of producing a quick bud sample is to take some fresh bud and put it into a sheet of paper. Fold the paper and press the bud down lightly. Place the paper on top of a working radiator and let the heat dry the bud. Check you bud later on in the day and it should be dry enough to smoke.

Expert Harvest Indication

There is a method that will allow you to determine precisely when to harvest. All you need is a magnifying aid and a little experience.

As the pistils grow out from the calyx they form resin glands (trichomes), which gradually change in color before they shrink and wither. This withering of the trichomes affects the look of the pistils, which in turn fade and tend to look burnt and dry. This 'unhealthy' appearance of the trichomes is perfectly natural. The plant has completed the blooming period and the trichomes are no longer needed to gather pollen. The cannabinoid content of these trichomes is not lost, however. It is simply converted into other psychoactive cannabinoid compounds. THC will also degrade as it is converted into other psychoactive compounds. Eventually, exposure to light will further degrade these cannabinoid compounds to next to nothing if the plant is not plant harvested.

The trichome withering process does not occur rapidly. It can take up to two weeks before the plant has withered its trichomes and pistils entirely, but even then new trichomes and pistils can be found growing in among the faded pistils. Eventually the old pistils will die to be replaced by the new pistils. The process will continue until there is a change in the photoperiod or a cellular breakdown in the plant and it dies.

As the plant reaches its peak bloom many of the pistils will change in color. Using a magnifying aid you can observe this change in the trichomes themselves, which affect the overall look of the pistils. By checking these trichomes daily you will be able to detect when the plant is nearing peak potency. The more trichomes change color, the more some will start to wither. The ones that wither first are usually in the minority because they were the first trichomes to form on the first pistils during the early days of flowering.

As some of these older pistils wither the other pistils begin a visible transformation in color from white to orange, red or brown. At this point, you should be anticipating the 'harvest marker' of 50 to 70 percent. When 50 to 70 percent of the pistils change color, the plant will have stopped producing new crystals (trichomes) and resin (cannabinoids secreted from the trichomes), the smell will have reached its peak and the bud mass will not have increased in a few days. At this stage any of the major bud masses on the plant can be theoretically observed as follows:

1. Less than 5% of the pistils are withering.
2. Approximately 90% of the pistils have reached maturity.
3. Less than 5% of the pistils appear to be in the early stages of growth.

The 90% group is the one that you should gauge your harvest with. Compare these to the ones that have gone past their peak bloom and harvest the plant just before they reach this stage. You should note that this usually corresponds with the breeders' flowering times. In the case of a plant with an unknown flowering time, you can use this expert method to predict when to harvest.

It's all about careful observation of the trichomes and their comparison to withered ones. Don't forget that trichomes can be harvested early or allowed to grow past their peak in order to affect the eventual high of the finished product.

Indica Harvest

Your one- to four-foot plant should be hacked at the base and picked up in its entirety. The weight of the Indica plant will probably amaze you if you have done everything right. Try not to let it touch the ground where the bud can gather up unwanted dirt or dust. The plant should then be hung upside down in a cool room with fresh air but no light.

When you hang the plants upside down the stems and branches automatically separate the buds, allowing space for air to flow around the freshly harvested flowers. The best temperature is between 60 and 75 degrees Fahrenheit. Relative humidity is best kept at around 55 percent. Light degrades the overall

THC quantity and quality. Light can also change the cannabinoid composition in your bud. Your room doesn't have to be light-proof, but you should take care not to expose your harvest to any direct light. Most growers use the bottom branches of the plant as support when hanging them up. By tying some fishing line to the walls, you can snag the bottom branch over the line to hang your buds upside down.

Next, take a pair of clippers and remove as many of the fan leaves as possible. Then remove the secondary leaves and put these into a separate pile. Last but not least gather some of the major trim leaf that can be removed easily from the bud. Trim refers to the small leaves that surround the bud and are usually covered in resin. This is a preliminary manicuring step only, designed to help ease the dry-

Some freshly manicured bud. Note that some the smaller leaf trim have been left intact because they are covered in trichomes.

ing process. The real manicuring comes later. Leave the trim areas that are hard to remove alone for now. The trim you need to remove right after harvesting should pull away with ease. If there is no branch on the trim area you are trying to remove then leave it alone. Chances are it will not pull free without taking some bud with it and you do not want to do this.

Now you have four different qualities of weed to choose from. The fan leaf will be an okay smoke, the middle leaves a little better and the trim will be very good. The bud is the prime stuff though and this will give you the best quality high.
Leave the plant like this until a branch can break easily between your fingers (it should literally snap between your fingers). This harvesting process takes about two to three weeks from start to finish, although some strains can take up to four weeks before the branches snap between your fingers.

The plant's branches naturally keep the bud separated to allow maximum airflow through them for drying after harvesting.

Sativa Harvest

Outdoor growers like to grow Sativa plants, which can grow up to 12 feet carrying more than 20 oz of bud. It is not uncommon for some Sativa varieties to produce over 2lbs of bud per plant. These large plants are not harvested easily.

The process is similar to Indica except the harvest itself can be quite labor-intensive. You need a canvas spread or another means of carrying the bud. The plant should be chopped at the base and spread out on the canvas. The canvas is then rolled up and tied tight for transport. Obviously, if you have more than one plant you might need more than one canvas sheet.

The plant should then be hung upside down in a cool room, with fresh air and no light. Because of the plant's size and bushiness you may have to cut the branches and hang these up separately. Take a pair of clippers and remove leaves and trim as suggested in the Indica harvest section.

Fan Leaves, Leaves and Trim

These are cured by letting them dry on a flat surface, away from direct light and with plenty of fresh air. The leaves will dry after three weeks and are easily smoked at that stage. Test them out to see what you like and what you don't like. Another thing you could do with the trim is to make hash from it. We'll talk about this in Chapter 17. Don't try to speed up your drying process with ovens or microwaves or heat. Let them dry out naturally and you'll cure yourself a much better smoke from the leaves. Cannabis connoisseurs will discard the leaves in favor of the more pleasing and potent bud that is also far less harsh to smoke. Remember though that even if you are a connoisseur the leaves can be used to make hash.

Manicuring

This is one of the most important parts of preparing your bud for the curing process. Manicuring is a type of aesthetic bud treatment that will also help you to separate the best from the rest. You will need a tray or two of some description depending on how much bud you have, a black plastic bag, a sharp pair of small fine scissors and some rubbing alcohol. Rubbing alcohol can be used to

A nice sized harvested branch awaiting manicuring.

remove resin strains from your scissors, which after awhile will become sticky, dull and even jammed with resin. The manicuring process can take a long time so some people like to set up their manicuring system in front of the television. Manicuring will get your fingers covered to resin so prepare everything that you will need beforehand — food, drinks, joints, bongs, etc.

Take as much of your hanging bud as possible and place it down in a heap on top of your black plastic bag. Try to keep the strains separate and even label each heap so that you remember which strain is which. During the manicuring process it is easy to get buds mixed up. Place another black plastic bag over this lot to avoid light degrading THC levels.

Get your first plant out from heap and use your fingers to remove as many of the branches and leaves as you can. This is your chance to remove trim matter that you may have missed during the preliminary manicure step. Chop the remaining branches into convenient workable sizes for hand-held manicuring. Repeat this process with all the other plants until you fill your tray with the first-round, hand-manicured plants.

Next you will start the more precise, second-round manicure. Pick up your first piece of bud and clip away as much of the branch or stem as possible. Now work your scissors in between the bud and leaf. In one quick pinch you should be able

Half the trim has been removed.

to separate the leaf from the bud by snipping the leaf at the base. Notice that the stem of the leaf is covered in trichomes? Hang onto these leaves as they are very high quality trim. Repeat the process until you have removed as much leaf as possible. If you find that you cannot get at the leaf then simply snip as much of the leaf away as you can by sheering them in half or as close to the bud as possible.

Rotate the plant by the stem to gain access to the other side of the manicured bud. This rotation movement is the quickest way to access all of the leaf sites on the plant.

Take care when cutting not to remove pistils or calyx along with the leaf. To avoid pistil removal, try using the very tips of the scissors when you snip so that the blades do not go past the piece you want to cut. Repeat this process with the other first-round, hand-manicured pieces and you will eventually end up with very nice manicured pieces of bud that are ready for curing.

All the trim has been removed and the branch is ready for drying.

How much you remove depends on what quality of manicured bud you want to end up with. Undoubtedly the method above produces the best quality manicured bud from your harvest, however the weight of the overall product will be reduced. By leaving on lots of trim leaves these will actually dry in with the bud to create a medium quality manicured bud that weighs more than the best quality manicured bud. Ultimately it is your choice: you can manicure your bud for maximum weight or quality.

You will end up with several separate piles of leaf, both from the preliminary manicure step and the more intensive manicuring process. Some people dump this leaf. Others smoke it. Still others will make hash from it. Most of the leaf will be harsh to smoke but will contain some cannabinoids. The better leaf will have visible trichomes. You can easily locate the leaf that is high in trichome content using a microscope. A microscope is a useful aid for separating the better leaf from the rest for hash making, especially if you are planning to use the cold water extraction technique using bubble bags described in Chapter 17. Of course, what you do with your leaf is entirely up to you.

The bud on the left will have more weight than the bud
on the right, which is manicured better.

CURING

As soon as the branches are brittle you should consider curing your bud using the canning method. Canning is a great way to get the most from your bud. Find a can with a removable lid. The more cans you have on-hand, the better.

Using a pair of scissors, clip your bud from the branch and place into the can. The branches and stems are not much good to you. They do contain THC, but only in small quantities. Most stems and branches go on the compost heap.

Now take the can and place it in a cool, dark room or cupboard.* Every day open the lid for a few hours (six hours is good) and then seal it again. Also, move the bud around a bit every couple of days. This is the most common curing technique, and it works best. Bud that is cured well smokes the best! I would give the canning process between three and four weeks before you should really sample your goods. Eight-week old bud can smoke extremely well and year-old bud is vintage stuff but can lose potency.

Fresh bud (eight-weeks canned curing) is the pinnacle point of cured bud. After that the THC cannabinoids rapidly change composition and lose potency. Fresh bud is far better than aged bud. You may hear of other curing processes, but canning does work wonders and is affordable too.

Canning also sweats the bud which causes it to retain its smell and flavor but also allows the bud to burn more effectively. By opening and closing the can at different intervals you can control how damp or dry you want your buds to be. Try and use cans that have a large opening at the lid — enough to allow your whole hand to fit inside. This is because some of the trichomes will fall from the bud into the bottom of the can. Use your fingers to get at these trichomes. You can gather these into a small mass that you can smoke later on.

Drying your bud helps to relax THC particles by removing water from the bud. This makes THC easier to burn and thus more psychoactive than when it is damp. Applying heat will also remove water but will affect the overall cannabinoid content of the bud. It is not a good idea to press bud or to pack bud tightly during the curing process as the bunching of THC particles makes them harder to burn.

---

* Make sure to store your canned buds in a cool, dry and dark place away from any direct light. Check occasionally for mold, which can build up on the buds due to humidity or age. If you find mold just clip it away to prevent it from spreading. Moldy buds should not be smoked.

Curing also helps to break down chlorophyll, which has magnesium-containing green pigments. Magnesium is responsible for the sharp and harsh taste in the back of your throat when you burn fresh bud. This is another good reason to cure your bud.

If you over-dry your buds you may loose too much moisture and this results in bud that has less taste and aroma than it should. The best way to add moisture back into your buds is to introduce new fresh bud to your cans. The new fresh buds will share their moisture with the dried bud, bringing them back to a more even level of moisture and restoring their aroma and taste. Some people*uses fruit slice to bring back moisture such as apple or orange slices. These fruit slices will also add their own aroma to the buds.

If you have dried your plants for three weeks hanging upside down you can sub-tract that time from the canning time. Although you can have good bud to smoke two weeks after your harvest it is better to wait for four weeks or more.

- Chop your plants at the base.
- Cut them into manageable amounts and hang them upside down in cool, dry and dark place.
- Clip/pull the major leaf away.
- Let dry until the branches snap between your fingers.
- Clip the trim from the bud.
- Store in cans in a cool, dry place away from direct light.
- Let the buds air occasionally and check for mold.

15 | HOW TO BREED MARIJUANA

IF YOU WANT TO CONTINUE GROWING A STRAIN that you enjoy, cloning is your best option. You could also continue the strain by breeding two plants to produce seeds. You won't completely replicate the strain again using the seed method, however, unless the two parent plants are from the same *IBL* (inbred line). Even if the two plants are not IBLs, they should produce seeds that contain most of the parents' features. If you want to create a plant with characteristics from two different strains, breeding the marijuana from seed is your only option. That is the subject of this chapter, which begins with an introduction to simple breeding procedures and then goes on to cover advanced techniques like breeding a true strain and backcrossing.

Making Seeds

How easy is it to make seeds? It's easy if you have healthy plants and a stable growing environment. When your male plants burst their pollen sacks in your grow room they'll pollinate the female flowers. You can also administer pollen directly to your females if you prefer.

Collecting and Storing Pollen

Pollen can be extracted from male flowers as soon as they open: you'll see the male flower open out from its calyx. It is best to gather pollen after it falls from the pod onto the leaves. You can shake the pollen onto the female flowers to pollinate them or grow your males separately and store their pollen for future use.

Film canisters are great for storing pollen. You can save pollen in a canister for the next harvest. Although it can be stored in the freezer for as long as 18

months, pollen is best used within six months of collection. Pollen has been
known to keep for longer than 18 months, but is usually not viable past this time.

Collecting and Storing Seeds
If you have pollinated your plants, at the end of the flowering stage the bud will
contain seeds. The seeds should be gray, tan or dark brown in color. They may also
be striped, banded or lined with different colored markings. If they are pale
cream or white in color, then they are probably not viable and you have harvested them too early. You should wait until the end of flowering to harvest your
seeds.

Your seeds will be mixed in with the bud and it can take quite a bit of time to
separate them from their sticky calyx pods. Do not squeeze the calyx directly
because you can damage the seed inside. Just tease the seed out from the calyx
with your fingers. If you do not want the bud you can brush a seeded flowering
branch against some fabric or a sieve to release the seeds from their respective
calyx pods. It is easier to remove seeds from dry, cured bud than from freshly
harvested plants.

If you plan to use the seeds in more than two years time, store them in an airtight container and place this in a freezer. If you plan to use the seeds within the
next two years, storing them in a standard film canister or similar container will
work well. Keep this canister away from heat and direct light and do not let it get
damp or your risk spoiling your seeds. Containers placed in the freezer should not
be opened until you are ready to use them. Allow the seeds to thaw at room temperature for at least 12 hours before use.

Simple Breeding
Your approach to breeding will depend on what you ultimately hope to achieve.
Do you want to create a new strain; create seeds that are similar to the parents;
or cross two plants to create a simple hybrid strain?

Continuing a Strain through Seeds
Say you purchased $120 worth of Silver Haze seeds and you want to make more
seeds without any interference from another strain. That's easy. Just make sure
that the male and female plants you breed with are from the same strain batch.
In this instance the same strain batch would be Silver Haze from the same breeder. If you use Silver Haze from different breeders then the offspring may express
a great deal of variation. This is because most breeders create their own versions

of a popular strain. Their variety may have dissimilar characteristics from those of other breeders who have bred the same strain.

If you only have Silver Haze from the same breeder in your grow room, then all you need are a group of males and a group of females. Let the males pollinate the females and you will get more Silver Haze seeds, but you will loose some of the features of the original parent plants unless the strain you have is an IBL or from a very stable inbred pure line.

Making a Simple Hybrid

Again, making a simple hybrid is easy. Just take a male plant from one strain and a female plant from another, for example Big Bud and Skunk. The result will be 'Big Bud x Skunk', but there will be differences in the offspring. Some of the plants will exhibit more Big Bud traits and some will exhibit more Skunk traits. Genes not expressed by each of the parents may also appear in the offspring.

If you want to breed for specific traits by eliminating variations, ultimately creating uniform plants or even an IBL, then you should start with a basic knowledge of plant genetics.

INTRODUCTION TO PLANT GENETICS

Genetics can be somewhat difficult to understand at first so we'll start by explaining a few rudimentary concepts and the basic terminology. The explanations for the words below can be treated as a glossary for your benefit.

++ Genes

Genes are the units of heredity transmitted from parent to offspring, usually as part of a chromosome. Genes usually control or determine a single characteristic in the offspring. There are genes responsible for each feature of your plant to be inherited, including leaf color, stem structure, texture, smell, potency, etc.

++ Gene Pairs

All of life is made up of a pattern of genes. You can think of this pattern as being similar to the two sides of a zipper. One side is inherited from the mother and the other from the father. Each gene occupies a specific locus, or particular space on the chain, and controls information about the eventual characteristics of the plant. So each gene locus contains two genes, one from the mother and one from the father. These gene pairs are usually denoted by a pair of letters, such as BB,

Bb, Pp, pp, etc. Capital letters refer to dominant genes while lower case letters refer to recessive genes. By way of example, B can represent Big Bud while b can represent small bud. Any letter can be assigned to any trait or gene pair when you are working out your own breeding program.

++ Chromosome
A threadlike structure of nucleic acids and proteins in the cell nuclei of higher organisms that carries a set of linked genes, usually paired.

++ Locus
A position on a chromosome where a particular gene pair is located.

++ Allele
Alleles are any of a number of alternative forms of one gene. For example the gene for purple bud color may have two forms, or alleles, one for purple and one for dark red.

++ Homozygous
Having identical alleles at one or more genetic loci, which is not a heterozygote (see below) and breeds true. Your plant is said to be homozygous for one feature when it carries the same gene twice in the responsible gene pair, which means both genes of the gene pair are identical.

++ Heterozygous
Having different alleles at one or more genetic loci. Your plant is said to be heterozygous for one feature when the genes of the responsible gene pair are unequal, or dissimilar.

++ Phenotype
The phenotype is the summary of all of the features you can detect or recognize on the outside of your plant, including color, smell and taste.

++ Genotype
The *genotype* is the genetic constitution of your plant, as distinguished from the phenotype. The genotype characterizes how your plant looks from the inside. It is the summary of all the genetic information that your plant carries and passes on to its offspring.

++ Dominant

Dominant is used to describe a gene or allele that is expressed even when inherited from only one parent. It is also used to describe a hereditary trait controlled by a gene and appearing in an individual to the exclusion of its counterpart, when alleles for both are present. Only one dominant allele in the gene pair must be present to become the expressed genotype and eventually the expressed phenotype of your plant.

++ Recessive

Recessive describes a gene, allele or hereditary trait perceptibly expressed only in homozygotes, being masked in heterozygotes by a dominant allele or trait. A gene is called recessive when its effect cannot be seen in the phenotype of your plant when only one allele is present. The same allele must be present twice in the gene pair in order for you to see it expressed in the phenotype of your plant.

++ Dominant/Recessive and Genetic Notation

Assume that the dominant 'B' allele carries the hereditary trait for Big Bud, while the recessive 'b' allele carries the hereditary trait for small bud. Since B is dominant, a plant with a Bb genotype will always produce Big Bud. The B is dominant over the b. In order for a recessive gene to be displayed in the phenotype, both genes in the gene pair must be recessive. So a plant with the BB or Bb gene will always produce Big Bud. Only a plant with the bb gene will produce small bud.

Now that we have explained the basic terminology of plant genetics, we can move on to the next step: rudimentary breeding concepts as laid out in the Hardy-Weinberg law of genetic equilibrium.

THE HARDY-WEINBERG MODEL OF GENETIC EQUILIBRIUM

An understanding of plant breeding requires a basic understanding of the Hardy-Weinberg law. To illustrate the value of the Hardy-Weinberg law, ask yourself a question, like: "If purple bud color is a dominant trait, why do some of the offspring of my purple bud strain have green buds?" or "I have been selecting Indica mothers and cross-breeding them with mostly Indica male plants but I have some Sativa leaves. Why?" These questions can be easily answered by developing an understanding of the Hardy-Weinberg law and the factors that can disrupt genetic equilibrium.

The first of these questions, reflects a very common misconception: that the dominant allele of a trait will always have the highest frequency in a population and the recessive allele will always have the lowest frequency. This is not always the case. A dominant trait will not necessarily spread to a whole population, nor will a recessive trait always eventually die out.

Gene frequencies can occur in high or low ratios, regardless of how the allele is expressed. The allele can also change, depending on certain conditions. It is these changes in gene frequencies over time that result in different plant characteristics.

A genetic population is basically a group of individuals of the same species (cannabis Indica or cannabis Sativa) or strain (Skunk#1 or Master Kush) in a given area whose members can breed with one another. This means that they must share a common group of genes. This common group of genes is locally known as the gene pool. The *gene pool* contains the alleles for all of the traits in the entire population. For a step in evolution — a new plant species, strain or trait — to occur, some of the gene frequencies must change. The gene frequency of an allele refers to the number of times an allele for a particular trait occurs compared to the total number of alleles for that trait in the population. Gene frequency is calculated by dividing the number of a specific type of allele by the total number of alleles in the gene pool.

Genetic Equilibrium Theory and Application

The Hardy-Weinberg model of genetic equilibrium describes a theoretical situation in which there is no change in the gene pool. At equilibrium there can be no change or evolution.

Let's consider a population whose gene pool contains the alleles B and b.

Assign the letter p to the frequency of the dominant allele B and the letter q to the frequency of the recessive allele b. We know that the sum of all the alleles must equal 100 percent, so:

$$p + q = 100\%$$

This can also be expressed as:

$$p + q = 1$$

And all of the random possible combinations of the members of a population would equal:

$$p2 + 2pq + q2$$

WHERE:

p	= frequency of the dominant allele in a population
q	= frequency of the recessive allele in a population
p2	= percentage of homozygous dominant individuals
q2	= percentage of heterozygous recessive individuals
2pq	= percentage of heterozygous individuals

Imagine that you have grown a population of 1,000 'Black Domina' cannabis plants from seeds obtained from a well known seed bank. In that population, 360 plants emit a skunky smell, while the remaining 640 plants emit a fruity smell. You contact the seed bank and ask them which smell is dominant in this particular strain. Hypothetically, they tell you that the breeder selected for a fruity smell and the skunk smell is a recessive genotype. You can call this recessive genotype 'vv' and use the formula above to answer the following questions.

QUESTION: According to the Hardy-Weinberg law, what is the frequency of the 'vv' genotype?

ANSWER: Since 360 out of the 1,000 plants have the 'vv' genotype, then 36% is the frequency of 'vv' in this population of 'Black Domina'.

QUESTION: According to the Hardy-Weinberg law, what is the frequency of the 'v' allele?

ANSWER: The frequency of the 'vv' allele is 36%. Since q2 is the percentage of homozygous recessive individuals, and q is the frequency of the recessive allele in a population, the following must also be true:

$$q2 = 0.36$$
$$(q \times q) = 0.36$$
$$q = 0.6$$

Thus, the frequency of the 'v' allele is 60%.

QUESTION: According to the Hardy-Weinberg law, what is the frequency of the 'V' allele?

ANSWER: Since q = 0.6, we can solve for p.

$$p + q = 1$$
$$p + 0.6 = 1$$
$$p = 1 - 0.6$$
$$p = 0.4$$

The frequency of the 'V' allele is 40%.

QUESTION: According to the Hardy-Weinberg law, what is the frequency of the genotypes 'VV' and 'Vv'?

ANSWER: Given what we know, the following must be true:

$$VV = p2$$
$$V = 0.4 = p$$
$$(p \times p) = p2$$
$$(0.4 \times 0.4) = p2$$
$$0.16 = p2$$
$$VV = 0.16$$

The frequency of the genotype 'VV' is 16%

$$VV = 0.16$$
$$vv = 0.36$$
$$VV + Vv + vv = 1$$
$$0.16 + Vv + 0.36 = 1$$
$$0.52 + Vv = 1$$
$$Vv = 1 - 0.52$$
$$Vv = 0.48 \text{ or } 48\%$$

Or alternatively, 'Vv' is 2pq, therefore:

$$Vv = 2pq$$
$$2pq = 2 \times p \times q$$
$$2pq = 2 \times 0.4 \times 0.6$$
$$2pq = 0.48 \text{ or } 48\%$$

The frequencies of V and v (p and q) will remain unchanged, generation after generation, as long as the following five statements are true:

1. The population is large enough
2. There are no mutations
3. There are no preferences, for example a VV male does not prefer a vv female by its nature
4. No other outside population exchanges genes with this population
5. Natural selection does not favor any specific gene

The equation p2 + 2pq + q2 can be used to calculate the different frequencies. Although this equation is important to know about, we make use of other more basic calculations when breeding. The important thing to note here is the five conditions for equilibrium.

Earlier we asked the question: "I have been selecting Indica mothers and cross-breeding them with mostly Indica male plants but I have some Sativa leaves. Why?" The Hardy-Weinberg equilibrium tells us that outside genetics may have been introduced into the breeding program. Since the mostly Indica male plants are only mostly Indica and not pure Indica, you can expect to discover some Sativa characteristics in the offspring, including the Sativa leaf trait.

THE TEST CROSS

Some of you may be asking the question: "How do I know if a trait, such as bud color is homozygous dominant (BB), heterozygous (Bb) or homozygous recessive (bb)?"

If you've been given seeds or a clone you may have been told that a trait, such as potency, is homozygous dominant, heterozygous or homozygous recessive. However, you will want to establish this yourself, especially if you intend to use those specific traits in a future breeding plan. To do this, you will have to perform what is called a test cross.

Determining the phenotype of a plant is fairly straightforward. You look at the plant and you see, smell, feel or taste its phenotype. Determining the genotype cannot be achieved through simple observation alone.

Generally speaking, there are three possible genotypes for each plant trait. For example, if Golden Bud is dominant and Silver Bud is recessive, the possible genotypes are:

HOMOZYGOUS DOMINANT: BB   = Golden Bud
HETEROZYGOUS: Bb   = Golden Bud
HOMOZYGOUS RECESSIVE: bb   = Silver Bud

The Golden and Silver Bud colors are the phenotypes. BB, Bb and bb denote the genotypes. Because B is the dominant allele, Bb would appear Golden and not Silver. Most phenotypes are visual characteristics but some, like bud taste, are phenotypes that can't be observed by the naked eye and are experienced instead through the other senses.

For example, looking at a mostly Sativa species like a Skunk plant you will notice that the leaves are pale green. In a population of these Skunk plants you may notice that a few have dark green leaves. This suggests that this Skunk strain's leaf color is not true breeding, meaning that the leaf trait must be heterozygous because homozygous dominant and homozygous recessive traits are true breeding. Some of the Skunk's pale green leaf traits will probably be homozygous dominant in this population.

You may also be asking the question: "Could the pale green trait be the homozygous recessive trait and the dark green leaf the heterozygous trait?" Since a completely homozygous recessive population (bb) would not contain the allele (B) for heterozygous expression (Bb) or for homozygous dominant expression (BB), it is impossible for the traits for heterozygous (Bb) or homozygous dominant (BB) to exist in a population that is completely homozygous recessive (bb) for that trait. If a population is completely homozygous for that trait (bb or BB), then that specific trait can be considered stable, true breeding or 'will breed true'. If a population is heterozygous for that trait (Bb) then that specific trait can be considered unstable, not true breeding or 'will not breed true'.

If the trait for Bb or BB can not exist in a bb population for that trait, then bb is the only trait that you will discover in that population. Hence, bb is true breeding. If there is a variation in the trait, and the Hardy-Weinberg law of equilibrium has not been broken, the trait must be heterozygous. In our Skunk example there were only a few dark green leaves. This means that the dark green leaves are homozygous recessive and the pale green leaves are heterozygous and may possibly be homozygous dominant too.

You may also notice that the bud is golden on most of the plants. This also suggests that the Golden Bud color is a dominant trait. If buds on only a few of the plants are Silver, this suggests that the Silver trait is recessive. You know the only genotype that produces the recessive trait is homozygous recessive (bb). So if a plant displays a recessive trait in its phenotype, its genotype must be homozygous recessive. *A plant that displays a recessive trait in its phenotype always has a homozygous recessive genotype.* But this leaves you with an additional question to answer as well: are the Golden Bud or pale green leaf color traits homozygous dominant (BB) or heterozygous (Bb)? You cannot be completely certain of any of your inferences until you have completed a test cross.

A test cross is performed by breeding a plant with an unknown dominant genotype (BB or Bb) with a plant that is homozygous recessive (bb) for the same trait. For this test you will need another cannabis plant of the opposite sex that is homozygous recessive (bb) *for the same trait.*

This brings us to an important rule: *If any offspring from a test cross display the recessive trait, the genotype of the parent with the dominant trait must be heterozygous and not homozygous.*

In our example, our unknown genotype is either BB or Bb. The Silver Bud genotype is bb. We'll put this information into a mathematical series known as Punnett squares.

	b	b
B		
?		

We start by entering the known genotypes. We do these calculations for two parents that will breed. We know that our recessive trait is bb and the other is either BB or Bb, so we'll use B? for the time being. Our next step is to fill the box in with what we can calculate.

	b	b
B	Bb	Bb
?	?b	?b

The first row of offspring Bb and Bb will have the dominant trait of Golden Bud. The second row can either contain Bb or bb offspring. This will either lead to offspring that will produce more Golden Bud (Bb) or Silver Bud (bb). The first possible outcome (where ? = B) would give us Golden Bud (Bb) offspring. The second possible outcome (where ? = b) would give us Silver Bud (bb) offspring. We can also predict what the frequency will be.

Outcome 1, where ? = B:
Bb + Bb + Bb + Bb = 4Bb
100% Golden Bud

Outcome 2, where ? = b:
Bb + Bb + bb + bb = 2bb
50% Golden Bud and 50% Silver Bud

RECALL:

Homozygous Dominant: BB = Golden Bud
Heterozygous: Bb = Golden Bud
Homozygous Recessive: bb = Silver Bud

To determine the identity of B?, we used another cannabis plant of the opposite sex that was homozygous recessive (bb) *for the same trait.*

OUTCOME 2 TELLS US THAT:

- Both parents must have at least one b trait each to exhibit Silver Bud in the phenotype of the offspring.
- If any Silver Bud is produced in the offspring then the mystery parent (B?) must be heterozygous (Bb). It cannot be homozygous dominant (BB).

So, if a Golden Bud parent is crossed with a Silver Bud parent and produces only Golden Bud, then the Golden Bud parent must be homozygous dominant for that trait. If any Silver Bud offspring is produced, then the Golden Bud parent must be heterozygous for that trait.

To summarize, the guidelines for performing a test cross to determine the geno-type of a plant exhibiting a dominant trait are:

1. The plant with the dominant trait should always be crossed with a plant with the recessive trait.
2. If any offspring display the recessive trait, the unknown genotype is het-erozygous.
3. If all the offspring display the dominant trait, the unknown genotype is homozygous dominant.

The main reasoning behind performing a test cross are:

1. When you breed plants you want to continue a trait, like height, taste, smell, etc.
2. When you want to continue that trait you must know if it is homozygous dominant, heterozygous or homozygous recessive.
3. You can only determine this with certainty by performing a test cross.

We should mention that, as a breeder, you should be dealing with a large popula-tion in order to be certain of the results. The more plants you work with, the more reliable the results.

Hardy-Weinberg Law, Part 2

The question may arise: "How do I breed for several traits, like taste, smell, vigor and color?" To answer this question, you will need to learn more about the Hardy-Weinberg law of genetic equilibrium.

If you breed two plants that are heterozygous (Bb) for a trait, what will the off-spring look like? The Punnett squares can help us determine the phenotypes, genotypes and gene frequencies of the offspring.

	B	b
B	BB	Bb
b	Bb	bb*

>>Take special note of this offspring and compare it with the parents.

IN THIS GROUP, THE RESULTING OFFSPRING WILL BE:

1 BB - 25% of the offspring will be homozygous for the dominant allele (BB)
2 Bb - 50% will be heterozygous, like their parents (Bb)
1 bb - 25% will be homozygous for the recessive allele (bb)

Unlike their parents (Bb and Bb), 25 percent of offspring will express the recessive phenotype bb. So two parents that display Golden Bud but are both heterozygous (Bb) for that trait will produce offspring that exhibit the recessive Silver Bud trait, despite the fact that neither of the parents displays the phenotype for Silver Bud.

Understanding how recessive and dominant traits are passed down through the phenotype and genotype so that you can predict the outcome of a cross and lock down traits in future generations is really what breeding is all about.

When you breed a strain, how do you know that the traits you want to keep will actually be retained in the breeding process? This is where the test cross comes in. If you create seeds from a strain that you bought from a seed bank, how can you be sure that the offspring will exhibit the characteristics that you like? If the trait you wish to continue is homozygous dominant (BB) in both parent plants then there's no way that you can produce a recessive genotype for that trait in the offspring, as illustrated in the Punnett square below.

	B	B
B	BB	BB
B	BB	BB

It is impossible for the recessive trait to appear. And if both parents contain the recessive trait then they cannot produce the dominant trait.

	b	b
B	bb	bb
B	bb	bb

In order to breed a trait properly you must know if it is homozygous, heterozygous or homozygous recessive so that you can predict the results before they happen.

Mendel and the Pea Experiments

Gregor Mendel (1822-1884) was an Austrian monk who discovered the basic rules of inheritance by analyzing the results from his plant breeding research programs. He noticed that two types of pea plants gave very uniform results when bred within their own gene pools and not with one another. The traits he noticed were:

Pea Plant #1	Pea Plant #2
Solid seed shells	Wrinkled seed shells
Green seeds	Yellow seeds
White flowers	Purple flowers
Tall plants	Short plants

He noticed that the offspring all carried the same traits when they bred with the same population or gene pool. Since there were no variations within each strain he guessed that both strains were homozygous for these traits. Because the pea plants were from the same species, Mendel guessed that either the solid seed shells were recessive or the wrinkled seed shells were recessive. Using the genotype notations SS for solid seed shells and ss for wrinkled seed shells, he knew that they couldn't be Ss because one lot didn't exhibit any of the other strain's phenotypes when bred within its own gene pool.

Let's illustrate this using two basic Punnett squares where SS is pea plant #1 with the trait for solid seed shells and ss is pea plant #2 with the trait for wrinkled seed shells.

PEA PLANT #1 RESULTS:

	S	S
S	SS	SS
S	SS	SS

All the offspring will be SS.

PEA PLANT #2 RESULTS:

	s	s
s	ss	ss
s	ss	ss

All the offspring will be ss.

The First Hybrid Cross (the F1 Generation)

Mendel made his first hybrid cross between the two strains and the results were all solid seeds as seen in the chart below.

F1 Cross	s	s
S	Ss	Ss
S	Ss	Ss

Up until this point, he didn't know which trait was recessive and which was dominant. Since all the seeds shells were solid, he now know with certainty that pea plant #1 contained the dominant genotype for solid seed shells and pea plant #2 contained the recessive genotype for wrinkled seed shells. This meant that in future test crosses with other pea strains, he could determine if a particular seed shell trait was homozygous or heterozygous because he had identified the recessive trait (ss).

The Second Hybrid Cross (the F2 Generation)

The offspring in the F1 cross were all Ss. When Mendel crossed these offspring he got the following results:

F2 Cross	S	s
S	SS	Ss
s	Ss	ss*

*Take special note of this offspring and compare with parents.

Mendel had mated two pea plants that were heterozygous (e.g., Ss) for a seed shell trait. In this group, the resulting offspring were:

25% of the offspring were homozygous for the dominant allele (SS)
50% were heterozygous, like their parents (Ss)
25% were homozygous for the recessive allele (ss)

In his first cross to create the hybrid plant, Mendel ended up with no recessive traits for seed shape. But when he crossed the offspring, because they were heterozygous for that trait, he ended up with some having the homozygous recessive trait, some having the homozygous dominant trait and some continuing the heterozygous trait. In correct breeding terms his first cross between the plants is called the F1 cross or F1 generation. The breeding out of those offspring is called the F2 cross or F2 generation.

Now since he has Ss, ss and SS to work with you could use Punnett squares to determine what the next generations of offspring will look like. Compare your results with what you have learned about ratios and you'll be able to see how it all fits together.

More on Genetic Frequencies

Take a look at the cross below between two heterozygous parents. If two heterozygous parents are crossed, the frequency ratio of the alleles will be 50% each. Remember the genotype can be Ss, SS or ss, but the allele is either 'S' or 's'.

	S	s
S	SS	Ss
s	Ss	ss

We can see S S S S (4 x S) and s s s s (4 x s). This means that the frequency of the allele 'S' is 50% and the frequency of the allele 's' is 50%. See if you can calculate the frequencies of the alleles 'S' and 's' in the following crosses for yourself.

	S	s
S		
S		

	S	s
S		
S		

Recall that the Hardy-Weinberg law states that the sum of all the alleles in a population should equal 100 percent, but the individual alleles may appear in different ratios. There are five situations that can cause the law of equilibrium to fail. These are discussed next

.

1. MUTATION. A mutation is a change in genetic material, which can give rise to heritable variations in the offspring. Exposure to radiation can cause genetic mutation, for example. In this case the result would be a mutation of the plant's genetic code that would be transferred to its offspring. The effect is equivalent to a migration of foreign genetic material being introduced into the population. There are other factors that can cause mutations. Essentially a mutation is the result of DNA repair failure at the cellular level. Anything that causes DNA repair to fail can result in a mutation.

2. GENE MIGRATION. Over time, a population will reach equilibrium that will be maintained as long as no other genetic material migrates into the population. When new genetic material is introduced from another population, this is called introgression. During the process of introgression many new traits can arise in the original population, resulting in a shift in equilibrium.

3. GENETIC DRIFT. If a population is small, equilibrium is more easily violated, because a slight change in the number of alleles results in a significant change in genetic frequency. Even by chance alone certain traits can be eliminated from the population and the frequency of alleles can drift toward higher or lower values. Genetic drift is actually an evolutionary force that alters a population and demonstrates that the Hardy-Weinberg law of equilibrium cannot hold true over an indefinite period of time.

4. NON-RANDOM MATING. External or internal factors may influence a population to a point at which mating is no longer random. For example, if some female flowers develop earlier than others they will be able to gather pollen earlier than the rest. If some of the males release pollen early and then stop producing pollen, the mating between these early males and females is not random, and could result in late-flowering females ending up as a sinsemilla crop. This means that these late-flowering females won't be able to make their contribution to the gene pool in future generations. Equilibrium will not be maintained.

5. NATURAL SELECTION. With regards to natural selection, the environment and other factors can cause certain plants to produce a greater or smaller number of offspring. Some plants may have traits that make them less immune to disease, for example, meaning that when the population is exposed to disease, less of their offspring will survive to pass on genetic material, while others may produce more seeds or exhibit a greater degree of immunity, resulting in a greater number of offspring surviving to contribute genetic material to the population.

HOW TO TRUE BREED A STRAIN

Breeding cannabis strains is all about manipulating gene frequencies. Most strains sold by reputable breeders through seed banks are very uniform in growth. This means that the breeder has attempted to lock certain genes down so that the genotypes of those traits are homozygous.

Imagine that a breeder has two strains: Master Kush and Silver Haze. The breeder lists a few traits that they particularly like (denoted by *).

Master Kush	Silver Haze
Dark green leaf	Pale green leaf *
Hashy smell *	Fruity smell
White flowers	Silver flowers *
Short plants *	Tall plants

This means they want to create a plant that is homozygous for the following traits and call it something like Silver Kush.

Silver Kush
Pale green leaf
Hashy smell
Silver flowers
Short plants

All the genetics needed are contained in the gene pools for Master Kush and Silver Haze. The breeder could simply mix both populations and hope for the best or try to save time, space and money by calculating the genotype for each trait and using the results to create an IBL.

The first thing the breeder must do is to understand the genotype of each trait that will be featured in ideal "Silver Kush" strain. In order to do this the genotype of each parent strain for that same trait must be understood. Since there are four traits that the breeder is trying to isolate, and 4 x 2 = 8, eight alleles make up the genotypes for these phenotype expressions and must be made known to the breeder.

Let's take the pale green leaf of the Silver Haze for starters. The breeder will grow out as many Silver Haze plants as possible, noting if any plants in the population display other leaf colors. If they do not, the breeder can assume that the trait is either homozygous dominant (SS) or recessive (ss). If other leaf colors appear within the population, the breeder must assume that the trait is heterozygous (Ss) and must be locked down through selective breeding. Let's look closely at the parents for a moment.

	S	SS
S	SS	SS
S	SS	SS

If both parents were SS there wouldn't be any variation in the population for this trait. It would already be locked-down and would always breed true without any variations.

	S	s
S	SS	Ss
S	SS	Ss

With one SS parent and one Ss parent, the breeder would produce a 50:50 population — one group being homozygous (SS) and the other heterozygous (Ss).

	S	s
S	SS	Ss
s	Ss	ss

If both parents were Ss, the breeder would have 25 percent SS, 50 percent Ss and 25 percent ss. Even though gene frequencies can be predicted, the breeder will not know with certainty whether the pale green leaf trait is dominant or recessive until they perform a test cross. By running several test crosses the breeder can isolate the plant that is either SS or ss and eliminate any Ss from the group. Once the genotype has been isolated and the population reduced to contain only plants with the same genotype, the breeding program can begin in earnest. Remember that the success of any cannabis breeding program hinges on the breeder maintaining accurate records about parent plants and their descendants so that they can control gene frequencies.

Let's say that you run a seed bank company called PALE GREEN LEAF ONLY BUT EVERYTHING ELSE IS NOT UNIFORM LTD. The seeds that you create will all breed pale green leaves and the customer will be happy. In reality, customers want the exact same plant that won the cannabis cup last year or at least something very close. So in reality, you will have to isolate all the 'winning' traits before customers will be satisfied with what they're buying.

The number of tests it takes to know any given genotype isn't certain. You may have to use a wide selection of plants to achieve the goal, but nevertheless it is still achievable. The next step in a breeding program is to lock down other traits in that same population. Here is the hard part.

When you are working on locking down a trait you must not eliminate other desirable traits from the population. It is also possible to accidentally lock down an unwanted trait or eliminate desired traits if you are not careful. If this happens then you'll have to work harder to explore genotypes through multiple cross tests and lock down the desired traits. Eventually, through careful selection and *record keeping* you'll end up with a plant that breeds true for all of the features that you want. In essence, you will have your own genetic map of your cannabis plants.

Successful breeders don't try to map everything at once. Instead, they concentrate on the main phenotypes that will make their plant unique and of a high quality. Once they have locked down four or five traits they can move on. True breeding strains are created slowly, in stages. Well known true breeding strains like Skunk#1 and Afghani#1 took as long as 20 years to develop. If anyone states that they developed a true breeding strain in one or two years you can be sure that the genetics they started with were true breeding, homozygous, in the first place.

Eventually you will have your Silver Kush strain but only with the four genotypes that you wanted to keep. You may still have a variety of non-uniform plants in the group. Some may have purple stems, while others may have green stems. Some may be very potent and others not so potent. By constantly selecting for desired traits you could theoretically manipulate the strain into a true breeding strain for every phenotype. However, it is extremely unlikely that anyone will ever create a 100 percent true breeding strain for every single phenotype. Such a strain would be called a perfect IBL. If you're able to lock down 90 percent of the plant's phenotypes in a population then you can claim that your plant is an IBL.

The core idea behind the true breeding technique is to find what is known as a donor plant. A donor plant is one that contains a true breeding trait (homozygous, preferably dominant for that trait). The more locked down traits are homozygous dominant the better your chances of developing an IBL, which does not mean that the line of genetics will be true breeding for every trait, but rather that the strain is very uniform in growth for a high percentage of phenotypes.

Some additional advanced breeding techniques that will help you to reduce or promote a trait in a population are discussed below. Using these techniques may not create a plant that is true breeding for the selected traits, but will certainly help to make the population more uniform for that trait.

ADVANCED BREEDING TECHNIQUES
Simple Backcrossing

Our first cross between the Master Kush plant and the Silver Haze is known as the F1 hybrid cross. Let's pretend that both traits are homozygous for leaf color: the Silver Haze is pale green and the Master Kush is dark green. Which is SS or ss? We won't know until we see the offspring.

F1 Hybrid Cross s	s	
S	Ss	Ss
S	Ss	Ss

This F1 cross will result in hybrid seeds. Since S is dominant over s, we'll know which color is more dominant and from which parent it came from. In this example, the overall results are pale green. Thus, the pale green allele is dominant over the dark green.

S = Silver Haze pale green leaf trait is dominant
s = Master Kush dark green leaf trait is recessive

We also know that because no variations occurred in the population that both parents were homozygous for that trait. However, all the offspring are heterozygous. Here is where we can take a shortcut in manipulating the gene pool for that population. By cloning the parent plant SS, we can use this clone in our cross with the Ss offspring. This is known as a backcross. Obviously, if our parent is female then we'll have to use males from the Ss selection in our backcross, and vice versa.

F2 Backcross	S	s
S	SS	Ss
S	SS	Ss

Now our first backcross will result in 50 percent homozygous (SS) offspring and 50 percent heterozygous offspring (Ss) for that trait. Here all the offspring will exhibit the pale green leaf trait. If we didn't backcross but just used the heterozygous offspring for the breeding program we would have ended up with 25 percent homozygous dominant (SS), 50 percent heterozygous (Ss) and 25 percent homozygous recessive (ss), as shown below.

F2 Hybrid Cross (without backcrossing)	S	s
S	SS	Ss
s	Ss	ss

Backcrossing seriously helps to control the frequencies of a specific trait in the offspring. The F2 Hybrid Cross produced some plants with the dark green leaf trait. The F2 Backcross did not.

The F2 backcross is an example of simple backcrossing. Let's see what happens when we do our second backcross (F3) using the same original parent kept alive through cloning. Our second backcross is referred to as squaring. Since we're dealing with only two types of offspring Ss and SS, we'll either repeat the results of the F2 backcross...

F3 Backcross with heterozygote	S	s
S	SS	Ss
S	SS	Ss

...or we will successfully lock down the desired trait as follows:

F3 Backcross with homozygote	S	S
S	SS	SS
S	SS	SS

In the F3 Backcross with the homozygote, all of the offspring are homozygous dominant (SS) and thus true breeding for that trait. These offspring are the result of squaring and can never produce the ss traits because the SS trait is now true breeding and stable. The F3 Backcross with the heterozygote has some Ss offspring. If we breed the Ss and Ss offspring we can produce the ss trait. This line would not be stable.

How to Generate a Clone Mother

The best way to generate a clone mother is to grow a large population of plants from the same strain. If the strain is an IBL then you should find that the plants do not exhibit much variation. It can be difficult to find a clone mother from an IBL strain, though, because IBLs are created to provide a population of plants from seed from the F3 Backcross with the homozygote, which all resemble the clone mother that the breeder enjoyed and wanted to share with you.

The best way to generate a clone mother is to select her from a large population of F1 hybrids. If you do not find a clone mother in the F1 population then allow random mating to occur and see if you can generate a good clone mother in the F2 population. If you do not find the clone mother in the F2 population then either grow a larger population or select different parents to create a new F1 population.

A clone mother is only as good as the environment she is grown in. The environment influences how the genotype is displayed in the phenotype.* Although indoor plants can grow outdoors and outdoor plants can grow indoors, the expressed phenotype of the genotype may change because of the diversity in growing conditions. This is why breeders urge that you grow their strains in the recommended environment.

Selfing

Selfing is the ability of a plant to produce seeds without the aid of another plant and refers to hermaphrodite plants that are able to self-pollinate. Hermaphrodite plants have both male and female flowers. This usually means that the hermaphrodite plant is monoecious. Most plants are dioecious and have male and female flowers on separate plants.

Monoecious cannabis strains will always display both sexes regardless of the growing conditions. Under optimal growing conditions a monoecious cannabis strain will still produce both male and female flowers on the same plant. Under optimal growing conditions a dioecious cannabis strain will produce male and female flowers on separate plants.

Stressful growing conditions can cause some dioecious cannabis strains to produce both male and female flowers on the same plant. Manipulating an irregular photoperiod during the flowering stage is an easy way to encourage the dioecious hermaphrodite condition. Not all dioecious cannabis strains can become hermaphrodites. The dioecious cannabis strain must have a preexisting genetic disposition to become hermaphrodite under stressful conditions in order for male and female flowers to appear on the same plant.

---

* The phenotype is the expressed genotype but this can be influenced by the environment. Remember your growing conditions influence the expressed phenotype. A purple hue color in the plant's stem may not be genetic at all but the result of lack of K in the nutrients or cold temperatures.

If you find a dioecious cannabis strain that has the hermaphrodite condition you can separate this plant from the rest and allow selfing to occur. If the male pollen is viable on this plant then the hermaphrodite will produce seeds. Selfed plants that produce seeds will eventually generate offspring that:

1. Are all female
2. Are all hermaphrodite
3. Produce male, female and hermaphrodite plants because the environment also influences the final sexual expression of the selfed plant
4. Express limited variation from the original selfed plant

Breeders should note that it is nearly impossible for a hermaphrodite to create male plants although the environment can influence males to appear. Hermaphrodites usually create female-only and hermaphrodite seeds. The female-only seeds often carry the hermaphrodite trait. Selfing has become popular among those who wish to breed all-female or feminized seeds. Unfortunately feminized seeds do very little for the cannabis gene pool as the hermaphrodite condition prevents growers from generating a sinsemilla crop.

Well-informed breeders tend to shy away from producing feminized seeds. Feminized seeds should only be used for bud production and not for breeding. Generating seeds from feminized plants is only advised for personal use and not for distribution.

Notes on Selfing by Vic High
These notes were taken from an online interview. Notes provided by Vic High, BCGA breeder.

++ 100% Female Seeds
POSTED BY THESILICONMAGICIAN ON FEBRUARY 13, 1999 AT 05:17:41 PT
As some of you may know I've been a regular in the chat room for a while and I spend a large amount of time in there. I have had the extreme pleasure of speaking to Mr. XX over the last few nights for many hours and have gotten to know him quite well via email and the chat. He has confided in me and in a few others about his process for coming up with 100 percent female seeds.

Mr. XX is a very nice guy, funny too and it's always a pleasure to speak with him. He doesn't speak English too well, but his wit comes through the rough language and he's a riot. He's a pure lover of cannabis and feels that everyone should share and share alike. He simply wants to share his knowledge with the cannabis community, and because he's spent 15 years researching this, I spoke about it with him in depth.

He has stressed literally hundreds of plants with irregular photoperiods. What he does is put the lights on 12/12 for 10 days. Then he turns the lights on 24 hours, then 12/12 again for a few days, then back to 24 hours for a day, then 12/12 again for a few weeks. If he does this and no hermaphrodites come up, he has found a 100% XX female that can't turn hermaphrodite naturally. He claims that your chances of finding a 100% XX female is vastly increased when using Indica genetics. He also informed me that the more Afghani or Nepalese genetics the plant has, the better the chances of finding a natural XX female. In his own words: "Where did nature give weed a home originally?" I tried to get him to narrow it down to a ratio, but he never specified just how many plants per are XX females. He claims there are plenty of XX females for everybody, and that's all he will say on the subject. It takes a lot of time and a lot of plants to find that one female.

He then uses gibberellic acid, mixing 30 centiliters of water with 0.02 grams of gibberellic acid and 2 drops of natruim hydroxide to liquefy the gibberellic. Then applies as normal and creates the male flowers. He has gotten down to the 4th generation without loss of vigor, and with no genetic deficiencies and hermaphrodites. He claims that the plants are exact genetic clones of one another, complete sisters. Basically it's cloned from seed instead of from normal cloning methods.

POSTED BY THESILICONMAGICIAN ON FEBRUARY 13, 1999 AT 05:17:41 PT
Mr. XX also says that it's easy for the home grower to find an XX female. It's a very time-consuming process but a straightforward one. He advises home growers to confine themselves to a single strain. Mr. XX used a Skunk#1 x Haze x Hawaiian Indica. He says to separate those plants from your main grow and stress them severely. Do this repeatedly with every new crop of seeds you get of that strain until you find the XX female. While this is time consuming it is by no means impossible.

CONCLUDING THOUGHTS ON BREEDING

Experimentation results in new hybrids. Stabilized hybrids result in new strains. It is far better to generate one excellent stable strain than to generate several unstable average ones. Breeding is a long-term commitment. Many breeders stop breeding after only a few years because of lack of time, space and money.

Although they may have learned something about breeding in that short a time, they will not have had the opportunity to put it into practice. If you want to breed cannabis then be prepared to spend a few grows getting the basics right first.

Breeding is all about recognizing which traits are worth continuing. Do not be afraid to admit that you do not have anything worth breeding. Some of the best breeders have gone through dozens of different populations before finding a plant that stands out from the rest.

There are many reasons to breed your own strain of cannabis. Try to find an original idea for breeding your own cannabis strain. Original ideas always seem to work out best.

16 | STRAIN INDEX

THIS SECTION CONTAINS A LIST OF CANNABIS STRAINS that you will more than likely come across if you shop around. These strains are also very popular with growers who like to post pictures of their crops on the internet. The majority of these strains are also featured in various cannabis plant competitions around the world and most of them have won awards.

We have compiled a top 10 list of these favorite strains arranged in alphabetical order per species type with a key denoting whether the plants are suitable for new growers, are true breeding, can be grown indoor or out along with a potency high type rating and the format that the strain is available in.

KEY

*	= A very good strain.
*	= Suitable for new growers.
***	= Not suitable for new growers.
TB	= Indicates an IBL strain or a strain that is stable with a lot of true breeding properties.
OUT	= Not suitable for indoors.
IN/OUT	= Suitable for both indoors and outdoors.
H	= High potency.
M	= Medium potency.

"TOP 10" INDICA

NAME	RATING	IBL	INDOOR/OUTDOOR	POTENCY	SEEDS/CLONE
Afghani	**	TB	IN/OUT	M	Seeds
Afghani #1	*, **	TB	IN	H	Seeds
BC Hash Plant	*, ***		IN	M	Clone
Black Domina	*		IN	H	Seeds
Champagne	*, ***		IN	H	Clone
G-13	*, ***		IN	H	Clone
Hindu Kush	**	TB	IN	M	Seeds
Masterkush	**	TB	IN	M	Seeds
Northern Lights	*, **	TB	IN	H	Seeds
Shiva	**	TB	IN	M	Seeds

Here are some other Indica strains that you might want to try out: Bazooka, Cream Sodica, Domino, Durga Mata, KC36, Kong, Kush, M-9, Mango, Mangolian Indica, Mazar, Pluton 2, Purple Star, Romberry, Shishkeberry, Slyder, Twilight, Williams Wonder.

"TOP 10" MOSTLY INDICA

NAME	RATING	IBL	INDOOR/OUTDOOR	POTENCY	SEEDS/CLONE
Big Bud	*	TB	IN	M	Seeds
Blueberry	*, **	TB	IN	M	Seeds
Chemo	*, ***		IN	H	Clone
Chronic	*		IN	H	Seeds
Early Girl	*, **		OUT	M	Seeds
Great White Shark	*, **		IN	H	Seeds
Matanuska Valley ThunderF*ck	*, ***		IN/OUT	H	Clone
Northern Lights #5	*, **	TB	IN	H	Seeds
Sweet Tooth	*, ***		IN	H	Seeds
Top 44	*, **		IN	M	Seeds

Here are some other mostly Indica strains that you might want to try out - Aurora Borealis, Big Treat, Buddha, Chitral, Early Bud, Eclipse, El Nino, Hawaiian Indica x Skunk #1, Hawaiian/Skunk, Himalayan Gold, Inca Spirit, K2, M39, MCW (Mighty Mite x Chemo x Widow), Mister Nice, Misty, Northern Lights #1, Northern Lights #2 (Oasis), Peak 19, Romulan, Sensi Star, Shiva Shanti, Texada Timewarp, Yumbolt.

"TOP 10" SATIVA

NAME	RATING	IBL	INDOOR/OUTDOOR	POTENCY	SEEDS/CLONE
Australian Bushweed	*, ***		OUT	H	Seeds
Cambodian	***		OUT	H	Seeds
Durban Thai	***		OUT	H	Seeds
Haze Strains	*, ***		OUT	H	Seeds
Malawi	***		OUT	H	Seeds
Mullimbimby Madness	*, ***		OUT	H	Seeds
Neville's Haze	*, ***		OUT	H	Seeds
Purple Haze	*, ***		OUT	H	Seeds
Swazi	***		OUT	H	Seeds
Thai	***		OUT	H	Seeds

"TOP 10" MOSTLY SATIVA

NAME	RATING	IBL	INDOOR/OUTDOOR	POTENCY	SEEDS/CLONE
Cinderella 88/99	*, ***		IN	H	Seeds
Durban Poison	*, ***	TB	IN/OUT	H	Seeds
Early Pearl	*, **	TB	OUT	M	Seeds
Haze #1	***		OUT	H	Seeds
Kali Mist	*, **	TB	IN	H	Seeds
Lambs bread Skunk	*, ***		IN/OUT	H	Seeds
Power Plant	*, **		IN	H	Seeds
Skunk #1	*, **	TB	IN/OUT	M	Seeds
Super Silver Haze	*, ***		IN/OUT	H	Seeds
Voodoo	**		IN/OUT	M	Seeds

Here are some other mostly Sativa strains that you might want to try out - B-52, Beatrix Choice, Durban, Durban X Skunk, Durban/Thai, Early Skunk, Haze #19, Haze Skunk, Mexican Sativa, Original Haze, Purple Skunk, Sensi Skunk, Shaman, Silver Haze, Skunk Passion, Skunk Red Hair, Super Haze, Swazi X Skunk.

"TOP 10" INDICA/SATIVA MIX

NAME	RATING	IBL	INDOOR/OUTDOOR	POTENCY	SEEDS/CLONE
AK-47	*, **	TB	IN	H	Seeds
BubbleGum	*, **	TB	IN	M	Seeds
California Orange	*, **	TB	IN	H	Seeds
Jack Herer	*, ***		IN	H	Seeds
Pole Cat	*, **		IN	M	Seeds
Purple Power	*, ***		IN	M	Seeds
Schnazzleberry	*, **		IN	H	Seeds
Super Skunk	*, **	TB	IN	H	Seeds
White Russian	*, **		IN	H	Seeds
White Widow	***		IN	M	Seeds/Silver

Here are some other Indica/Sativa mix strains that you might want to try out - Apollo 11, Aurora, Blue Heaven, California Indica, C4, Dutch Dragon, Early Riser, Euphoria, Flo, Frost Bite, Fruit Loop, Green Spirit, Hawaiian Indica, Holland's Hope, Jack Flash, Juicy Fruit, KC 33, Killer Queen, Leda Uno, Malibu Blue, Mighty Dutch, Nebula, Night Queen, Orange Crush, Orange Strains, Plum Bud, Purple #1, Rosetta Stone, Shiva Skunk, Silver Pearl, Skunk Indica, Space Queen, Special K, Trance, White Rhino.

SENSI SEEDS

BIG BUD®

One of Sensi's most popular strains. A plant for professional cash croppers. Even experienced growers continue to be amazed and come back to fill their garden with these heavy ladies. It is advisable to tie up the bottom branches as they have a tendency to break under their excessive weight.

FLOWERING: 50-65 days, HEIGHT: 110-150 cm, YIELD: up to 150 gr.

SUPER SKUNK®

This plant is especially developed for Skunk lovers. We have crossed our best Skunks back to their Afghani ancestors. Brush against this plant and the room immediately becomes filled with a powerful Skunk aroma. Despite the smell a very pleasant high with more body to it than the Skunk #1®.

FLOWERING: 45-50 days, HEIGHT: 120-150 cm, YIELD: up to 125 gr.

MEXICAN SATIVA®

The Mexican Sativa® is a hybrid containing a Mexican Oahakan, a Pakistani Hashplant® and Durban®. A great mix of international flavours from the fusion cuisine of The Cannabis Castle.

FINISHING: September-October, HEIGHT: 200-300 cm, YIELD: up to 250 gr.

SENSI SEEDS

AFGHANI #1®

Our top Afghanis have been used for this variety. Characteristic are the big, dark Indica leaves, their strong aroma, sturdy stems and high yield. A must for the Indica connoisseur.
FLOWERING: 45 days, HEIGHT: 100-130 cm, YIELD: up to 125 gr.

NORTHERN LIGHTS #5® x Haze®

This hybrid is the pinnacle of achievement in Cannabis breeding today. The result: an extremely potent plant with a great Sativa high. At the Harvest festivals in the early nineties this strain was already years ahead of its competitors. Even today, it has not been surpassed. The high yields compensate for the slightly longer flowering period. Hybrid vigour results in lush growth, heavy bud formation and abundant resin. A true champion!
FLOWERING: 65-75 days, HEIGHT: 150-180 cm, YIELD: up to 150 gr.

FIRST LADY®

True to its name, this is one of the fastest flowering varieties available. These dominant Indica ladies will bloom rapidly and grab your attention in the way that only a lady can. Originated in the high valleys near Mazar-I-Sharif, Chitral, and Kandahar, in Afghanistan and Pakistan; this Indica cross will remind our older growers of the good old days when the first ladies were introduced in the western world. This strain is characterized by broad plants with short, woody stems and internodes, and large dark green leaves.
FLOWERING: 45-50 days, HEIGHT: 100-130 cm, YIELD: up to 100 gr.

SAGARMATHA SEEDS

MANGOLIAN

A Sister to Slyder, this variety produces a mostly pure Indica with a fantastic mango bouquet and savory taste. She is similar to Slyder in potency, but she is much more fragrant. Serrated, sativa-like leaves and beautiful orange pistils dot the crystallized Indica buds.

FLOWERING: 55 - 60 days, HEIGHT: 1 meter, YIELD: 300 - 325 grams / m" (dried, indoor)

SPECIAL K

Special K (Kali) was the first cross using Western Winds. With a high THC rating 18% and large girthy colas, she proved to be a favorite of many of our (Hazy) customers. Flowertops are long, containing giant, crystal-covered calyxes endemic to Western Winds, however, tops are of a higher density. Trimming is a short pleasure since the number of side leaves and close cutting are few. The buzz is long and cerebral with a strong onset.

FLOWERING: 65 - 75 days, HEIGHT: 1.2 - 1.5, YIELD: 325 - 375 grams per square meter

YUMBOLT

Yumbolt brings back that old-fashioned flavor from the fabled hills of Humboldt Co. California. Possessing a sedative stone with an outdoor aroma, she will often induce heavy eyelids with a satisfying smile. A producer of large succulent flowers, this girl will qualify for every grower's wants and desires. She is believed to have originated from Himalayans of Afghanistan and climatized in the mountains of Humbolt County California in the late 70's. Several generations later in the early 90's we were blessed with the seeds and then propagated them in Holland.

FLOWERING: 60 days, HEIGHT: 1 meter, YIELD: 350 grams / m2 (dried, indoor)

17 | HOW TO MAKE HASH

HASH IS A COMPRESSED FORM OF CANNABIS, but it isn't just compressed bud. In fact, contrary to what many people think, compressed bud has nothing to do with hashish.

Earlier in this book, we discussed capitate trichomes and how these tiny stalked resin glands contain cannabinoids — the major compounds produced by the cannabis plant, which include the THC. THC is found in the male leaf, but the female produces THC in her leaves, trichomes and calyx. THC is rarely extracted from the male leaf because it is contained inside the leaf but since the resin glands can be wiped from the female plant it is much easier to perform THC extraction from a female. The *gland* heads, or rounded tips of the trichomes, secrete the major cannabinoids in an oil-like substance, often referred to as resin, in order to gather fallen pollen from the male plant. This resin can be removed by rubbing your fingers over the bud.

The stalks that support the gland heads are second to the gland heads in the amount of cannabinoids produced. Under certain conditions, the glands and stalks can burst. In the case of a strain like Afghani#1 that is thick with resin, this explosive action of the gland is automatic. Strains that are prone to bursting their trichomes form ball-shaped pistil clusters rather than the usual straight or curled pistil shapes. These ball-shaped clusters are a good indication that a strain is a suitable candidate for resin extraction.

GATHERING THE STALKED CAPITATE TRICHOMES

Hash is made primarily from the collection of the stalked capitate trichomes. When the collected trichomes are compressed, they form the blocky mass that is referred to as hashish. There are many ways to do this, ranging from bulk hash production to rolling small finger-size quantities. Each method produces a different quality or grade of hashish. Some methods gather only the trichomes, while other methods gather trichomes and other subsidiary elements like leaf particles and branch shavings.

Water extraction is the best way to achieve trichome-only extraction. We won't discuss older methods used for mass production, as these are somewhat standard to the home methods mentioned below. The quality of your hashish is determined to a large degree by the genetics you started with in the first place. If you used plants that weren't very potent, don't expect to produce very potent hash.

SKUFF

When you harvest your bud you will have trimmed the leaves away from the bud. This trim is referred to as *skuff*. Skuff should be sticky; so whether it's on the stem, branch, leaf or bud; if it feels sticky then you can use it to extract the resin. If you really want to be a connoisseur, then you should examine your skuff for trichomes with a microscope. If none of the skuff parts have trichomes, discard them. You must take the remaining skuff and store this for 3 to 6 weeks, in much the same way as you would canned bud, before using the basic and advanced extraction methods detailed below.

SCREENING
BASIC METHODS
Flat Silk Screening

Screening is a process much like grating cheese, but on a far finer level. A silk screen is stretched across a square wooden frame and nailed tightly to it. The screen typically has a pore size of between 120 and 180 microns. The smaller the microns, the higher the quality, but the less you will produce. Larger micron pores will result in larger sieved amounts but will allow some leaf matter and branch trim to drop through, degrading the quality of hash you smoke. Typical street hash is not nearly as fine or high in quality as the large pore screening method.

Here's how it's done: The bud is placed over the screen and can either be dragged across the screen manually or using a roller. Manual screening is much easier if you're using smaller quantities of bud, but for large quantities you should consider another method, like automatic tumbling in a drum machine. A sheet of glass placed under the screen is the best way to catch the matter that falls through. After the screening process is complete, the screen can be patted down to shake off any powder that sticks in the pores.

Flat Metal Screening

This is done much like the flat silk screening method but before the flat silk is used, the bud is subjected to a grating process. The grate is usually made from tough nylon or stainless steel and is of equal proportion in pore size to the silk screen. By first using the metal grate, you can remove more matter from the bud than the single silk screen would. The bud matter that passes through the metal screen can then be sieved through the silk screen by shaking the screen back and forth over a glass surface. You end up with two grades of sieved bud residue this way.

Multiple Screening Method

This is a refined version of the above two methods. Any number of screens can be used in this method but the average is four or five. Each screen running from start to finish should have a different micron measurement starting from the largest and running down to the smallest silk screen. The bud matter is sieved through the first screen, then down onto the second screen. The process is repeated with each new screen until most of the matter has passed through. You should end up with several screens that contain bud matter running down to the finer trichomes on the last screen. This is an excellent way to achieve the best results. You end up with several screens each containing different qualities of cannabis residue.

Advanced Screening

Now that you have an idea of what screening is about, we can look at it in closer detail. The following advanced technique can be applied to all of the above screening methods.

We stated that a metal or nylon screen could be used first, followed by a silk screen. Nowadays steel fabrics can be bought in sizes that have much smaller pores than even the finest silk screen. You should typically look for a metal or nylon screen that ranges somewhere between 100 to 140 lines per inch. The screen most commonly used by home hash makers has 120 lines per inch. A wooden frame is constructed to hold the screen in place and can be glued or nailed into position.

Take four small wooden blocks and place them over a sheet of glass or a mirror.

Place the screen over the blocks, leaving a gap of an inch between the mirror and the screen. Place a small amount of skuff on the screen and gently role it back and forth across the screen using a credit card or similar object. Do this very gently, over and back, over and back and over and back with very little pressure. You may have to push the skuff as many as a hundred times before you can see the tiny resin glands gather on the mirror below.

Once you have collected as many resin glands as possible, use the card to sweep them off the mirror and onto another surface. Take the used skuff and, this time, apply a bit more pressure as you roll it back and forth across the screen. With this little bit of extra force you'll be able to remove any resin glands that didn't fall through the first time, but you may also push through some material, such as branch shavings and leaf particles. This second round of pressing will result in a lower quality grade of skuff.

Skuff is skuff; from the time you cure your trim to the point where you sieve it through, it is still skuff. Your objective is to try and collect as much resin from the skuff as possible. You won't end up with hash, but you will end up with different grades of skuff that can be used to make hash later.

You can smoke the different grades of skuff there and then, but you may notice that it's hard to do so. Since this powder is so fine, it will easily fall from a joint or pass through the pores of a pipe screen. In order to solve this problem you must compress the skuff into hashish. This is covered later in the Chapter, after we've outlined three other advanced extraction techniques.

Drum Machines

A drum machine is an automatic screening device. You will probably have to build one yourself, but this is easy enough to do with the right materials. The size of the unit depends on how much cannabis you wish to sieve at a time. Most drum machines have a 1.5- to 2-foot diameter.

The screen is placed in between the two wooden cylinders and the cannabis trim is placed inside this screen. A small motor attached to the side rotates the drum. As it slowly rotates (at a rate of about two rotations per minute), the trichomes drop through the sieve onto the surface stand between the legs of the drum. A simple mirror or sheet of glass is used to catch the skuff. You can keep the tumbler rotating for up to one hour to get the most from your skuff without applying any pressure.

If you want to apply more pressure, simply place a small wooden ball (or any-thing that is slightly heavy with a smooth, rounded surface) inside the barrel of the drum. As the drum rotates, the object inside will add a little more pressure to the skuff as it comes in contact with the screen. Different sized screens can be used to extract different qualities of skuff.

BASIC WATER EXTRACTION

Resin glands can be removed from the cannabis plant by agitating the trim in cold water — typically ice cold water or water that has been chilled in a fridge overnight. The trim is placed in a bucket, which is then filled with cold water. The water and trim are swirled and mixed with a wooden spoon or an electric whisk. Let the mixture sit for a few minutes before scooping out the skuff floating on the surface. The remaining liquid is strained through a coffee sieve to collect most of the trichomes, as they won't pass through with the water. Let the coffee sieve dry and you've got excellent grade trichome extract to use to make hash. The basic idea behind this is that cold water breaks the glands away from the leaf matter. The glands eventually sink to the bottom of the bucket because they are heavier than water. The bulk leaf matter should stay afloat and can be easily scooped away.

ADVANCED WATER EXTRACTION

Developed by Bubble Bags, www.bubblebag.com, in Vancouver this is an excel-lent kit that results in some of the best quality hash. The kits come in four variations: one gallon - seven bag kit, five gallon - seven bag kit, twenty gallon - seven bag kit and five gallon - three bag kit. Whichever one you buy it will certainly be one of your best investments.

SUPERCRITICAL FLUID EXTRACTION
The ultimate way of making high quality hash oil with butane.

Solvents can also be used to extract *raw cannabis oil* from harvested cannabis flowers. Raw cannabis oil contains:

- Psychoactive cannabinoids in high percentages
- Plant tissue in low percentages
- Chlorophyll in low percentages
- Trace elements in low percentages (non-psychoactive water soluble matter)

Raw cannabis oil is best extracted from highly resinous strains like the Afghani cannabis plant. Strains that have a semi-dry or dry floral trait should *not* be considered candidates for cannabis oil extraction because the amount of oil extracted does not necessarily justify the procedure, although the end material is a very high-grade form of hash oil. With these dry strains you may have to perform the extraction process several times before a substantial amount of psychoactive oil is produced. Like any other cannabinoid extraction process, you are better off using a resinous strain to rationalize the end results.

Isopropyl, ethanol and acetone used to be popular solvents for hash oil extraction but the process for each one is time consuming, costly and material-intensive. They often result in smaller amounts of lower grade than you hoped for. There is a much easier and more affordable way to enjoy a purer form of cannabis oil. The process known as *butane extraction* produces better results in a much shorter time frame.

Butane extraction is the most popular form of raw hash oil extraction because it is based on an industrial process known as SFE (supercritical fluid extraction) and is very easy to perform. You should only use butane fuels that are recommended for flameless lighters (jet torch will also do). These types of butane are much cleaner and extract raw hash oil better than other butane fuel types that you commonly find at the drugstore or fuel depot. A good tobacconist shop should stock flameless lighter butane.

Butane is a very good solvent for hash oil extraction because it separates cannabis oils from most other useless plant/bud matter. This type of filtered oil is sometimes nicknamed 'Hash Honey Oil' because the results are like an amber honey. SFE can produce a very fine and pure cannabis oil from resinous strains. It simply separates cannabis oils from plant tissue, chlorophyll and the other trace elements that we find in most raw hash oils. You can imagine the final weight of the butane extracted oil to be the equivalent of the total weight of anything sticky or oily on the plant separated from the rest of it.

Once you have obtained the butane, you need a pipe that measures 1.5 to 2.0 inches in diameter, is 16 to 24 inch long and is made from either polypropylene (PP) or polyethylene (PE). Basically, the bigger the pipe, the more bud it can hold. Do not use PVC piping because it can be a health hazard. Either PP or PE piping works best and can be found in any good DIY store. Each end of the pipe will need a cap. You should be able to get some PP or PE caps at a home improvement store or someone can make them for you. If you cannot find any suitable caps, you can try using large bottle caps and 'blue tack' to hold them in place.

You need a stand to hold this pipe. A lab stand is perfect for the job but anything that will hold the pipe up off the ground is fine. You also need a filter. An extreme-ly fine cloth filter, like a bandage wrap with pores or a fine pipe gauze, will work well. Any filter that will allow oil to drop through but leave the plant matter in the pipe is ideal. Coffee filters will not work very well unless they have a large pore size. You also need a clear plastic measuring cup, a clean wooden stick (like a medical tongue depressor) and some nicely manicured bud. You should be able to use 1 oz or more of bud in the above pipe design.

In the diagram below you can see the parts in alignment without the stand. The parts are as follows: 1) Butane canister, 2) Top cap with hole for canister, 3) Tube for holding the bud, 4) Filter, 5) Bottom cap with perforations, 6) Cup to catch the oil and butane.

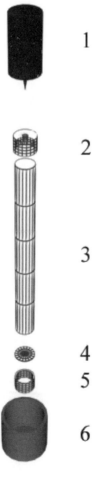

Butane Filter*

Butane Filter

The whole unit should snap into place as follows.

NOTE: Butane is a fuel and will combust when ignited by anything like a spark. If you do not have a professional SFE unit with the proper ventilation, then use butane SFE extraction carefully, outdoors, away from any buildings and other people. Avoid inhaling butane or the exhaust from butane extraction by wearing a facemask.

PROCEDURE:

1. Drill a hole in the end of the first cap that allows the nozzle of the butane canister to fit neatly into it.
2. Drill six small holes near the center of the second cap.
3. Place the filter in this second cap.
4. Attach the second cap to the pipe.

5. Fill up the pipe extremely loosely (never cram it in) with finely ground bud.

6. Attach the first, or top, cap to the pipe.

7. Mount your pipe on your stand and place it over your clean measuring cup.

8. Open the butane can and turn it upside down placing the nozzle in the top cap. Fill the pipe up slowly, allowing the butane to draw the oils down through the tube.

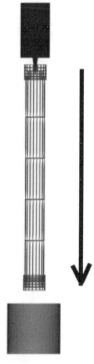

Butane Filter

9. Remove the butane canister when its weight stops decreasing (meaning it is empty) and move a safe distance away.

10. Wait fifteen to twenty minutes before approaching the apparatus even if the top cap has given up any viable signs of fume release. The butane should have evaporated away, leaving an oil/butane mixture in the cup.

11. Open the top cap to allow all fumes to escape. Butane will still be active in the cup and bud in the pipe so leave these two alone for another twenty minutes. The remaining oil in the cup is raw hash oil with some butane.

12. Any remaining butane can be evaporated by placing the cup into a dish of hot water.

13. You now have made raw hash oil. It should be ready to smoke in a few hours.

Tips for butane extraction

I have heard of numerous SFE accidents caused with butane. All of them happened the same way. Most SFE butane extraction accidents occur when the pipe is full of bud and butane is dripping down into the cup below. Any flame, spark or ignition will cause that butane to become unstable. Almost all of the accidents I have heard about occurred because a flame or spark ignited the butane. In most cases it was a smoker who caused this. **Do not smoke when you are performing SFE with butane, period.** If you can do that then butane extraction is actually one of safest methods of hash oil extraction available to the home grower.

During the SFE process the butane must be left alone to drain down into the plastic cup along with the raw hash oils that it collects on the way down. Vapor and fumes will come out through the top of the cap and the cup.

After about fifteen minutes, most of the butane will have passed through. There may be some remaining butane/oil extract near the filter and end cap but forcing this through (by either blowing, tapping or pushing) into the tube may add unwanted matter to your extract. A brief shake is all that is needed to help the remainder into the cup. Use the wooden stick to wipe away any oil/butane mixture from the base of the filter. This butane/oil extract in the pipe and cup is still part of the SFE process and the butane will continue to evaporate.

Butane has a low boiling point (even evaporates at room temperature) and if you need to boil off any excess butane in the cup simply place the cup into a bowl of hot water (not boiling!) and watch the butane evaporate. This is why butane extraction is best done outdoors. Butane will eventually evaporate into the atmosphere instead of into your home where it can become a fire hazard. You should eventually be left with an amber-colored substance in the cup. This is your high-grade hash oil!

The butane should be completely evaporated by heating the cup of raw hash oil/butane in hot water. Your high-grade hash oil is sticky to touch and best smoked in small quantities because of its quality. Oil is best enjoyed by placing a small glob of oil on some foil and heating the foil lightly from beneath, causing the oil to boil and vaporize. This vapor should be then consumed using a Pyrex straw (plastic straws burn and inhaling burning plastic is not good). As a note: Cannabis oil is an excellent format for medicinal use because it is very pure. By vaporizing cannabis oil, the user can enjoy a pure form of cannabis without carbon monoxide.

Here are some other tips for butane extraction:

- After you remove the hash oil from the cup you can use some isopropyl (90 percent minimum content) to collect any residual oil that may by still in the cup. Add a small amount of isopropyl to your cup and swirl it around. Heat the cup at a very low heat (less than 200 degrees to avoid THC evaporation) to evaporate the isopropyl, leaving the remaining hash oil collected from the rim of the cup.
- You can perform a second extraction using the same procedure with the used bud to remove any excess oil that is still left in the bud. The bud should be mostly devoid of any cannabinoid compounds and should be disposed of.
- A slow release of butane into the pipe allows sufficient time for the SFE to take place, improving the quality of the process and the final amount. Try not to force all your butane in too quickly.
- The butane you use must be as pure as possible. Bottled butane is usually mixed with chemicals so that when it leaks you smell it. These chemicals can interfere with the butane/cannabis SFE process.
- Use a bud grinder to make sure that your bud is powered down as much as possible. The finer the mix the better the extraction results.
- You should be able to get between 5 and 10 grams of hash oil for every 1 oz of good quality resinous bud that you use.
- You can also process leaf or trim using butane SFE. You can expect about 0.5 to 2 grams of hash oil for every 1 oz of trim used. This depends on the quality of the trim.

PRESSING RESIN INTO HASH

Again, the quality of the resin glands will determine the quality of hash that you will smoke. In the first chapter we talked about Zero Zero. Recall that hashish can be graded, based on quality, from high (00) to low (3). This is calculated based on a simple ratio of cannabinoids to vegetable material. Good quality hashish has a high ratio of cannabinoids to vegetable material. In Morocco, 00 is used to describe hash that has the highest level of cannabinoids to vegetable material achieved by the extraction process. You can well imagine that this is the finest resin available compressed into hashish. You may be pleased to know that compressing hashish is simple.

Take your extracted resin glands and put it into a cellophane bag. Fold it into a flat block shape and tape the ends of the cellophane to create the package. Try to create the best flat block you can by pressing it with your hands to make it more even. Using a pin, make a few holes on both sides of the bag. One hole per square inch is a good measurement to go by.

Get two or three newspaper pages and dampen them down with a clean cloth that has just been rinsed. Don't saturate or break the paper, just dampen it. Set an iron to low heat and place the newspaper over the cellophane bag. Hold the iron over the paper and press it down with medium pressure for about fifteen seconds. Turn the bag over and place the newspaper on top again. Dampen the paper again, as needed. Repeat the pressure for the same amount of time. You should only have to do this once or twice per side.

Let the bag cool for five minutes and remove the cellophane. You should have a nice block of hash. In addition, your hash will be of a much better quality than the street hash you find on the market. Street hash tends to be made from the less fine skuff material in order to make more blocks of hash. If you smoke homemade hash then you'll probably understand why 90 percent of street hash is sold at rip-off prices. Those big ounce chunks probably only contain 10 percent of the good stuff, if any at all!

This technique of screening and pressing is used to make hash in many countries. As you can imagine, in order to produce bulk amounts you would need to use a lot of skuff in conjunction with numerous drum machines working around the clock. If you harvest more than ten plants then it is worth using one of two to make a nice chunk of hash or some oil for yourself. Since good homemade hash is devoid of leaf matter and other foreign elements it is a very pure smoke which guarantees a hit every time. Cannabis connoisseurs regard homemade hash as one of the best ways of getting the 'best' from the plant. Treat yourself to a little homemade hash at harvest time if you can. It is well worth the experience and who knows, you may just decide to produce a load of homemade hash instead of bud! Give it a whirl — you should be pleased with the results.

18 | IMPORTANT CANNABIS ISSUES

THIS CHAPTER DEALS WITH SOME IMPORTANT questions surrounding the health risks and social issues associated with cannabis use. It should be the endeavor of every cannabis user to learn as much as they can about the plant, its immediate effects and the long-term consequences of use. If you encourage yourself to learn more about these aspects of cannabis, you may eventually encourage other users to do the same. Educating yourself is your best defense against cannabis misinformation.

We are currently in an era of cannabis pseudo-science, in which scientists, documentary makers, doctors and other 'cannabis experts' speak extensively on the subject and impose their own interpretations, which are rarely supported with factual data. You must ask why some mainstream cannabis researchers use doctors as the only authority for their cannabis research? A doctor's authority is in medicine. Cannabis has other uses besides being a medicine, yet most people seem to think that doctors are the only answer to the cannabis question. This is a false assumption. Some doctors and medical authorities have made names for themselves by supporting cannabis prohibition; others have made names for themselves by supporting cannabis legalization. Unfortunately, we seem to hear from the former most often, while the latter are often silenced.

Here are a few of the pseudo-scientific claims that are commonly used to support the argument for cannabis prohibition due to the presence of stronger, more potent cannabis on the market.
• Cannabis is getting stronger
• The stronger the cannabis, the greater the health risks

- Hydroponics makes cannabis stronger
- New lighting technology means stronger cannabis
- Feeding products and growth hormones make cannabis stronger
- New extraction techniques make hashish stronger
- More crystals means more THC and stronger cannabis

In the pages that follow, we examine each of these claims, or myths. Growers will also learn something from this discussion.

Myth #1: Cannabis is Getting Stronger

The concept that "Today's cannabis is stronger than the cannabis of the 60s or 70s" is unsubstantiated by fact. Open any seed bank catalogue that has strains from the 60s and 70s in stock. Order them, grow them, sample your results and you will learn why they are still some of the most expensive seed lines on the market. Strains developed in the 60s and 70s are arguably still the most potent cannabis strains around.

Not only are people more informed as to what constitutes bad cannabis nowadays, but low potency plants are also less likely to be available and/or purchased. This does NOT imply a potency increase. What it does suggest is that people might need to USE LESS cannabis to get the SAME EFFECT as using a lot of bad cannabis. When you think about use in terms smoking it is easy to see that smoking less is far better than smoking more.

Consider this: If the cannabis of the 60s were weaker than the cannabis of the 21st Century, why would internationally known seed banks still advertise some of the oldest stabilized cannabis plants of the 60s and 70s as their most potent?

Haze strains, Thai and other Sativa (species of cannabis) strains of the 60s (imported largely from Asia) are landrace strains that were cultivated by locals for their high cannabinoid content and hemp material. They were bred for hundreds, maybe even thousands, of years.

The suggestion that hybridizing these plants in conjunction with breeding techniques has somehow made cannabis stronger is a false notion. What has happened is that a new species of cannabis has emerged on the market that was not previously widely available. This species is called Cannabis Indica and is the reason why cannabis may seem different, but is not necessarily stronger or more potent.

Cannabis Indica and Cannabis Ruderalis where not common in 60s America and Europe, which was then a mostly Sativa market. Cannabis Sativa by its nature gives a head high effect. Cannabis Indica gives a body down effect. This has to do with the plants' flowering times and cannabinoid contents. Cannabis Sativa and Cannabis Indica can be bred together to produce a hybrid plant that is a 50/50 mix, mostly Sativa or mostly Indica. However this does not increase potency. Potency is genetically determined—you cannot GENERATE new genes that where NOT THERE in the first place.

New breeding techniques give growers and breeders more control over plant characteristics but this does not lead to a potency increase. If seed banks could breed plants that were even double in potency of the strains of the 60s, they would be selling them. What we have gained over the years are strains that pro-duce more flowers, and therefore higher yields, but this has nothing to do with the intoxicating properties of the plant.

Fact: Big plants do not equal more potent plants quite simply because the traits for yield and potency are governed by different genes.

Myth # 2: The Stronger the Cannabis, the Greater the Health Risks

Cannabis is a very controllable recreational and medical drug to use. The effects of cannabis are not as unpredictable as some 'authorities' may have you believe. Calculating how much to take is easy because similar amounts from the same strain should produce the same effects. In fact most experienced cannabis users can recognize the subtle variations of the different cannabis species.

Long-term users experience something called tolerance. If you smoke cannabis every day your tolerance level will increase within a few days. You will notice that you will need to take slightly more to get the same effect that you experienced when your tolerance level was at its lowest—when you first started using cannabis. This does not mean that you will have to keep increasing the amounts that you take in order to experience an effect. Your tolerance levels will eventu-ally peak and the amount that you need to take in order to experience the effect will remain at this fixed level. Increasing the amounts that you take will no longer heighten the effects, but merely sustain them for longer. Usually, cessation of use for a week or two is enough to bring your tolerance back down to its initial level.

Other recreational drugs, like alcohol, can be pushed past your peak tolerance by consuming more. The effect of alcohol consumption increases vigorously with the amount taken and it is possible to exceed tolerance levels to the point at which users can even develop 'alcohol poisoning.' The effect of cannabis consumption is very much dependant on your tolerance levels. Through experience you learn to respect your limits for cannabis.

So what is the worst possible scenario with regards to taking too much cannabis? Even using large amounts of the strongest cannabis strain on its own (without alcohol) will only result in apathy followed by sleep for the novice user: Sweet dreams!

Another health-related misconception is that "high THC levels mean higher volumes of smoke being held in the lungs for longer, which is equivalent to smoking lots of cigarettes".

THC levels, percentages and concentrations do not equate to more smoke. In any given volume of smoke there is a ratio of THC-related compounds to other gases, such as carbon monoxide, that are released during the burning process. One ounce of poor quality cannabis will give off the same volume of smoke as one ounce of high-quality cannabis. Also many people do not smoke cannabis in joints but take the healthier carbon-monoxide-and-tar-free route by using vaporization techniques. Smoke-free vaporization is discussed in detail later in this chapter.

Myth #3: Hydroponics Makes Cannabis Stronger

Hydroponics is a method of cultivation whereby soil is replaced by a soil-less substrate, such as rockwool, Oasis, perlite or vermiculite. The plant is placed in this soil-less substrate and fed an aerated nutrient solution. This method allows the plant to receive the optimal levels of water, air and nutrients it needs in order to survive and thrive.

The very nature of hydroponics allows the plant to expend less energy in the pursuit of nutrients, air and water, and to divert more energy towards plant growth. This results in increased plant size, better health and bushiness (plants grown in hydroponics tend to produce more nodes because of the optimum growing conditions involved). This does not result in increased potency.

Why? Because potency is determined at a genetic level. The environment may influence the final expression of the gene but it certainly does not change the gene to increase potency. Potency cannot increase past the gene's threshold with any known type of growing method, growth hormone or stimulant.

A plant's genotype (what is encoded as the plant's D.N.A.) is expressed in the plant's phenotype (what you can see, smell, taste, etc.) when the plant is growing. Phenotypes are genetically governed but are also influenced by the environment. Even in optimum growing conditions the plant will never increase past its threshold for potency levels, or size contained in its genotype.

It is also worth noting that hydroponic growing does not guarantee that you will automatically increase your overall yields. Many new soil-based methods can achieve the same or better results. The notion that hydroponics somehow increases cannabis potency.

Myth #4: New Lighting Technology Means Stronger Cannabis

HID lighting has indeed changed the world of indoor growing over the past twenty years. HID lighting like MH (Metal Halide) lights and HPS (High Pressure Sodium) are the choice of professional indoor cannabis growers the world over. However, all these lights do is provide the optimal lighting conditions plants require in order to live up to their full genetic potential. It does NOT improve potency, which is genetically determined.

Also, HID lights may be a good replacement for natural light but natural light is still the best light you can use for cannabis cultivation. Geographical and environmental conditions prevent growers from having complete access to this light for at least six months of the year. Some Sativa plants require up to six months flowering before they reach their full potential—which, after three months of vegetative growth, adds up to nine months growing time! Lighting is clearly important to achieving optimal growth, but the notion that new lighting technology had led to stronger cannabis is flawed.

Myth #5: Feeding Products and Growth Hormones Make Cannabis Stronger

Most feeding products contain primary nutrients, secondary nutrients and micronutrients. None of these nutrients, in any combination, will increase a plant's potency. They are simply elements that the plant needs in order to grow and thrive.

The only way in which a growth hormone can affect cannabis potency is if the hormone causes D.N.A repair malfunction, which can lead to a mutation of the plant's D.N.A. However this type of mutation is not controllable and the chances of it happening and resulting in increased potency are very slim. In addition, the plant may exhibit other side-effects that could be negative. So even if you did succeed in increasing the potency via a growth hormone or a D.N.A. repair mutation, you could end up with a sickly or inferior plant on your hands that is hard to grow or reproduce. The notion that feeding products and growth hormones make cannabis stronger is flawed.

Myth #6: New Extraction Techniques Make Hashish Stronger

The reason why hash may seem stronger is because it is not always pure. In fact most mass-produced hash contains traces of adulterates like tranquillizers, opium, heroin and even commonly purchased medicines to help add spice to the product. This is very common with imported cannabis products but does not mean that cannabis produced at home is not adulterated too.

The black-market creates an incentive to produce and sell adulterated cannabis products. Remember that there are absolutely no content restrictions on illegal cannabis and most people have no way of knowing what it is they are taking. Hashish can be cut just like other drugs during production so that the drug manufacturer can sell its product for more money because it is better. Cannabis prohibition fuels that!

In Amsterdam, where cannabis is legal, nearly 100% of all cannabis consumed comes from local, regulated cultivation companies. The bud and hash they produce is not contaminated with any foreign drugs.

New hashish extraction methods, like cold water bubble hash extraction (the best of methods), do not increase potency; they simply reduce the amount of foreign bodies (leaf, stem, dirt) in the hash. The objective of the extraction method is to try to produce almost pure THC. This does not make the product stronger, or more potent, per se. It makes it more concentrated and pure, so that smaller doses are needed to achieve an effect. The notion that new extraction techniques make cannabis stronger is flawed.

Myth #7: More Crystals Means More THC and Stronger Cannabis

Crystals are simply indicators of trichome development on the flowering pistils and its surrounding leaves and stems of the female cannabis plant. Under close observation these crystals look like mushroom heads on a long stalk. That is why they are also known as stalked capitate resin glands. The head of the trichome and stalk contain the highly prized cannabinoids.

Trichome growth and potency levels are two very different traits. You could have an extremely frosty plant with low cannabinoid content in the trichomes or you can have a plant with hardly any trichomes that are extremely high in cannabinoid content.

Although high trichome numbers do not mean high potency levels, breeders generally try to stabilize high trichome numbers with high cannabinoid levels for aesthetic and manicuring purposes intended for the final product's presentation. The notion that more crystals means more THC and stronger cannabis is also flawed.

SO, IS CANNABIS GETTING STRONGER?

Hopefully I have made some headway in explaining how cannabis has changed since the 60s and 70s. The bottom line is that, to-date, nothing on the market has proven to beat the potency levels of the strains of the 60s and 70s. However this does not mean that plants with hyper-cannabinoid levels do not exist. They do "if you can find them" and then set about either cloning the strain or stabilizing them.

THE TRUTH ABOUT HYPER-POTENT CANNABIS

Random mating of plants may eventually lead to the emergence of a plant with the right genetics to contribute to a breeding program for hyper-increased potency.

- Most new traits are discovered accidentally, and not always by people with breeding knowledge who can harness the trait and continue it.

- If you did discover this trait, you would have to grow extremely large selections of test offspring to breed such a plant. You would have to test each and every plant to find the trait and stabilize it so that all of its offspring would produce the same hyper-potent trait. This could take a matter of months or a number of lifetimes to achieve.

- Sometimes the authorities get to it first, bringing your hyper-cannabinoid breeding program to an abrupt halt.

- The strains of the 60s and 70s still have not been beaten for cannabinoid levels because these old strains have been selected by generations of local growers compared to our mere 40 years of cannabis cultivation and breeding agendas.

• It is less common to find poor strains being produced by breeders these days. This means that nearly all commercial cannabis is potent in some way shape or form.

• Only a handful of cuttings (clones) in the world exist which have proven to be hyper-potent—Cali O, MTF, Champaign, Chemo and G13, to name a few.

• Clones are not sold by internationally known seed banks, perhaps because clones are difficult to ship around the world.

• Only good (not to mention lucky) breeding techniques or GM (genetically modified) crops can make cannabis genetically stronger, or more potent.

• The only group to claim to have truly hyper-potent cannabis plants is the U.S. government, which conducts experiments into genetically modifying cannabis. They have never released them to the public.

So, What Has Actually Changed?

Maybe now would be a good time to list some actual changes that have taken place over the years.

1. The introduction of Cannabis Indica species has led to the development of hybrid plants that combine the head high effect with the body down effect.

2. Good cannabis breeders have eradicated poorer forms of cannabis from the gene pool in their breeding programs. This includes hermaphrodite plants that can never produce sinsemilla crops. The net effect is that there are less poor cannabis plants on the market so nearly every type of home grown cannabis is good to some degree as long as it has been grown, flowered, harvested and cured correctly.

3. Sinsemilla crops are flowering female plants that do not bear seeds because the males have been removed before pollination occurs. This does not increase potency. It does increase yield because the plants can divert energy from seed production towards flower production.

4. There are many variations of cannabis on the market with different tastes, smells and high types. The Sativas of the 60s and 70s are very strong and are not really suitable for the novice smoker.

5. Imported hashish usually contains adulterates. It is rarely, if ever, just cannabis.

The bottom line is that since the cannabis plant first started being used by humans the gene pool has not undergone some form of a major potency increase. What has changed is our ability to stabilize traits in a plant population and to ensure that traits are continued in the offspring.

Laws against cannabis have also brought about serious and harmful change. If you look at the facts you will learn that we humans have been using the plant for thousands of years without any major problems. Cannabis prohibition also prevents people from accessing a useful crop and potential fuel source. It also fuels terrorism, extortion, misinformation, scare tactics, murders, beatings and child labor. It allows criminals to control the cannabis black market where they sell their own inferior or adulterated product to adults and children. It puts innocent people all over the world in jail or in jeopardy. These are major problems and we need to get cannabis back under our control. Prohibition does not improve lives—it destroys them...and this FACT cannot be disputed. Given these negatives, how can there be a logical reason for cannabis prohibition?

Having said this, there are some health risks and social issues associated with cannabis that should be part of a healthy, open discussion on the subject. Some of the issues are addressed in the section that follows. These should not be treated as reasons for cannabis prohibition, because regardless of cannabis prohibition these issues still exist. A few key issues are addressed in the section that follows.

How to Avoid Taking Cancer Causing Agents
Is cannabis a carcinogen? The answer is yes if you smoke it using a flame directly in contact with the cannabis, which causes a process called combustion. This is because carbon monoxide is released during combustion and carbon monoxide can be deadly to humans.

Whatever way you look at it, regular inhalation of carbon monoxide will eventually destroy your lungs. If there is a history of cancer in your family then chances are that constant, prolonged inhalation of carbon monoxide will cause cancer to develop in you. The risks are staggering if you think about it. Most people who breathe in a lot of carbon monoxide die from carbon monoxide-related diseases. Of course, pollution from modern society (cars, industry, etc.) has produced much more carbon monoxide than cannabis smokers ever have or will.

Nicotine was also recently discovered to be a carcinogen. It was thought for a long time that it was just the tar and carbon monoxide that were carcinogens, but the more we look at less suspicious substances, the more we find that they are indeed carcinogens as well.

At the moment it is not known if cannabis is a carcinogen because cannabis is made up of so many different types of materials, including cannabinoids and their thousands of related gases that are released during combustion. The number of compounds we need to analyze to be able to say for sure probably runs in to the ten of thousands.

So before anyone discovers carcinogens in these compounds, we might as well assume that some of them are bad, and are actually the result of the combustion process. It makes good sense to remove the risk of contact with carbon monoxide from the equation. This is easy to do: you can either cook with cannabis or use a process known as vaporization.

Cooking with Cannabis

Non-smokers can enjoy marijuana without the effects of carbon monoxide. The Marijuana Chef Cookbook by S. T. Oner, is a great cannabis cooking guide for all marijuana lovers. It covers the basics of cooking, cannabis drinks, desserts, vegetarian marijuana meals, main marijuana courses, starters and soups. It contains quite a number of recipes for you to choose from.

Cooking with cannabis is a healthy way to enjoy cannabis. Many cannabis users have found that cannabis foods are just as delightful as smoking a joint or using a vaporizer. If you like cannabis you should give cooking a try.

VAPORIZATION

Vaporization is the key to the future of smoking cannabis. The vaporization technique simply uses heat instead of a flame to convert your cannabis matter into a fume rather than smoke that contains carbon monoxide.

Imagine placing a small amount cannabis on a knife and gradually heating the knife over a stove. As the knife heats up, the cannabis begins to heat up as well, but it does not burn or catch fire right away. As the knife heats up, a vapor drifts out from the bud. After a while the knife will become very hot and the cannabis will catch fire (if there is still some matter left) and give off a plume of gray and blue smoke.

There is a point at which the cannabis is converted into fumes without releasing carbon monoxide. It will only start to release the cancer-causing agent when the temperature of the knife increases to the point at which cannabis reaches its combustion threshold and starts to burn. In other words, you do not need to burn cannabis in order to smoke it. All you need to do is heat the knife to the point at which THC vaporizes. This is what a vaporizer does.

Like a bong, hookah or any glass pipe, the vaporizer holds the vapor or fumes in an enclosure before you inhale. Most vaporizers are electric and require charging before the heating element is ready for the application of cannabis. Since the temperature of the heating element never rises above the threshold of THC combustion you do not release carbon monoxide. The boiling point of THC is 200°C (392°F). Between 200°C and 300°C will release THC more quicker. Between 300°C and 400°C carbon monoxide may be released along with THC. Between 400°C and 500°C carbon monoxide will be released along with THC. Temperatures of 500°C and above result in complete combustion with maximum carbon monoxide emissions. Everything burns up, leaving very little ash. Vaporizer users stick with 200°C (392°F) to achieve the desired effect of keeping carbon monoxide levels either at zero or to natural levels present in air.

Vaporizers can be bought in all sizes, shapes and forms. Pharmaceutical companies spend hundreds of thousands on industrial vaporizers in order to reduce carbon monoxide emissions from their factories. Make sure that your vaporizer has an adjustable temperature function so that you can choose how hot you want the element to get.

Before you buy a vaporizer you may want to check out the low-cost, do-it-yourself method described below. Remember though, that you are much better off buying a professional vaporizer to ensure that no carbon monoxide is released.

The Light Bulb Vaporizer
The light bulb vaporizer is a simple vaporizer that you can make using common household products. It allows the user to smoke cannabis without inhaling carbon

monoxide in the process. This is one of the safest ways you can consume marijuana.

ITEMS NEEDED:
1. A screw-type 100-watt domestic light bulb
2. A normal plastic screw-type bottle top
3. Two straws or a 10 cm glass tube and a 3 cm glass tube
4. A multipurpose pocket knife
5. Water

PREPARATION:
Be careful when you hold the bulb that you do not break it. Very little pressure is needed to complete this procedure. Hold the bulb in a thick cloth or use padded gloves for protection if you need too.

Step 1. Prepare the items as shown in the above picture.

Step 2. Use the knife to cut the base of the bulb at the last screw-threading groove. The knife should sink in easily because this metal is very light.

Step 3. After cutting the base of the bulb it should come off easily.

Step 4. If you look into the bulb you will notice some glass in the way of the element.

Step 5. Push down on this area very gently with a knife, turning the knife as you do so.

Step 6. With very little pressure, the glass inside will crack and the element will become dislodged. The knife will pass all the way through.

Step 7. Empty out the contents. There will be broken glass here so be careful. If you have trouble getting the element out, keep tipping the bulb back and forth until a wire protrudes through the opening. Catch this wire and you will be able to pull the element out.

Step 8. Using the knife, churn out any remaining glass still present on the rim of the opening.

Step 9. You now have a bulb which has the end cut away and all the inside contents removed. Look inside to make sure that all the glass has been tipped out.

Step 10. Give the bulb a rinse with water to remove any of the remaining dust particles or glass. If your bulb is not the clear type, then this process will wash away the inside coating, making your bulb transparent. Make sure to let the bulb dry before using it again.

Step 11. Take the plastic bottle top and make two holes in it using the pocket knife. By using the screwdriver part of the knife you can easily make a hole.

Step 12. Insert your straw or glass tubes into the holes in the bottle cap.Glass tubes last longer than plastic tubes.

Step 13. Screw the bottle cap with the straws attached into the bulb. The bottle cap should easily screw onto the bulb's grooves.

Step 14. If you are using straws you can cut them down to size to match the example. You will notice that one of the straws is smaller than the other. This smaller straw is just an air-flow straw. It simply allows air to enter the bulb as you inhale cannabis fumes through the top straw.

Step 15. Unscrew the cap and put some bud in before sealing.

Using your light bulb vaporizer:

Use a naked flame to heat the bulb just under the bud. Swirl the flame around in a circular motion like a scientist. Inhale through the longer tube. After about fifteen to thirty seconds you will taste some vapor. This vapor contains various cannabinoids without carbon monoxide. You can inhale this without inhaling carbon monoxide. As you continue to heat the glass, more vapor will be released. However the longer you heat the glass, the more the temperature will increase— eventually passing the boiling point of THC so that carbon monoxide is released. You will see this clearly in the glass because it will begin to fill with smoke. You will also taste the difference. The taste of carbon monoxide mixed with cannabinoids is like hay. Do not inhale this if you want to stay healthy. Although this smoke does contain cannabinoids, it also contains carbon monoxide. Have a tissue nearby to wipe the glass after you are finished. Unscrew the cap and dump out the used bud. A black residue will develop on the outside of the bulb. This is the result of the flame coming into contact with the glass. You can wash your bulb out after a few uses and start all over again.

Conclusion

Vaporization is a safe and effective method of smoking marijuana as long as you do not release and inhale carbon monoxide. Regulating the flame can also help prevent the bud reaching temperatures that cause carbon monoxide to be released. Professional vaporizers are more controllable than the light bulb method because the temperature of the heated bud can be kept well below the point of carbon monoxide release.

CANNABIS LEGALIZATION AND SOCIAL ISSUES

Cannabis and Young Adults

Many parents and teachers are opposed to cannabis decriminalization and legalization because of concerns about risks to the health, the wellbeing and future of children. This is very understandable.

Most adults agree that children should not use drugs and most cannabis users and enthusiasts recognize this. In fact many shops, web sites and message board forums related to cannabis actively seek to prevent children from using or growing cannabis.

Although this cannot achieve 100% effectiveness, it does demonstrate that many cannabis users take the issue seriously. Sadly though the same cannot be said for some of those who deal cannabis on the black market, which is a result of pro-hibition. This is yet another reason to bring cannabis back under our control.

If you have seen the Academy award-winning film Traffic then you will probably understand that there is also a need for closer parent/child communication with regards to drug education. The concept that cannabis decriminalization or legal-ization will lead to more (or less) children using cannabis is flawed. But then, the illegality of cannabis doesn't seem to stop them from using it either. Cannabis is a very popular recreational drug.

So ask yourself this basic question: if my child is determined to get hold of cannabis would he be better off procuring it from the black market or from a controlled, regulated manufacturer or retailer?

We should be dealing with the cannabis issue in terms of REALITY and not in terms of myths that are propagated by anxiety or fear, most of which is the result of pseudo-scientific or political misinformation. Too many people let their emotions be their guide instead of relying on reason where marijuana is con-cerned. The fact is that your child can buy drugs whether or not cannabis pro-hibition exists. A storefront does not make cannabis any more or less accessible than it already is to your child, right now, in reality. It does, however, make it less dangerous.

CANNABIS IS A REALITY

Cannabis does not disappear because it is prohibited. Cannabis is a very common illegal drug, and most users who experiment with illegal drugs are bound to try cannabis at one point. Most of these users are totally unaware of its effects because cannabis prohibition stifles proper education and research. There are well over 15,000 scientific papers on cannabis and a lot of them explain how cannabis is used and what effects it has on the user without using scare tactics or fear to induce a psychological block with regards to cannabis information. Scaring people can prevent people from doing something, however it does so by controlling them, not educating them.

Some people suggest that cannabis is only taken for euphoria. However there are many other reasons why people take cannabis. Some take it for medical use. Others take it to feel more relaxed and not for its euphoric properties. Cannabis is a substance that has many more uses than getting you high.

THE ALCOHOL VS. CANNABIS DEBATE

Even though Alcohol is water-soluble and is cleared from the body at the rate of one unit per hour (the amount in half a pint of beer, a single whisky, or a glass of wine) it can still kill you.* A drop of pure alcohol is enough to send any grown man to the local ER ward. Some will even die if the problem is not treated soon enough. That is why there is a legal limit on how much percentage of alcohol is allowed per bottle. Go above this limit and you can seriously hurt people if not kill them outright.

Alcohol poisoning is common. Upward of 5,000 people die from alcohol overdoses every year in the United States alone. People die because of alcohol poisoning.

50% of THC is still present in the body five days after use and 10% after a month. Traces can be detected in hair and urine for months after that. However this does not mean that the psychoactive effects of cannabis are still active in the brain. It simply means that the body is disposing of THC in its own way, over time.

Cannabis does not directly kill people. Unlike alcohol, pure, concentrated THC will not kill you unless you have some rare allergy to it. There are more deaths associated directly with alcohol than there are indirectly with cannabis. The only deaths associated with cannabis are either indirect (cancer from smoking) or avoidable (car crashes or other accidents), and even the chances of getting cancer from THC can be avoided by using alternative medical smoking methods or eating cannabis.

Animal testing has shown that extremely high doses of cannabinoids are needed to have a lethal effect on the animals. At this moment the hypothetical toxicity amount needed to cause death derived from these studies is 1:40,000 for cannabis. That means that you would have to consume 40,000 times as much cannabis as you normally would in order to reach the hypothetical toxicity amount that causes death.

In the annals of medical history no one is ever reported to have died from a cannabis overdose. In the annals of medical history hundreds of thousands have died from alcohol overdose or alcohol poisoning. Alcohol abuse will damage more vital organs in the body than cannabis use. In most cases cannabis-related damage (mainly lung disease) can be reversed by discontinuing the use of the drug or taking it in another form (unless cancer is contracted in which chemotherapy is

* In 2003 the UK Department of Health's "Alcohol Concern" foundation revealed that 13 in 100,000 men and 7 in 100,000 women died directly from alcohol related deaths in 2001. Alcohol Concern's Chief Executive, Eric Appleby, explained: "These figures are based on death certificates where alcohol is actually mentioned as a cause of death." http://www.alcoholconcern.org.uk/legalbutlethal.htm

usually the treatment option).* With alcohol, most damage cannot be reversed and damaged organs can only be replaced via a transplant operation (if you can afford one or afford to wait for one).

Deaths recorded in the United States** in any typical year are as follows:

Tobacco deaths	400,000
Alcohol deaths	80,000
Workplace accidents that result in death	60,000
Automobile accidents that result in death	40,000
Cocaine deaths	2,200
Heroin deaths	2,000
Aspirin deaths	2,000
Cannabis deaths	0

The Califano Report from The National Center on Addiction and Substance Abuse (CASA) at Columbia University is also worth noting.

Far more people are hospitalized for alcohol-related illness than cannabis-related illness even though we know that cannabis is the third most commonly used drug in the Western world. Also there are more types of alcohol-related illness than cannabis related illness to deal with. The burden on taxpayers to solve alcohol related-illness is significantly higher than cannabis-related abuses, even in countries that have decriminalized or tolerate cannabis use.

Any type of drug abuse can cause a different personality to emerge. Abusers can become stubborn, cannot manage themselves properly, find it hard to deal with disapproval and feel misinterpreted. This is common to all types of drug abuses and should not be singled out with cannabis alone. Mobile phone addiction, Internet addiction, computer game addiction and television addiction can also cause these types of personality disorders to emerge and yet mobile phones, computer games, the Internet and television are not illegal. All these things have suspected or proven health risks associated with them too.

With regards to cannabis addiction there are no signs or evidence of physical addiction. Many major pharmaceutical companies have tried to develop pills, to help cure cannabis physical addiction, however these drugs have never been approved by medical boards because the pharmaceutical companies have been

---

*Cannabis also has medical uses for cancer treatment.
** National Institute on Drug Abuse. NIDA
Joseph A. Califano, Jr., President and Chairman of The National Center on Addiction and Substance Abuse at Columbia University (CASA) and former U.S. Secretary of Health, Education and Welfare.

unable to prove any physical addictive properties associated with cannabis. There are many pills, on the market however that help deal with the physical addiction of other drugs like tobacco, alcohol and hard drugs.

Psychological addiction* is treated by psychiatrists and not doctors of internal medicine (who are used in the treatment of other drug abuses like alcohol and hard drugs) and for personalities who express psychological cannabis addiction, treatment is administered through psychotherapy and perhaps occupational therapy alone.

DRIVING WHILE UNDER THE INFLUENCE
Cannabis has been brought into the intoxicating driving debate. The bottom line to any debate is that you should not do drugs and drive, period. Even though some people have suggested that cannabis causes more road accidents than alcohol, this is certainly not reflected in reality where the majority of DUI road accidents are the result of the driver's use of alcohol. This is why the government actively uses alcohol detection methods in its attempt to prevent driving related crimes.

LIBERATE THE HERB, LIBERATE THE INNOCENT, AND FREE SOCIETY
The Federal Bureau of Prisons estimates that they have house roughly 170,000 inmates for any given month. Out of these roughly 84,000 (55%) are in their drug related offenses. This is more drug-related incarcerations per capita than any other nation in the world. Since 1965 America has arrested more than ten million people for marijuana-related offences.**

In 2002 the annual report on the state of the drug problem in the European Union and Norway concluded that: "Use of illegal substances is concentrated among young adults and particularly males in urban areas, although some spreading to smaller towns and rural areas may be taking place."***

Recent cannabis use (last 12 months) was reported by 5 to 15% of young adults in most countries. Recent amphetamine use was reported by 0.5 to 6%, cocaine use by 0.5 to 3.5%, and ecstasy use by 0.5 to 5%.

Lifetime experience of cannabis is reported by 10 to 30% of European adults,

* In 2001, Drug Abuse Substance Abuse and Mental Health Services Administration. Treatment Episode Data Set (TEDS): 1994-1999, National Admissions to Substance abuse Treatment Services reported that 220,000 entered drug abuse treatments programs between these dates. However 99.99% of those who entered drug abuse treatment programs for 'marijuana addiction' did not do so of their own free will but by the order of a judge.
** U.S Department of Justice - Federal Bureau of Prisons. http://www.bop.gov
*** European Monitoring Centre for Drugs and Drug Addiction (EMCDDA) http://www.emcdda.org/

while amphetamines, cocaine and ecstasy have been tried by about 1 to 5%.

Cannabis use increased markedly during the 1990s in most EU countries, particularly among young people, although in recent years its use can be leveling off in some countries. Cocaine use may have increased in recent years in some countries, although this trend is less clear.

There is an incentive for individuals who are subjected to drug tests to choose harder drugs as their form of recreational drug because these substances disappear from the system more quickly. Again another indication that drug testing does not help the cannabis problem in any way.

Cannabis remains one of the most confiscated drugs in the world and makes up almost a whopping 80% of all illegal confiscations even though it is considered a less problematic drug than alcohol or harder drugs. If cannabis were legalized tomorrow drug enforcement agencies would automatically loose 80% of their figures, which are used as a basis for government budgeting on drug enforcement programs. On many levels, cannabis prohibition could be more about money than most government officials would care to admit.*

CANNABIS AND VIOLENCE
This is the original myth used to support cannabis prohibition (think Reefer Madness). Cannabis prohibition has not reduced acts of violence or crime. It has increased after cannabis prohibition. No study has shown a link between cannabis use and crime. Likewise no study has shown a link between cannabis use and violence.

A notable incident occurred in the UK. A British member of parliament and labor government minister, Johnathan Prescott, debated the issue that cannabis causes people to become violent and should therefore remain illegal. He did this on national television and without any evidence to support his claim. Shortly after making this statement Minister Prescott punched a man twice for throwing an egg at him during a political rally. Since then he has earned the nickname "Two-jabs" Prescott from the media and surprisingly managed to retain his position as a government Minister.

CANNABIS AND BRAIN DAMAGE
There is no scientific evidence to suggest that THC damages the brain** in any

---

* European Monitoring Centre for Drugs and Drug Addiction (EMCDDA) http://www.emcdda.org/
** On 27th June, 2003. Dr. Igor Grant a professor of psychiatry at the University of California at San Diego (UCSD) reconfirmed that cannabis does not cause permanent brain damage after conducting an extensive study of cannabis users for his research into marijuana and brain damage for the IOM.

way, shape or form. Animal asphyxiation experiments, using monkeys, were conducted in the 70s and subsequently used to prove that cannabis kills brain cells. Monkeys were gassed to death with cannabis smoke over a long period of time. The monkeys had electrodes implanted in their brains to monitor the effects of the exposure to cannabis smoke. The monkeys died and the brain cells were counted. A healthy monkey was also killed as a control experiment and its brain cells where counted. The U.S. government was brought to court on this issue to reveal the experiment under the "Freedom of Information" act. When the hoax was exposed (and the unnecessary animal deaths) the U.S. government never used these findings again. The study was harshly condemned for its inadequate sample size of only four monkeys, its complete failure to manage experimental prejudice, and the misidentification of the monkeys brains as "damaged".

Two noteworthy studies were conducted in 1977 and published in the Journal of the American Medical Association (JAMA). These studies showed no evidence of brain damage in heavy marijuana users. These facts have never been disproved. In the same year as these studies were released, the American Medical Association (AMA) officially proposed decriminalizing marijuana—a proposal that was ignored by the American DEA.

MEDICAL CANNABIS SHOULD NOT BE A LEGAL ISSUE

In cancer terms one joint is thought to be the equivalent of five cigarettes. However joint smoking is a mostly western phenomena. Prohibition prevents good scientific investigations into the prohibited substance from occurring unless it is considered acceptable for medical use. Many fear that the medical use of cannabis will result in good scientific investigations of cannabis, which will result in many of the current cannabis prohibition laws being repealed.

Cannabis prohibition is currently a very profitable business for some but not all! Many jobs would be lost if cannabis prohibition was discontinued. However far more jobs would be created in the scientific, agricultural and production sectors if prohibition were lifted.

Also, there is nothing new about medical cannabis. Medical cannabis has its roots in western civilization dating back to the 1700s and even before. It is only in recent times that medical cannabis has been prohibited but only because of legal issues and not its medicinal values.

Cannabis and the Immune System

Cannabis use may affect the immune system. For some illnesses it is advised that you discontinue cannabis use until the illness has passed. Consult your doctor for further information. This is because cannabis may cause fewer white blood cells to be produced, which are used in the fight against some diseases. Discontinuing cannabis use will restore the immune system to its previous condition before cannabis was used.

Cannabis and Sexual Dysfunction

Sperm production may also be decreased with cannabis use. Discontinue cannabis use and sperm production should return to normal levels again. There is no scientific evidence to suggest that young men will develop breasts if they use cannabis. This is a red herring associated with a testosterone decrease in some individuals who use cannabis. There is absolutely no evidence to support a case that this decrease is permanent. Cannabis tolerance can also occur, bringing levels back to normal again even though cannabis has not been discontinued.

Cannabis and Pregnancy

Babies that are born to cannabis-using mothers may have some abnormalities like being small, hyperactive and show certain types of behavioral problems. There may also be an increase in leukemia with children born to cannabis using mothers, however none of this is definitively proven. However, the bottom line here is the same advice that has always been administered to pregnant women: only take drugs that your doctor recommends when pregnant. It is your duty to discontinue cannabis use if you are pregnant.

Cannabis and Human DNA Repair Malfunction

There is no scientific evidence to support the case that cannabis directly causes D.N.A repair malfunction in human beings. D.N.A repair malfunction results in a mutation at the cellular reproduction level. A D.N.A repair malfunction type mutation is usually random and can result in anything. There are no specific conclusions to random D.N.A repair malfunction although scientists can cause certain types of malfunctions to appear using specific techniques. However these techniques may result in other types of uncontrollable mutations from occurring alongside the controllable one. The notion that cannabis can cause a certain type of, or any type of, D.N.A repair malfunction in human beings is not scientifically proven.

SO WHY IS CANNABIS ILLEGAL THEN?

With the underwhelming amount of evidence to support the fact that cannabis is dangerous, you might wonder why it is then illegal. Cannabis is illegal because the U.S. government incorrectly classed cannabis as an opiate during the opium wars and this notion has been adopted throughout most of the rest of the world.

The prohibition campaign was also backed by the cotton industry, which wanted to see an end to the cannabis hemp industry for its own gain and profit. The cotton industry financially backed politicians who made statements to the newspapers and public about cannabis.

Cannabis-related violence was used as the main reason for cannabis prohibition. Violent crimes did not decrease after the prohibition of cannabis. They increased if anything. During WW2 the prohibition of cannabis was lifted so that cannabis could again be used to help the war effort. George Bush Senior's parachute was made from cannabis when he ejected safely from his burning plane.

Shortly after WW2 cannabis was again prohibited because it was claimed that it would make men docile and unable to fight the communist threat. There has been a complete turnaround in the reasons for cannabis prohibition over the last 60 years. This is because there have never been logical grounds for cannabis prohibition. This is the very reason why intelligent people can see through the hoax while others are fooled by it.

Consult the book The Emperor Has No Clothes by Jack Herer, for a full disclosure on the real reasons for cannabis prohibition and how the hoax has been maintained. The book contains lots of information with regards to the inaccuracies of some pseudo-scientific approaches to cannabis prohibition.

PEOPLE ARE NOT SCIENCE EXPERIMENTS

It is a lie to suggest that in all of history, no young people have ever taken marijuana regularly on a mass scale. This occurs all the time in countries that have never prohibited cannabis use. Therefore the implication that our youngsters who use cannabis are somehow guinea-pigs in a tragic experiment is absolutely flawed. THC receptors evolved naturally in the human brain and are proof of our long-term association with the cannabis plant. We have been using cannabis throughout our entire evolution.

It is only in the past 80 years that cannabis has been prohibited in some countries. Most of those who have taken cannabis all their lives will attest to the fact that they have not been adversely affected. Some believe that the Netherlands is a good example of how cannabis tolerance leads to an increase in crime. This completely misses the mark. The rate of marijuana use among Dutch teenagers is actually lower than that among American and European teens from countries in which cannabis is illegal.

CANNABIS AND THE INSTITUTE OF MEDICINE (IOM)

In 1998, 109 distinguished scientific researchers held a discussion on medical marijuana in New York. Their documents and deductions were published in 1999. They said that marijuana or THC do not qualify as safe or effective medication which aim at restoring or maintaining physiological functions of cells, organs and organisms. They have no place in a modern pharmacopoeia from which cannabis was eliminated in the first part of the century. However these 109 distinguished scientists' findings where voided by the Institute of Medicine soon after.

In March 1999, the U.S. government-sponsored Institute of Medicine (IOM) Report concluded that: "Until a nonsmoked rapid-onset cannabinoid drug delivery system becomes available, we acknowledge that there is no clear alternative for people suffering from chronic conditions that might be relieved by smoking marijuana, such as pain or AIDS wasting..." The U.S. DEA ignored this and has said: "Any determination of a drug's valid medical use must be based on the best available science undertaken by medical professionals. The Institute of Medicine (under the National Academy of Sciences) conducted a comprehensive study in 1999 to assess the potential health benefits of marijuana and its constituent cannabinoids. The study concluded that smoking marijuana is not recommended for the treatment of any disease condition." This is a lie and in direct conflict to the IOM findings.

CANNABIS AND HARDER DRUGS: THE GATEWAY THEORY

The suggestion that marijuana use leads to hard drugs is flawed from the outset. Most hard drug users have taken cannabis, however out of the 100s of millions of people worldwide who have tried cannabis, we do not find 100s of millions of hard drug users. In fact 1 in 100 cannabis users will likely try a harder drug however this is not because of cannabis use. How many bicycle riders grow up to become motorcycle drivers? The thing to note is that the majority of people who use cannabis will never do another illegal drug.

If a cannabis user cannot get cannabis then they may take a harder drug that is more readably available from a dealer. This is why drug dealers are also called drug pushers. The cannabis user may be pushed to buy something else because the dealer does not have cannabis available. This is very important and we find that most cannabis users come in contact with hard drugs as a result of contact with the same source who does not have any cannabis available. Drug dealers can also use this tactic to sell the user stronger and more expensive drugs. This is a major reason why cannabis should be disassociated with other forms of harder drugs. It is a problem that springs from prohibition.

In 1993 the Rand Corporation cannabis study concluded that hard drug abuse emergency room situations decreased in places that had decriminalized marijuana in contrast to places that did not. This has a name. It is called the "negative gateway" effect. It is a fact that cannabis legalization results in less hard drug abuse.

CANNABIS AND MEMORY
Cannabis does affect short-term memory until you terminate its use. Cannabis use does not affect short-term memory permanently, which is a misconception derived from the statement that cannabis impairs the short-term memory.

CANNABIS AND PAPER PRODUCTION
Most cannabis prohibition campaigners advocate that paper from trees is much cheaper than paper made from cannabis. Do you see the obvious lunacy in the suggestion that we should continue cutting down trees for paper instead of using a plant that takes a minimum of 3 months to grow to full maturity as opposed to 50 years for most trees?

The same argument goes for most types of linen too which are made from chemical and waste producing factories. In the long term it is far cheaper and more natural to use cannabis in many different types of fabric production.

CANNABIS AND ILLEGAL DRUG CLASSIFICATION
Incorrectly classifying cannabis as a hard drug has led some of the 1 out of every 100 cannabis users to believe that they can handle any hard drug because they can handle cannabis. This is a totally false notion caused by cannabis prohibition.

High percentages of hard drug users also use soft drugs however their preference is for hard drugs. 1 in 100 soft drug users may use hard drugs. 99 out of 100 soft drug users prefer to stick with soft drugs and will never use a hard drug.

The illegal drug classification system is nonsense in itself. Even doctors would admit that the drug classification system is only there to support incarceration and sentencing laws. It actually means nothing scientifically.

CANNABIS AND MIND CONTROL

That idea that "Drugs take control of your mind. No person can do that—no parent, no teacher, and no friend. You can't make rational decisions" is flawed. Most companies, governments, education systems have policies in place that are geared towards controlling an individual or a population of people. Prohibition is used to control people's minds! The War on Drugs, Just Say No. What are these if not a form of propaganda and mind control?

To prevent cannabis from having an effect on your mind you simply discontinue using the drug. The effect goes away. This does not change your mind or personality in any way unless you develop a psychological dependency to cannabis. Very few people will develop this dependency because long-term cannabis use usually leads to boredom. Most people stop using cannabis because they get bored with it or do not have the time to use the drug anymore.

CANNABIS PROHIBITION HAS FAILED

With regard to alcohol and tobacco the idea that "If discovered today they would certainly be controlled drugs. Do we really want another legal drug like cannabis?" is flawed. Cannabis is clearly already there and being used by people even though it is prohibited. Prohibition sweeps the problem under the carpet and decentralizes control of the drug and hands it over to the black market instead.

We know that prohibition is a failed concept because all types of drug use are on the increase with all kinds and type of people of all ages. In 80 years, drug prohibition has done nothing to help this in any way shape or form. People use drugs irrespective of prohibition. People can easily acquire drugs irrespective of prohibition. People take drugs irrespective of prohibition. In some cases the very fact that something is illegal makes some people want to do it! This is one reason why cannabis is used more by people in America and the UK than in Holland. The Netherlands partially legalized marijuana with some restrictions in the 1970s. Since then, hard drug use has declined so substantially that the argument that marijuana is a "gateway" drug that leads to hard drug use has been proven invalid.

Reports on cannabis never seem to be consistent. Some will claim the drug is harmless, others will claim that it is dangerous and should not be legalized. Many scientists, doctors and cannabis users have come out and said quite openly that cannabis is not as dangerous as alcohol or tobacco. In fact such statements caused the Home Secretary in the UK to lower the classification of cannabis to a class C drug instead of a class B drug.

The War on Drugs was lost long ago. The war on drugs began by using jail as a deterrent. The reason for mixed messages, confusion and bewilderment in our youth is the fact that the war against drugs like cannabis has changed back and forth from "it will make you violent" to "it will make you docile."

Its reasons have always changed because science has pointed out the validity of pro-cannabis legalization statements. It changes to suit its own agendas and not to suit scientific facts. In the majority of cases, like the ones mentioned above, the war on drugs seeks to actively ignore scientific fact in favor of legal law enforcement agency statements on the issue which, in most cases, are in direct conflict with scientific advice and knowledge. See the IOM statement under the heading "Cannabis and the institute of Medicine (IOM)" in this chapter .

Harm Reduction is important. The very knowledge that a vaporizer exists will stop large numbers of cannabis users from smoking joints or inhaling carbon monoxide for the remainder of their lives. The idea that "teaching young people about how to use cannabis is bad because it is introducing people who will never use cannabis into cannabis" is flawed. In school, 85% of what we teach our children will never be used by our children again. It is there to educate them, to get them to think for themselves; not to brainwash them into doing what we preach as some would have you believe. In fact teachers who support the idea that teaching young people about how to use cannabis is bad are likely more concerned about making the student do whatever they tell them to do, rather than teaching the student to think for themselves.

No two politicians, doctors, scientists will ever cite the same reasons for cannabis prohibition. This is because there are no reasons for cannabis prohibition. This is the root cause of all mixed messages that people are receiving as a result of the cannabis prohibition hoax.

CANNABIS PROHIBITION AND LAWSUITS
Your hard-earned tax money is extremely vulnerable to cannabis prohibition

compensation claims (there are lawyers waiting on every corner to give this a shot).

The government can end up owing cannabis prohibition criminals damages because of a hoax which may seem real at the moment but as it is exposed for the hoax that it is (currently happening now) things will eventually change. Should cannabis prohibition be deemed illegal based on scientific findings in the legal/political arena then your tax money may go to pay for compensation claims for those who have suffered any legal consequence of cannabis prohibition.

It is worth a thought that the professionals who deliver false, misleading and often downright incorrect pro-prohibition information should be the first to pay out for compensation claims before anyone else does because THEY are the perpetrators behind the hoax. Would they support their cause if they where held accountable for the hoax?

Most cannabis prohibition campaigners currently enjoy diminished responsibility. Your hard-earned tax money is currently paying for their support of cannabis prohibition. In turn, your tax money is also going to pay for cannabis prohibition compensation claims should cannabis be legalized. Do you see how cannabis prohibition has totally made a mess of everything? You lose money either way. Prohibition is the cause of this. That is why cannabis prohibition is the wrong method of management for the cannabis issue. It always has been and always will be.

CANNABIS AND THE AUTHOR

I am a cannabis user and have been able to still write and compile this book for you to read. Does this look like the work of a disorganized/violent/docile mind?

I have never been involved in a crime other than using/growing cannabis. I have never even received a parking ticket. I have only met a police officer once in my lifetime and this was because he thought I was doing 40 mph in a 30 mph zone. I pointed out to him that I was wrong and that I was sorry and that I genuinely try to adhere to rules of the road, which I do. He understood and let me go. Fair play to that man.

I have never profited from growing cannabis either and I would advice you to do the same. Teach people how to grow cannabis but do not grow just for profit. You should be growing for yourself so that you do not have to engage in the black market. This is one of the reasons why I wrote this book. This is all about producing high-quality non-adulterated cannabis for yourself. Do this for yourself on your own property and you will jump over the heads of those fighting among themselves over this non-issue.

I have never seen a violent cannabis-related incident except where black market hard drug money was concerned! I see far more violent alcohol-related crimes than cannabis ones. In fact I can safely say that I have never met a true stoner who wished another harm. I have seen black market hard drug dealers crack a few heads open though. I am sure many black market hard drug dealers have been killed or kill because of who they choose to be and what they choose to do. There is absolutely no reason that cannabis needs to be associated with this black market violence, yet many people still support cannabis prohibition! Cannabis prohibition is a human error without any justified scientific, moral or societal grounds.

Supporting cannabis prohibition is a sure-fire way to fail society. If you still have any doubts then reread everything again.

Individuals have the author's permission to copy this section of the book and to send it to your local politicians, doctors, school teachers, pharmacists, municipal leaders, publicans, writers, journalists, artists, newspapers, magazines, shops, etc.

If you read this and think that it makes sense then please forward it to someone else.

The author hopes that you will join him in the most logical conclusion to everything that can be learned here.

It's only cannabis!
Yours Sincerely,

Author of *THE CANNABIS GROW BIBLE: THE DEFINITIVE GUIDE TO GROWING MARIJUANA FOR RECREATIONAL AND MEDICAL USE* published by Green Candy Press.

19 | THE CANNABIS GROW BIBLE CHECKLIST

Through practical application of the information contained in this book the journey from novice grower to guru is attainable. This final chapter is designed to serve as a checklist summarizing the most important factors in achieving superior cannabis growth results. These factors are listed and discussed briefly below:

+ Good Genetics
+ Proper Lighting
+ An Ounce of Prevention
+ Air Circulation and Ventilation
+ The Right Medium
+ Optimal Pot/Container Size
+ Safe Fertilizers
+ 12/12
+ Avoiding Plant Stress
+ Carbon Dioxide (CO_2)
+ Labeling

Good Genetics

It goes without saying that a plant with genetic traits for low bud production and potency will not produce an outstanding crop. If you start with bad genetics you'll only end up with poor results, no matter what you do or how skilled a grower you may be. To obtain good genetics you should get your seeds from a seed bank that advertises strains from reputable breeders. A number of quality breeders enter competitions, such as the Cannabis Cup in Amsterdam. You should pay a visit to Amsterdam and sample what the breeders have to offer in the coffee shops. The coffee shop owners may tell you where you can purchase seeds from bud that you enjoy smoking. Most of the cannabis pictures in this book come from well-known strains that breeders have produced and can be bought through seed banks.

Selecting good clone mothers is also important. By selecting a good mother plant you can create a population of clone mothers that increases your overall yield. Obtaining good genetics is crucial for good growing results.

Proper Lighting

Light is a very important factor in plant growth and bud production. If you aren't getting the bud sizes that this book highlights, you should consider upgrading your lighting system.

Although results can be achieved using a 250-watt HID or fluorescent tubes, a 400-watt HID is better. A 600-watt HID will produce a much better crop than a 400-watt HID and a 1000-watt HID is the absolute best light available on the market. Of course, not everyone wants to grow large amounts of bud and a 1000-watt HID can be expensive to run. However, a 1000-watt HID light will improve your results.

Conserving light is also important. Use reflectors, white walls and Mylar to keep the spread of light even and contained in your grow room. Any light leaks mean that usable light is being lost and you are paying for it, so try and use as much of it as possible. Your plants will love you for it.

Try to keep lights as close to the plants as possible without burning them. Keeping the distance from bulb to plant to a minimum is very important. It increases over-all yield and reduces internode length development. Keep those internode lengths down and you will get much better results.

An Ounce of Prevention

Prevention is better than cure. Any problem will stunt plant growth to some degree. Anticipating and preventing the problem before it happens entails know-ing what problems to expect and being adequately prepared through advance planning. This book has explained some of the problems common to cannabis. Healthy plants are rewarding plants, so take good care of your plants' health and you will reap the rewards for doing so.

Check on your plants regularly. Spend time checking them for fungi and pests.

This is what cannabis gardening is all about and can quickly turn into a routine that you enjoy as you watch your plants grow strong and healthy.

Air Circulation and Ventilation

Air circulation is very important. Outdoor plants don't have this problem but growth of indoor plants can sometimes be stunted or slowed if they don't receive enough fresh air. Fresh air is important to replace any impurities that build up in your grow room. The percentage of different compounds that make up air can change or fluctuate if new air isn't introduced into the grow room and can cause problems with your grow. Heat can also build up in spaces that don't have good air ventilation, and a rise in temperature can cause stunted plant growth. Try to keep fresh air moving around your grow room at all times for the best results.

Air circulation brings a mild wind to your grow and this is very important for stem and branch growth. By stressing it slightly, the wind will cause the plant to react with thicker stem and branch growth. This is important for bud production, and the plant will be thicker, stronger and healthier overall. I've witnessed growers use fans in their grow rooms that can triple the width of a stem. On more than one occasion I've seen indoor stems that are two inches thick on a plant that is only four feet tall. These plants tended to produce the most bud in the same strain population too. The reason for this was because they were located very near to the main fan and placed directly under the light. In other words, the growing conditions were optimal for that plant.

Dust is also a problem for indoor growers. In a grow room you need to use ventilation to keep dust from settling on your sticky bud. Those tiny pistils are producing the resin that you want. A big blob of dust on a pistil will stunt its growth and reduce the overall effect the bud has when sampled.

The Right Medium

Soil is the most popular choice of medium. If the soil isn't suitable for growing cannabis, no matter how skilled a grower you are, your plants will not reach their optimum potential. You may have to experiment with soils before you find one that suits your cannabis plants. Never underestimate the importance of soil. Make sure the pH is right and the nutrients that your plant requires are present in the soil. Soils should hold a bit of water, but should also drain well — you don't want muddy or fast-draining soils. Aim for the middle ground and choose a soil that does both well.

Hydroponics is an important development in plant horticulture but requires more maintenance than soil growing. Growing in hydroponic systems can improve yields and speed up the growing time considerably. If you have the time and money give hydroponics a shot. It can be a wonderful way to improve your yields.

Optimal Pot/Container Size

A four-inch-square pot may be suitable for clones or SOG-type growing situations, however anything less than this can stunt growth because the plant roots will not be able to develop fully. 'Pot bound' or 'root bound' plants can experience nutrient deficiencies as well. For these reasons most growers prefer to use three-gallon buckets, which are also commonly called three-gallon nursery pots. Three-gallon pots tend to permit enough root growth to allow the plant to flourish. To achieve even more effective results you should try using five-gallon nursery pots. Five-gallon nursery pots will help to produce very sturdy and strong plants with thick stems and plentiful node development. The problem with five-gallon pots is that they take up quite a bit of space, so less plants will fit into the grow room.

I once saw a plant in a five-gallon pot that was left in the vegetative growth stage for an additional three weeks after calyx development to encourage increased branch and node development. When flowered, the plant became a monster bud manufacturer and produced a much larger yield than any other plant in that particular crop. If you have the right genetics and the time to veg your plants a little longer, a five-gallon pot can make all the difference in the final yield.

Cannabis also tends to do most of its rooting during the vegetative stage of growth. As soon as flowering begins root development slows down considerably. Try to allow for good root development in the initial stages of growth by giving the roots plenty of room to grow. It is possible to produce colossal two-pound yielding plants in five-gallon pots with the right genetics, light and grow time.

For hydroponic set-ups you can buy net pots that usually range from between two and eight inches square. The most common net pot is the five- or six-inch type. This size net pot is suitable for simple hydroponics systems like 'The Bubbler'. For large Sativa plants, an eight-inch net pot is more suitable. Make sure that if you plan to grow a plant to yield more than one ounce, you should choose at least the five-inch type net pot to ensure adequate support for the stem and root mass.

Safe Fertilizers

If you provide the food that your plants require they will provide you with good results. Cannabis plants like food but not too much food. You should also note that some fertilizers could change the taste of your bud. Many people claim that this is a myth, but if you smoke enough varieties from different grow techniques, you'll be able to taste the difference between natural outdoor bud and indoor bud that has been chemically treated. Some people have complained about headaches from smoking indoor cannabis that has been burnt through overfeeding. There are many potential reasons for this, but the main reason is that instead of using a feeding solution for food plants, the grower used one for plant appearance, like the kind used for roses. Some of these non-food plant fertilizers contain ingredients beyond the standard primary, secondary and micronutrients. These extra ingredients can often be toxic and a warning label on the side of the fertilizer container should indicate this. The same goes for pest sprays — another good reason to grow your own bud.

However if you have read this book then you know to stick to food fertilizers and sprays that can be used on food plants. If you get your feeding mixtures right you'll boost the overall performance of your plants and keep them healthier too.

Hormones can also increase the overall yield and vigor of your plants, but they can be expensive. In some countries hormones are banned because of the risk that they might interfere with a plant's genetics and yours. Research hormones thoroughly before using them, but note also that many growers have used reputable brand name hormones and achieved larger bud quantities.

Keep notes of feeding times and amounts to help you gauge your feeding routines. It is sometimes easy to forget when you last fed your plants and what mixtures you used. Keep these notes safely hidden from prying eyes.

12/12
If you use 12/12 and keep your flowering room completely lightproof, you will improve your overall yield. A 100 percent lightproof room will increase yields by as much as 30 percent more than a room that is only 99 percent lightproof. That is how important total darkness is to your plants during the flowering stage of the life cycle. Avoid interrupting this schedule and you will reap the rewards for doing so.

Avoiding Plant Stress
Multiple transplants should be avoided in order to minimize plant stress. By solving problems quickly and taking good care of your plants you will achieve much

more effective results. Stress-related disorders are often responsible for lowering yields.

This book has covered many aspects of plant stress that can be avoided by simply implementing the good growing practices covered within these very chapters.

Carbon Dioxide (CO₂)

CO_2 supplements boost yields and should be employed if you have the resources. My experience has shown that CO_2 can naturally enhance yields to almost double that of a similar grow that does not include a CO_2 supplement.

Although you can produce great results without using CO_2 it does make all the difference. Growers who use CO_2 rarely ever turn away from it. It is a wonderful way of achieving very high yields with the right genetics.

Labeling

Never underestimate labeling. Label everything you can. This includes labeling seeds, seedlings, vegetative plants, flowering plants, clones, your harvest, your manicured bud and your stored end products.

Labeling prevents mix-ups from occurring. If you mix up your plants, you are left with the problem of trying to guess correct flowering times and strain type. Labels can be bought in most good grow stores. Plastic labels should be used in conjunction with a non-permanent pen so that they can be reused again.

My experience as a grower has taught me that the cannabis plant is so diverse that no one country, seed bank or breeder can claim to have all the best genetics. In fact the majority of high-quality genetics are available to ANY grower through the right seed bank. Not all seed banks send their seeds everywhere in the world but you will be able to find a few that do. There is nothing preventing good growers from obtaining what they need by checking a few things out.

If you understand and control the above points then you will achieve the goal of growing superior bud. We hope that this book has helped in some way and that you will continue to refer to it in the future.

Producing your own bud has never been easier. Hundreds of thousands of people grow all over the world both indoors and outdoors. Many of them have been doing this for decades and have kept it a secret by simply not telling people that they grow. They also only grow for themselves and this makes all the difference in keeping their pastime confidential. People who do not sell their produce are rarely ever discovered.

If you know people that have an interest in cannabis then tell them about this book. This is the kind of information that they need to make their own high-quality bud. The results are cheaper and better as you will see!

Remember: Do not break the law. Before you get seeds, clones or grow cannabis check your country's laws to ensure that your actions are not illegal. We would like you to grow cannabis but we do not want you to get into legal trouble.

Have fun and thanks for reading this book.

Greg Green

LIBERATE THE HERB

++ | RESOURCES

CANNABIS WEBSITES

http://www.hightimes.com -- High Times Magazine
http://www.marijuananews.com -- Marijuana News and Legal Information
http: //www.cannabistimes.com -- Cannabis Times Newspaper
http://www.cannabis.com -- General Cannabis Information Website
http://www.yahooka.com -- General Cannabis Information Website
http://www.cannabisculture.com -- Cannabis Culture Magazine
http://www.overgrow.com -- Cannabis Growing Website
http://www.cannabisworld.com -- Cannabis Growing Website
http://www.growadvice.com -- Cannabis Growing Website
http://www.cannabishealth.com -- Cannabis Health Website
http://www.erowid.org -- Drug Information Website
http://www.lycaeum.org -- Drug Information Website

HASH AND PROCESSING

http://www.bubblebag.com
http://www.pollinator.nl
http://www.mixnball.com

HYDROPONICS AND LIGHTING

http://www.hydroponics101.com -- Hydroponics Shop Locator USA
http://www.hydroponic-shop.com -- Greenfields Hydroponics UK
http://www.greenthings.co.uk -- Green Things Hydroponics UK
http://www.allamericanhydro.com -- Online reseller Michigan USA
http://www.bchydroponics.com -- BC Canada

http://www.blunt.co.uk -- Esoteric Hydroponics, Surrey UK
http://www.hydrogrowth.co.uk -- Hydrogrowth Wigan UK
http://www.hydroponics.com -- Ontario Canada
http://www.hydromall.com -- Worldwide Store Search (Over 500 entries)

MEDICAL CANNABIS INFORMATION

Now that you are able to grow your own medicine why not join up with the International Association for Cannabis as Medicine (IACM). They can be contacted at the following address below.

Arnimstrasse 1A
50825 Cologne
Germany
Phone: +49-221-9543 9229
Fax: +49-221-1300591
E-mail: info@cannabis-med.org
Website: http://www.cannabis-med.org

The members of the board of directors is composed of eight medical doctors. Ask them to send you information on medical cannabis and they will invite you to become a member of the International Association for Cannabis as Medicine. This is an excellent resource for updates on medical cannabis information which includes a publication called the Journal of Cannabis Therapeutics.

SEEDBANKS

http://www.geocities.com/stonedas72/AussieSPC.html -- Australian Seeds
http://www.africanseeds.com -- African Seeds Canada and Europe (Breeders)
http://www.hempdepot.ca -- Hemp Depot Canada
http://www.hempqc.com -- Heaven's Stairway Canada
http://www.eurohemp.com -- Heaven's Stairway UK
http://www.hemcy.com -- Hemcy Seeds Holland
http://www.legendsseeds.com -- Legends Canada
http://www.emeryseeds.com -- Marc Emery Direct Marijuana Seeds Canada
http://www.peakseeds.com -- Peak Seeds Canada
http://www.seedsdirect.to -- Seeds Direct UK
http://www.worldwideseeds.com -- World Wide Seeds Switzerland
http://www.sensiseeds.com -- Sensi Seed Bank (Breeders)
http://www.cannabisworld.com/cgi000/auction.cgi -- Seed Auction Worldwide

http://ssc.gq.nu/invite/ssc.html -- Seed Swap Club Worldwide
http://www.greenhouse.org -- Green House Seeds Amsterdam (Breeders)
http://www.dutch-passion.nl -- Dutch Passion Seeds Amsterdam (Breeders)
http://www.seriousseeds.com -- Serious Seeds Amsterdam (Breeders)
http://www.flyingdutchmen.com -- The Flying Dutchman Seeds (Breeders)
http://www.homegrownfantasy.com -- Homegrown Fantasy (Breeders)
http://www.kcbrains.com -- KC Brains Amsterdam (Breeders)

VAPORIZERS

http://www.xijix.com -- Digital Herbal Vaporizers
http://www.plasticsmithbc.com -- The BC Vaporizer
http://www.vaportechco.com -- Vapor Tech Vaporizer
http://www.vriptech.com -- Vriptech Vaporizer

++ | GLOSSARY OF TERMS

A

ACIDITY: The state, quality or degree of being acid, indicated by a pH value below 7.

AERATE: To loosen or puncture the soil in order to increase water penetration.

AFGHANI STRAIN: A short, highly resinous strain of Indica from Afghanistan.

AIR LAYERING: A specialized method of cloning a plant, which is accomplished by growing new roots from a branch while the branch remains connected to the parent plant.

ALKALINITY: The alkali concentration or alkaline quality of an alkali-containing substance; having a pH value above 7.

B

BACTERICIDE: A chemical compound that kills or inhibits bacteria.

BALLAST: A transformer used mainly with HID lighting equipment.

BLIGHT: Any of numerous plant diseases resulting in sudden conspicuous wilting and dying of affected parts, especially young, growing tissues.

BLOTCH/BLOTCHING: Any of several plant diseases caused by fungi and resulting in brown or black dead areas on leaves or fruit.

BRACT: A small leaf or scale-like structure associated with and surrounded by an inflorescence or cone.

C

CALYX: Outer whorl of flowering parts; collective term for all the sepals of a flower.

CANNABINOIDS: The psychoactive compound found in cannabis

CHILLUM: A small fat pipe made of clay.

CHLOROPHYLL: The green pigment in leaves. When present and healthy usually dominates all other pigments. Chlorophyll is important in the conversion of CO_2 and H_2O into glucose, which plants feed on.

CHLOROSIS: Chlorosis is the yellowing of normally green plant tissues due to the destruction of the chlorophyll or the partial failure of the chlorophyll to develop.

CLONE: To reproduce or propagate asexually; rooted cuttings, normally considered female in the context of this book.

CO_2: The chemical formula for carbon dioxide.

COLA: Refers to the main branch of cannabis flowers located at the top of the stem.

COMPOST: An organic soil amendment resulting from the decomposition of organic matter.

COROLLA: Inner whorl of floral parts; collective name for petals.

COTYLEDON: Leaf of the embryo of a seed plant, which upon germination either remains in the seed or emerges, enlarges and becomes green.

F

FAN LEAVES: The largest leaves of the cannabis plant that gather the most available light.

FERTILIZER: A plant food, which, when complete, should contain all three of the primary elements N P K.

FLOWERING STAGE: The peak period of development of a plant, when the cannabis plant displays its sex and produces flowers and bud.

FOLIAGE: A cluster of leaves.

FUNGICIDE: A compound toxic to fungi.

G

GENOTYPE: The genetic constitution of an individual, especially as distinguished from the phenotype; the whole of the genes in an individual or group.

GERMINATION: The process of the sprouting of a seed.

GLANDS: Refers to resin-producing part of the cannabis plant.

H

HASH/HASHISH: Compressed cannabis resin.

HASH OIL: Refers to cannabis resin when it is in a liquid state.

HEMP: This is the stalk and stems produced from the cannabis plant, often used to make fabrics.

HERMAPHRODITE: A trait of a plant where both the male and female flowers are found on the same plant.

HID: high intensity discharge.

HPS: high pressure sodium.

HUMUS: The brown or black organic part of soil resulting from the partial decay of leaves and other matter.

HYBRID: The offspring of two plants of different species or varieties of species.

HYDROPONICS: The science of growing plants in mineral solutions or liquid, instead of in soil.

I

IBL: Abbreviation for inbred line. An inbred line is a nearly homozygous line produced by continued inbreeding, usually through self-fertilization.

INDICA: A species of cannabis plant.

INFECTIOUS DISEASE: A disease that is caused by a pathogen which can spread from a diseased to a healthy plant.

INFLORESCENCE: The flower cluster of a plant.

INTERNODE: The distance between branches along the stem of a plant.

L

LANDRACE: An ancient or primitive cultivated variety of a crop plant.

LOAM: A rich soil composed of clay, sand and organic matter.

LUMEN: A scientific measurement for luminosity from a light source.

M

MARIJUANA: Another term for cannabis.

MH: Metal halide.

MACRONUTRIENTS: Elements, such as carbon, hydrogen, oxygen or nitrogen, required in large proportion for the normal growth and development of a plant.

MICRONUTRIENTS: Mineral elements that are needed by some plants in very small quantities.

MILDEW: A powdery growth on the plant's surface.

MOTHER PLANT: A plant kept for its vigor or likable characteristics by the grower to be used for cloning and breeding.

MUTATION: A change in genetic material brought about by an abnormal influence such as radiation.

N

NECROTIC: from necrosis, meaning death of cells or tissues through injury or disease, especially in a localized area of the body.

NODE: Position on a stem from which one or more structures (especially branches) grow.

NPK: Abbreviation for nitrogen (N), phosphate (P) and potassium (K), the three primary nutrients for plants.

O

ORGANIC: This refers to a method of gardening utilizing only materials derived from living things and not from synthetic material.

OSMOSIS: The process by which a solvent passes through a semi-permeable membrane into a region of greater solute concentration, so as to make the concentrations on the two sides more nearly equal.

P

PARASITE: An organism living on or in another living organism (host) and obtaining its food from the latter.

PATHOGEN: An entity that can incite disease.

PERLITE: A form of obsidian consisting of vitreous globules expandable by heating and used for insulation and as a plant-growing medium.

pH: A measure of the acidity or alkalinity of a solution, numerically equal to 7 for neutral solutions, increasing with increasing alkalinity and decreasing with increasing acidity. The pH scale commonly in use ranges from 0 to 14.

PHENOTYPE: The observable physical or biochemical characteristics of an organism, as determined by both genetic makeup and environmental influences.

PHLOEM: The food-conducting tissue of vascular plants.

PHOTOPERIOD: The duration of an organism's daily exposure to light, considered especially with regard to the effect of the exposure on growth and development.

PHOTOSYNTHESIS: The chemical process in plants in which carbon dioxide and water are converted into glucose by the influence of light energy.

PHOTOTROPISM: The inclination, which plants have, to grow towards light.

PISTIL: The ovule-bearing organ of a flower.

POLLEN: The male gametes or microspores of a seed plant, produced as a fine granular or powdery substance in the anthers of a flower or the male cone of a gymnosperm and usually transported by wind or insects.

POLLINATE: Convey pollen to or deposit pollen on a stigma, an ovule, a flower, a plant and so allow fertilization.

POT BOUND: See root bound.

POTENCY: The strength of the cannabis drug, usually measured by the THC levels in a plant.

PRUNING: The cutting and trimming of plants to remove dead or injured material, or to control and direct new growth.

R

rH: Abbreviation for relative humidity; rH is expressed in a percentage and measured with a hygrometer.

ROOT BALL: The network of roots along with the attached soil of any given plant.

ROOT BOUND: A condition that exists when a potted plant has outgrown its container.

ROOTS: The colorless underground part of a vascular plant, which serves to anchor it and convey nourishment.

ROT: Rot is the disintegration, discoloration and decomposition of plant tissue.

RUST/RUSTING: Rust is a plant disease that gives a rusty appearance to the infected surface of the plant.

S

SATIVA: A species of cannabis plant.

SEPAL: Can mean a leaf or segment of the calyx.

SINSEMILLA: Refers to non-pollinated female cannabis plants.

SKUFF: Sifted resin from the cannabis plant.

SKUNK: An old strain of cannabis that has a strong smell and sour taste.

STIGMA: The receptive part of the pistil.

SUBSTRATE: A surface upon which an organism grows or is attached.

T

TETRAHYDROCANNABINOL (THC): The psychoactive cannabinoid in marijuana that is responsible for the high or drug effect.

THC: See Tetrahydrocannabinol

THINNING: In gardening, the act of removing some plants to allow sufficient room for the remaining plants to grow.

TRANSPLANTING: The process of moving one plant from it's medium to another medium or another location.

TRICHOMES: A hairlike or bristlelike outgrowth, as from the external surface of a plant.

V

VASCULAR: Term applied to a plant tissue or region consisting of conductive tissue.

VEGETATIVE GROWTH STAGE: The stage in the life cycle of the marijuana plant that occurs before flowering and after the seedling stage.

VERMICULITE: A moisture-holding medium for plant growth or a protective covering for bulbs made from hydrated silicates.

W

WHORL: Group of three or more structures of the same kind (generally leaves or flower parts) at the same node.

WILT: Any of various plant diseases characterized by slow or rapid collapse of terminal shoots, branches or entire plants.

Z

ZERO ZERO: An extremely pure and potent grade of Hashish.

++ | INDEX

R

Rabbits, 181
Recessive gene, 211
Reflectors, 60–61
Regeneration, 172
Rejuvenation, 172
Resin, 5, 176–177, 195, 197
    pressing into hash, 251–252
Re–veging, 172
rH. See Humidity
Rockwool, 136
Rodents, 183
Root rot, 187–188, 192
Rooting hormone, 167, 169
Ruderalis, 9, 17, 172

S

Safety, 44–45, 61. See also Security
Sampling, 197
Sand and silts, 67
Sativa, 8, 13, 17, 63, 80, 115, 117,
    147, 161, 229–230
    harvesting, 200–201
Scale (pest), 181
Scales (mineral), 142
Screen. See ScROG
Screening hash, 240–244
ScROG (screen of green), 116–121,
    158
Scuffing seeds, 29
Security, 41–46, 114
Seed(s)
    bad, 193–194
    banks, 20–22, 42
    counterfeit, 21
    germination, 25–30
    obtaining, 4, 20–22
    planting outdoors, 148–149
    production, 12–13, 208
    propagation, 27–28
    scuffing, 29

selecting, 18–20
storing, 22–23, 208
varieties, 16–18
Seedling(s), 10
    transplanting, 31–33, 147–148
Selfing, 230–232
Sexing plants, 108–109
Sexual dysfunction. See Hermaphrodite
Shock, transplant, 32–33
Single pack hydroponics nutrients, 135
Sinsemilla
    condition, 13
    growing, 110
    hermaphrodites, 171
    plant, 7–8
Skuff, 240
Slugs, 181
Smelly plants. See Odor control
Snails, 181
Soapy pesticides, 176–177
Social issues of cannabis use, 268–282
Soil, 64, 67–69, 150–151, 285
    control, 80–83
    flushing, 78, 80, 95–98, 193
    nutrients, 65
    pH, 65
    propagation in, 27–28
Soil-less mixtures, 138
SOG (sea of green), 112, 115–117,
    119–120, 158
Solvents for hash oil extraction, 246
Species of cannabis, 8–9, 234–240
Special clone mother, 112–114,
    229–230
Spider mites, 181–182, 186
Spiders, 185
Stem, weak, 30
Strains of cannabis, 8-9, 234–240
Sulfur, 77
Super
    critical fluid extraction, 245–246

AVAILABLE AT YOUR LOCAL BOOKSTORE

CANNABIS CULTIVATION
MEL THOMAS

The easy-to-follow, step-by-step directions enable anyone to grow and harvest the highest quality marijuana using simple techniques and inexpensive, everyday gardening tools. An experienced grower, Mel Thomas pens a comprehensive manual that is both interesting and informative. Don't know the difference between soil and hydroponic gardens? Thomas will walk you through it. The book covers all of the important factors which can influence growth rate, yield and potency: lighting, planting mediums, pH, nutrients, water systems, air and temperature, and CO_2. CANNABIS CULTIVATION will help you turn almost any space into a high-yielding garden. $16.95

THE MARIJUANA CHEF COOKBOOK
BY S. T. ONER

THE MARIJUANA CHEF COOKBOOK gives a whole new meaning to cooking with herbs. With more than 40 first-rate recipes, this wonderful cookbook offers a multitude of ways to turn humble leaf into culinary treats that everyone can enjoy. In the mood for something sweet? Try Decadent Chocolate Bud Cake washed down with a delicious Mary Jane's Martini. A heady blend of theory and technique, THE MARIJUANA CHEF COOKBOOK is filled with delicious easy-to-follow recipes that will take you and your dinner guests on a natural high. $12.95

THE GRINGO TRAIL
MARK MANN

ASIA HAS THE HIPPIE TRAIL. SOUTH AMERICA HAS THE GRINGO TRAIL. Mark Mann and his girlfriend Melissa set of to explore the ancient monuments, mountains and rainforests of the southern continent. But for their friend, South America meant only one thing...drugs. Funny, shocking and revealing, THE GRINGO TRAIL is an On the Road for the Lonely Planet generation. A darkly comic road-trip and a journey of drama and discovery through South America's turbulent past and volatile present. $12.95

GREETINGS FROM CANNABIS COUNTRY
ANDRE GROSSMAN

GREETINGS FROM CANNABIS COUNTRY is a must have for enthusiasts! The book contains a collection of 30 beautifully detailed photo-postcards, taken by Andre Grossman at Trichome Technologies—the world's most sophisticated and largest marijuana growing operation. Fourteen of the potent strains of marijuana are displayed in both a colorful and playful way. The safest way to send pot through the mail! $11.95

ABC BOOK: A DRUG PRIMER
STEVEN CERIO

Steven Cerio's ABC BOOK: A DRUG PRIMER is a must-have for Ravers and Stoners alike. Come along for the ride from A-Z, and read the poems that accompany Steven's colorful psychedelic illustrations. Each letter represents a different type of drug, and its effects are stated in an accompanying poem. A lighthearted and amusing piece of work, this ABC book is pure fun! $12.95

ONLINE AT WWW.GREENCANDYPRESS.COM